AMERICAN DEMOCRACY
AND WORLD POWER

AMERICAN DEMOCRACY
AND WORLD POWER

ROBERT A. ISAAK

St. Martin's Press   New York

Library of Congress Catalog Card Number: 76-28133
Copyright © 1977 by St. Martin's Press, Inc.
All Rights Reserved.
Manufactured in the United States of America.
0987
fedcba
For information, write St. Martin's Press, Inc.,
175 Fifth Avenue, New York, N.Y. 10010

cover design: Mies Hora

cloth ISBN: 312-02205-0
paper ISBN: 312-02240-9

for Gudrun

PREFACE

The basic problem of America is that Americans no longer think of this country as the New World. As America became rich and powerful, its policy makers deserted their liberal, democratic tradition and humanitarian social ideals for the sake of cynical Old World values and desperate power manipulations. This book explores the seeming incompatibilities between America's democratic ideals and its present world power status and suggests an alternative political economy that might help to restore pride in those ideals at home and abroad.

Part one first examines what America has stood for in the past and what it appears to stand for at present, and then explores the tensions between capitalism and socialism on the one hand and democracy and elitism on the other. Part two traces the value conflicts America has with other nations—Old Rich allies, New Rich oil producers, and Poor opponents. The global political economy, public opinion, foreign aid, *détente*, isolationism, and interventionism are all analyzed in this light. Part three suggests what America should stand for in the future, and outlines a program for countering the decline of Western culture, reforming the educational system to make Americans into more effective democratic elites, and transforming America's old ideology of *laissez-faire* liberalism into a new political economy of social liberalism that is more appropriate for the times. Part four speculates on how America's future will probably develop given the Old World policies of those in power, and what the price is apt to be if New World reforms are neglected.

It is a pleasure to acknowledge my indebtedness to those who helped to refine the arguments made here. Professor John Stoessinger made helpful comments on the entire manuscript, while Charles Kindleberger, John Spanier, Joan Spero, Dietrich Noske, Norman Graham, and Steve Berry responded frankly to one or more chapters. Simon Whitney was particularly generous with astute observations on chapters dealing with economics. Student and faculty reactions to seminars I gave on social liberalism at Columbia University, the future of American foreign policy at the New School for Social Research, and the role of corporations in society at Pace University's Graduate School of Business further enriched my ways of thinking. Wilfrid Kohl's faculty seminar on international political economy and Zbigniew Brzezinski's conference on liberalism and force, both at Columbia, helped to focus my thoughts. Last but not least, the supportive atmosphere of Columbia's Institute on Western Europe made the completion of this work possible.

R.A.I.

CONTENTS

1 THE AMERICAN PREDICAMENT

Foreign politics demand scarcely any of those qualities which a democracy possesses; and they require, on the contrary, the perfect use of almost all those faculties in which it is deficient. . . . Almost all the nations which have exercised a powerful influence upon the destinies of the world, by conceiving, following up, and executing vast designs—from the Romans to the English—have been governed by aristocratic institutions.
—*Alexis de Tocqueville*, Democracy in America, *1835*

Americans are torn between their democratic ideals and their conservative empire. The conflict between America's liberal ethos and America's position as a superpower in world politics threatens to divide the American people internally and to lead to national decline externally. In a world of over 150 countries, only slightly more than two dozen are democracies, and many of these are dominated by short-sighted regimes that pursue their own national gain despite the international consequences. As the largest, wealthiest, and most powerful Western democracy in absolute terms, the United States faces a predicament that has more than just domestic implications: its resolution may help to determine whether the Western democratic form of government can be saved short of another world war.

Though this country's dilemma had been long in the making, Americans became acutely conscious of it only after the jolting experiences of the 1970s: the American defeat in the Vietnam War, the Watergate affair, the breakdown of the old international economic system with the spread of world-wide inflation and recession, national reaction to the violent changes and frustrated idealism of the 1960s, and citizens' increasing awareness of the limits of growth and of personal expectations. The optimism with which the New World was founded seemed to fade. People adopted an Old World cynicism based upon an acceptance of limits and class inequities, and focused upon possible losses rather

1

than potential gains. At home many Americans felt not like leaders but like pawns of social change. They dwelled upon their own uncertainty rather than setting high goals for themselves and took things as they came rather than trying to steer events.

As Americans withdrew from their commitments abroad in Cambodia and South Vietnam and hedged on their commitments elsewhere, people all over the world began to ask themselves what America really stands for. Where was this country going as a superpower, a democracy, and a peacemaker? Which allies could count on its support?—and which were being written off? Would the shadow cast by the apparent lack of American will power obscure the promise of the American Dream?

Rarely was the future of American social and foreign policy more in doubt. Opinion surveys showed that Americans were becoming more fiscally conservative and were turning inward, away from foreign involvement. Despite the significant decline in the proportion of national income devoted to military purposes, the desire to reduce defense spending even further became widespread. [1] The shift in federal spending from defense to welfare needs in the past decade has also served to remove capital from the productive sectors of the economy that increase the Gross National Product and channel it into the nonproductive sectors of transfer payments. [2] This shift has critical implications for an American political economy that depends upon economic growth to expand democratic and economic opportunities for all. Some even speak of the coming American age of "welfare pension socialism" because the federal government's capital is becoming increasingly tied to social security and pension funds, which grant automatic cost-of-living increases with every turn of the inflationary spiral. Any lack of economic growth limits domestic options for future American policy makers.

The options for American policy makers are becoming even more limited in the foreign policy arena. The Vietnam War and Watergate affair have greatly undermined the confidence of the American people in the executive branch of their government exactly when their support is most needed by foreign policy makers to secure American interests abroad. While the power of the secretary of state declines because of adverse events abroad and congressional restrictions at home, no individual or group appears to be gaining enough power to make a strong American foreign policy possible in the future. The *Pax Americana* is coming apart, and many are afraid to speculate on what might replace it.

American foreign policy does not contradict the internal structure and values of the country but rather expresses them. To change this country's foreign policy, its internal structure must change. Old World conservative, imperial policies help to generate the very kinds of threats they are designed to prevent. But effective New World policy alternatives require grassroots changes in American values and society: the replacement of materialistic rugged individualism with social liberalism, which gears individual incentives to social needs. Without such a philosophical shift at home and a positive, activist foreign policy based upon it abroad, the best of Western democratic civilization represented by the American nation is likely to decline sharply relative to other cultures and ideologies. In short, American moral and ideological vitality must be restored and American foreign policy reversed to stem the tide of the decline of the West.

It is not so much that Aleksandr Solzhenitsyn is right in declaring that moral and spiritual bankruptcy has led to Western retreat and the imminent danger of Soviet domination of the world. Rather, the argument here is that the West, and America in particular, cannot afford the luxury of assuming that Solzhenitsyn is totally wrong. Americans cannot dismiss his words as merely the frantic warnings of an escaped concentration camp prisoner who desperately struggles for the freedom never before allowed him. Solzhenitsyn has pessimistically noted that perhaps we are fated to understand only by experiencing everything for ourselves.[3] To learn only by one's experience is the *reductio ad absurdum* of the American creed of individualistic pragmatism. But viewing the American commitment to individual freedom positively, Americans cannot risk failing to take such sensitive warnings about threats to their democratic way of life seriously.

Yet, throughout the land one senses not concern as much as despair, not anger at frustrated ideals and social inequities as much as uncertainty. insecurity, and individual feelings of powerlessness. Battered by Vietnam, mocked by Watergate, and drained by the economic recession, Americans often seem content to struggle only to maintain what they have, to lower their sights, to come home and leave world problems to others. The temptation to pursue isolationism abroad and withdraw from social concerns at home is understandable but may constitute the single greatest psychological threat to the future of Western civilization in general and to America's influence and security in particular. The image of sitting by Siddhartha's river seems hauntingly attractive until the river suddenly fills with pollution or is infested by nuclear submarines and one awakes from passivity too late to head off the nightmares to follow.

Rarely have Americans had a greater challenge or opportunity to seize their moment in history. They have a chance not just to hold their position—which, *alone*, is a self-defeating historical strategy—but to reform themselves in their own best image and to solve the world's critical problems with their considerable capabilities.

It may be wholesome as Peter Schrag has suggested, that Americans have become somewhat "Europeanized" in accepting a sense of their own limits, in anticipating the end of the American future. The Nixon era, for example, had much that was European in flavor: the wage and price controls of a managed economy, the Metternichian conduct of foreign affairs, a call for the end of permissiveness, and the recovery of self-discipline.[4] But these programs and policies suggest an Old World acceptance of the way things are. Their object was to stabilize the existing class structure by helping to maintain the poor rather than to transform them; to seek peace by maintaining existing world arrangements rather than leading nations toward a new system; to convince individuals of their limitations rather than their capacity for higher self-development. If this Europeanization goes too far, America could end up as decadent as the Old World with its passive acceptance of a rigid class system and barriers to social mobility.

Ironically, to recover their New World spirit, Americans may have to look to the New World movements in Old Europe that Americanization helped to inspire: recent political movements for social justice, a balance of freedom and equity, an urge in the Mediterranean basin for increasing democratic controls. This country's sophisticated task is to restore its New World heritage using its recently acquired Old World skills. Maturity, in this sense, is always somewhat contradictory: it is all very well not to put the cart before the horse (as the 1960s taught us); but first one must have a cart (as the 1970s are teaching us). And the choice between horses has become more crucial than ever.

The past ideals and future hopes of Americans have been colored to a great extent by what they have *not* experienced. In the nineteenth century, the observant French nobleman Alexis de Tocqueville toured the United States and noted: "The great advantage of the Americans is that they have arrived at a state of democracy without having to endure a democratic revolution; and that they are born equal, instead of becoming so." The import of these words was lost until Louis Hartz spelled out their meaning clearly in *The Liberal Tradition in America*. Hartz noted that America skipped the feudal stage of history and the revolutionary reaction to feudalism. Americans, therefore, could really never understand the meaning of the socialist left's rebellion against feudalism or the reactionary right's opposition to socialism. In short, rugged, individualistic liberalism was all Americans knew, and their liberalism became rigid and dogmatic, defining itself in the simplistic New World categories of Puritan morality and the Protestant ethic that were radically different from the Old World ways of decadent Europe. Since Americans were "born equal," their experience could never tell them what it would be like to have to overthrow a feudal tradition, to *be* revolutionary in order to *become* democratic. The British left without much of a struggle and an alternate group of British dissenters set up their democracy with a more or less clean slate, moving westward to escape social problems as they came up.

Americans, argues Hartz, regard all ideologies apart from their own democratic liberal ethos as alien and unintelligible. Those steeped in the absolute moral ethos of "Americanism" in world politics either withdraw from "alien" ideologies or things abroad or try to transform them to fit their own dogmatic image. America's messianism is the opposite of its isolationism. As diplomat George Kennan has noted, Americans seem to oscillate between fleeing from the rest of the world and embracing it with too ardent a passion.

To a great extent, Secretary of State Henry Kissinger was able to avoid the pitfalls of this country's dogmatic liberalism because of his European heritage and intellectual models. He became adept at the cynical, Old World diplomatic manipulations typical of a great empire threatened by dissent from within and opposition from without. In terms of the American predicament, he became a hero of mainstream Americans who wanted an essentially conservative "peace" that promised to preserve America's military and economic interests abroad and material life style at home. But, by the same token, Kissinger became anathema for many who, believing in America's liberal, democratic ethos, considered this powerful intellectual immigrant a threat to domestic freedoms and to the check-and-balance, consultative rules of the game that kept America democratic. Kissinger's secrecy and ambiguity—so effective in maintaining his cherished *détente*—totally contradicted the grassroots American democratic creed and the Wilsonian idealism of open covenants openly arrived at. Kissinger's Old World elitism inevitably brought about a democratic reaction from Congress and from people who were determined to revive their liberal democratic ethos regardless of the temporary costs to America's power.

Indeed, despite American territorial expansion and growing world influence in the twentieth century, Americans have never fully accepted that they are citizens of an *empire*—a state having vast territories and a variety of peoples under a single rule. Our forebears had no such illusions. They thought America was born an imperial republic. George Washington called it a "nascent empire." To its founders, this nation was an *imperium* or sovereign state, that sought expansion. Yet curiously, after America expanded as far as possible on the North American continent, took control of Hawaii, the Philippines, and Puerto Rico, and spread troops and businesses throughout the world, Ameri cans, in general, still did not see their country as an empire. The United States became a superpower almost without its people being aware of it. Americans accepted it as part of their "Manifest Destiny" as the nation of nations, the people of peoples. *E pluribus unum*—one out of many—is the country's motto, stamped on its smallest coins. This was to be a New World where immigrants from everywhere could come and start a new life with equal opportunity. What could be more natural than that this New World should succeed, should become the richest and most powerful nation in the world, a paradigm for others?

When Americans finally did discover that they had imperial interests to defend, global responsibilities to bear, they did not always like it. That position seemed to detract from the country's uniqueness, to make it just another great power, with all the weary responsibilities that entails. To justify the nation's superpower status to themselves as much as to anyone else, American policy makers used a self-righteous liberal democratic rhetoric to describe all imperial actions. Americans entered World War I, "the war to end all wars," in order to "make the world safe for democracy." Americans entered World War II to save the world from Hitler. They entered Korea and Vietnam to save those countries from communism. And they never quite understood why the self-righteous messianism behind such actions did not taste as sweet after the fact. Afterward they often turned from an outward interventionism to an inward nationalism, viewing each experience abroad as unique rather than as part of a pattern, refusing to be burned further by experience. Americans have begun to regret their country's superpower status, to wish perhaps that they were part of a smaller, less successful national enterprise. But it appears to be too late.

The question now is: if America must be a great power in the world, upon what principles should this power be based and for which goals should it be exercised? Recently, a conference on liberalism and force at Columbia University posed the related question, "What is meant by a liberal foreign policy?" To this, philosopher Charles Frankel responded, noting that three assumptions of a "liberal foreign policy" are that liberty is the prime value, that peaceful change is stimulated even while weighed against security costs, and that transnational common interests are encouraged to help international peace and cooperation. These criteria give national policymakers a way to assess probable risks in uncertain situations, to put their dice one way rather than the other.[5]

Although useful, such principles are too abstract to resolve many real world foreign policy dilemmas. It is well to promote liberty, but whose liberty comes first? Who benefits most from certain kinds of peaceful change or opposition to revolutionary change? And are there not antagonistic coalitions within the transnational brotherhood such as the First, Second, Third, and

Fourth Worlds (i.e., the Old Rich capitalist democracies, the Middle-class communist powers, the New Rich oil producers and their lower-middle-class dependents, and the Poor totally without the resources for self-sufficiency)? Each of these classes of nations would define a "liberal foreign policy" quite differently.

Before Americans can work out a coherent liberal foreign policy, they must be clear on their democratic ideals. The tragedy of Vietnam, in terms of the American liberal creed, was not that the Thieu army was too weak to resist the onslaught of the communist attack from the North, but that the Thieu government was not democratic. No positive ideological American principle, therefore, could be raised to justify our support for the regime. All that remained was the negative, and therefore ultimately self-defeating, rationale of anticommunism and the domino theory. Dice were not being thrown *for* something, but *against* something (or more accurately, they were tossed in a hole). Kissinger's approval of the Central Intelligence Agency's subversion of the democratically elected socialist government in Chile through $11 million paid to striking workers was another political action that seemed to contradict Americans' domestic liberal beliefs. That action raises one of the most difficult questions of the American predicament: Is a "democratic" intervention possible? Or, put another way, is a "democratic superpower" a contradiction in terms?

Similarly, American diplomatic support for Latin American military dictatorships as well as for Franco's regime in Spain and the authoritarian Shah of Iran is also comprehensible only in the Old World light of diplomatic alliances to shore up American strategic and economic interests in the world regardless of any moral or liberal considerations. American liberalism, as it is practiced in foreign policy today, seems to have a nonliberal basis: American foreign policy supports conservative stability as a foundation for economic growth and investment abroad and as the key to alliance reliability. The peoples of other countries see such liberalism for what it is: an American ideology used to promote this country's economic and military interests. American liberalism seeks to preserve *American* freedom. And those countries that are stable or rich enough (not withstanding their undemocratic nature) may join the American club and become a part of Western enterprise. Has democracy become a luxury in the late twentieth century that only stable, bourgeois societies can afford?

Just as America became a democracy almost unconsciously because of the lack of obstacles in the eighteenth century, so it became an empire unconsciously as it was reluctantly drawn into world affairs in the twentieth, emerging as the only country whose power had increased and whose homeland had not been touched in World War II. The resulting split between America's conservative behavior as an empire and her deep-seated liberal ethos has given the United States a glaringly hypocritical image in the world. American policy makers speak as if they represented liberal democratic freedom throughout the world, while they use power as an instrument to support American strategic and economic interests regardless of democratic principle.

The success or failure of American foreign policy in the future depends upon developing value priorities, that are realistic in the context of America's role as an empire or superpower. Without such a coherent American position, supported by a democratic consensus, the schizoid inconsistencies in America's image in the world are apt to undermine both democratic processes at home and American interests abroad. The question of where America's vital interests are involved abroad has become a subject of political debate in the post-Vietnam and post-Watergate era. Both Congress and the voters are no longer willing to leave national security matters to the executive branch of government or to technological experts. The economic recession and breakdown of the international economic system have made this connection between foreign policy and domestic interests even more explicit: arms sales abroad means jobs at home, grain sales to Russia mean happier American farmers, increasing American energy independence means lower gas prices. In the late twentieth century foreign and domestic policies have become inseparable, and citizens are becoming increasingly aware of this interdependence in their everyday lives.

In this era of rapid social change and self-examination, Americans have a unique opportunity to restore their liberal, democratic tradition—the tradition symbolized by Thomas Jefferson and Benjamin Franklin. These two sophisticated Enlightenment statesmen were humanistic pragmatists who believed that reason and science could help human beings to satisfy their needs and to overcome the mistakes and injustices of the past. They based their New World optimism on a skeptical empiricism, not on revolution and nihilism for their own sake. Indeed, they accepted many Old World traditions, including Roman law and English constitutionalism. But they did so only after a critical analysis of which aspects of the old traditions would be helpful in America's unique position. To the extent that the rational assumptions of the eighteenth century have broken down and been replaced by the indeterminism of the modern age, it may be even more important for the American nation to replace its present politics of ambiguity with a set of clear-cut social values.

In the developing nations of the world, Jefferson's call for a revolution every ten years is sometimes quoted. Jeffersonian democracy could well become a credible creed through which American policy makers might appeal for Third World support at home and abroad. To make this plan viable, Americans would have to carry out democratic reforms at home—perhaps drawing on Ben Franklin's recommendation of the pragmatic social conscience applied to local community problems. The American people must again begin to believe in their government and its principles before they can give enthusiastic support to executive policy makers or to increases in foreign aid and defense budgets. Why not restore America's New World image? Why not create a humane vision of political economy and development that can compete with Soviet and Chinese models in the Third World? The alternative appears to be an Old World cynicism, polarization at home, and a defensive American policy of withdrawal and reaction abroad.

The present tendency toward a skeptical nationalism (which can, *in effect*, become isolationism) seems less an attempt to resolve the American predicament than an effort to escape from it. Americans seem unwilling to admit that their dilemma in the world will require compromise, and may involve tragedy. Compromise is the basic rule of the American domestic game of politics, but it is perceived as weakness internationally, and tragedy is generally lacking from the American experience and philosophy. Threatened with complexity and future shock, the typical pragmatic American is tempted to pick up his chips and go home, to flee into a simplistic nationalism, hoping optimistically for the storm to pass before playing the game of nations again. The perception that American economic prosperity depends to some extent upon constant interactions with other nations counters this temptation somewhat. But America's vast resources and ability to meet the basic economic needs of its people make the ostrich alternative extremely attractive in times of crisis, as symbolized by President Nixon's "Project Independence" in response to the quadrupling of oil prices by the oil producers. Thus the conflict between America's democratic ethos and conservative imperialism is also apparent in the antithesis between independence and interdependence.

The Jeffersonian democratic ideals became increasingly difficult to implement as America became a superpower. Yet as difficult as it is to actualize the possibility of independent, sovereign states that promote equal rights for all citizens in a world of increasing scarcity and a population explosion, the ideal may well be the only possible coherent basis for an American policy that seeks to serve the free world. Viewed positively, the American struggle in the last part of the twentieth century should be like the noble, but impossible, task of Sisyphus, who, for his excessive pride, was sentenced eternally to push a stone up a mountain and watch it roll back each time as he neared the top. The hubris of the American creed seems to have fated us to push states (including our own) toward democracy, while knowing full well we will fail, more or less, in the end. As Albert Camus noted, it is the *process* of struggling toward the heights that must make the ethical man happy. America needs a rich resource of selfless, ethical citizens to make a democratic policy for the New World even a possibility. Unfortunately, to date, many citizens have avoided becoming involved with national politics.

Oswald Spengler predicted the decline of the West over fifty years ago, and many people in the world believe his prediction is coming to pass. But such a pessimistic vision of historical inevitability, of empires withering and dying like plants, goes against the optimistic American belief in free will and progress through individual actions. In this critical philosophical debate in America today, the two sides are represented by Henry Kissinger on the one hand, who pessimistically implied the inevitable decline of Western democratic states, and by the secretary's idealistic, democratic critics, on the other hand, who accuse him of Old World cynicism typical of imperial statesmen corrupted by power. Kissinger contradicted the Spenglerian view in practice by using his free will at every opportunity to make diplomatic arrangements according to his values. Realists use power to run to death in circles, while idealists, on the sidelines, stroke their ideas like flowers.

The ultimate confrontation between idealists and realists in our era is in economics. The realists argue for a new mercantilism, an economic nationalism of self-sufficiency whereby each nation tries to increase exports, reduce imports, and cut down unemployment at home. The idealists argue that such economic nationalism has led to protectionism and war in the past, the exporting of the problems of the rich nations to the poor nations, and the destabilization of the world economic system by encouraging dog-eat-dog behavior. They argue for a new international economic order, perhaps even a world currency to replace the dollar and gold. The American predicament here is that the liberal world economy advocated by the United States since World War II has also been an imperial economy; the United States has had the "privilege" of being allowed to carry large balance-of-payments deficits because of the domineering role of the dollar as the world's reserve currency. This country's position in the world economy raises several questions: If a liberal, democratic empire is, indeed, possible, can there be only *one* in the world? If so, who will support the other countries and their right to democracy? Or is democracy reserved for the world's richest countries alone?

One of the most unrecognized aspects of the American predicament is that the citizens of the richest democracy in the world constitute an elite. Americans have tremendous technological, educational, and economic advantages over those in the rest of the world. In a very real sense, Americans do not have to struggle to become equal or to remain equal throughout their lives. This does not mean that great differences between the very rich and the very poor, the successful and the failures do not exist in America. Still, even the very poor in the United States would be considered well off in many countries of the world where people are without the basic necessities of life. Futhermore, America provides opportunities for upward mobility for its poor, however critical one may be of the unjust distribution of such opportunities throughout American society. To be born American, therefore, means to be born with the heavy responsibilities that accompany privilege, to be born with less justification or excuse for failure, and ultimately, to be obligated to attain the highest state of moral achievement and self-realization possible in this fertile environment.

As an elite group, the ultimate American adventure and moral responsibility is to help others to help themselves in other cultures—not imperialistically, not chauvinistically, but humanistically. We must learn the languages of others rather than forcing foreigners to learn English; we must learn to step into the shoes of those not given our educational opportunities, our leisure time, and our prosperous experience. Out intervention must be a sensitive, selfless one that sets an example, not a materialistic, self-righteous ideological stance.

The more sophisticated elites become, the more they exercise their power and privilege by understatement, by an apparent denial of their own self-interest. The extreme example of this maturity is Socrates who knew so much that he claimed to know nothing—a most seductive political posture. As a people who have only recently discovered their elite position relative to others in the world, Americans have been more naïve than innocent. Their leaders have exercised power on their behalf, often in crudely self-righteous and self-interested terms. But the experience of the failure of this country's foreign policy in Southeast Asia has shed some of the American naïveté concerning power and its limits.

The threat of Western decline, the contraction of the American empire abroad, and the frustration of American democracy at home may be countered by a clear-cut New World policy that advocates an open-ended political system of "democratic elitism" domestically and supports the democratization of regimes internationally. Americans must recover respect for their own ideals if they are collectively to maintain their leadership of the Western liberal tradition.

Notes

[1]Bruce Russett, "The Americans' Retreat from World Power," *Political Science Quarterly*, 90, 1 (Spring 1975), 1-21. Also see William Watts and Lloyd A. Free, "Nationalism Not Isolationism," in *Foreign Policy*, No. 24, Fall, 1976.

[2]Samuel Huntington, "The United States," in "The Governability of Democracies," Report to the Trilateral Commission, May 1975. Published as *The Crisis of Democracies*, by Michel Crozier, Samuel Huntington, and Joji Watanuki (New York: New York University Press, 1975).

[3]BBC interview with Aleksandr Solzhenitsyn, broadcast on William Buckley's "Firing Line," Channel 13, March 31, 1976, in New York City.

[4]Peter Schrag, *The End of the American Future* (New York: Simon and Schuster, 1973), pp. 287-306.

[5]This conference was sponsored by the Research Institute on International Change, directed by Zbigniew Brzezinski, at Columbia University on April 7, 1976.

Part I

WHERE AMERICA STANDS

O I see flashing that this America is only you and me,
Its power, weapons, testimony, are you and me,
Its crimes, lies, thefts, defections, are you and me,
Its Congress is you and me, the officers, capitols, armies, ships, are you and me,
Its endless gestation of new states are you and me,
The war (that war so bloody and grim, the war I will henceforth forget), was you
   and me,
Natural and artificial are you and me,
Freedom, language, poems, employments, are you and me,
Past, present, future, are you and me.

I dare not shirk any part of myself,
Not any part of America good or bad. . . .
                                    —*Walt Whitman, "By Blue Ontario's Shore,"*
                                    Leaves of Grass, 1855-1892

2 AMERICAN VALUES AND THE AMERICAN IMAGE

Here are no aristocratic families, no kings, no bishops, no ecclesiastical dominion . . . no great manufacturers employing thousands, no great refinements of luxury . . . not the hostile castle, the haughty mansion . . . a pleasing uniformity of decent competence appears throughout our habitation.

—J. Hector St. John de Crèvecoeur,
"What Is an American,"
Letters from an American Farmer, 1782

and I am waiting
for the American Eagle
to really spread its wings
and straighten up and fly right.

—Lawrence Ferlinghetti,
"A Coney Island of the Mind," 1958

Take care of yourself.

—American colloquialism

Defining what it means to be American has important implications for future American policy at home and abroad. The New World has aged since the early frontier days. The American way of life is now characterized by haughty mansions and great corporations rather than rough-hewn homes and small, independent farms. Technology and wealth have made Americans increasingly dependent upon elites in all aspects of social life. Have these changes in the material conditions of life also affected American values? What *does* it mean to be American today and how do others perceive the American culture and its power?

Traditionally speaking, to be American is to be a rugged individualist through and through, fighting fiercely for one's self-interest and independence and defending the rights of other individuals everywhere to do the same.

Individual freedom, material interest, and self-determination were translated into a political ideology of national freedom, the maximization of capitalist interests, and democratic self-determination. The promise of the American creed became its biggest political problem: to create a society that maintains individual liberty while promoting the equality of opportunity necessary for all to share in this freedom.

The American Dream is a profoundly *individual* dream: every American has the right to create or buy his or her own personal Walden, which will then be protected by the federal government. But for those living in a technological society during an era of economic scarcity, the old American Dream appears to be hopelessly simplistic and outrageously expensive. Only the rich can afford their Waldens. The poor have a hard time finding a job, much less buying a house. And the large middle class is caught between the dream of total independence and the social reality of high taxes, inflation, and the possibility of unemployment. Americans now seem to value individual security more than individual freedom.

Foreigners often misinterpret what it means to be American, seeing the question only from a single-minded, and therefore distorted, point of view. For example, in *The Revolt of the Masses*, philosopher José Ortega y Gasset wrote:

> The characteristic of the hour is that the commonplace mind, knowing itself to be commonplace, has the assurance to proclaim the rights of the commonplace and to impose them wherever it will. As they say in the United States: "to be different is to be indecent." The mass crushes beneath it everything that is different, everything that is excellent, individual, qualified and select. Anybody who is not like everybody, who does not think like everybody, runs the risk of being eliminated.[1]

Here, from a European perspective, Ortega mistakes the image and effects of American democracy for its meaning and values. While correctly noting that the twentieth century has become the age of the masses, he fails to note that America stands for the masses *as individuals*. Superficially, to the foreigner, a certain commonplace bourgeois homogeneity, a group conformity in praise of the average respectable citizen seems to characterize American life. But probing more deeply, one finds a surprising range of opportunity for individual self-expression, development, and nonconformity. In America, conformity is more often a question of choice than of necessity. In their quest for security over individual freedom, many Americans choose not to risk nonconformity. Yet in American society, the penalties for nonconformity are not nearly so great as to rule it out. Indeed, many Americans make successful careers out of criticizing standard American culture and its values. Americans *like* their conformity just as they like their apple pie and evening cocktail. But they *respect* individual distinction, defiant individuality, the successfully different person.

There is, of course, some truth to George Santayana's contention that being American is a career. Most Americans are terribly busy in the process of changing themselves as opposed to taking themselves for granted or accepting a certain state of being, as people in less mobile cultures do. The cultural need to get somewhere—to do something—is ingrained in Americans from birth. But they feel the need to "make it" because their society promises them they can. They are born free to make it, and so most of them set about trying. In other cultures where the social class system is more rigid and social norms more restrictive, individuals often do not have the opportunity to become what they want to become. I remember speaking with a Russian fisherman several years ago in a cafe in Leningrad. He wanted to become a philosopher. In Russia, his chances were slim indeed, but in the United States he might have made it. Eric Hoffer, after all, is a longshoreman three days a week and a philosopher and writer the rest of the time. Many Americans even have the ultimate freedom of choosing not to try to make it. Other peoples are not so fortunate.

Although they look after their individual security in everyday life, Americans are still concerned with freedom. The national split between imperial and democratic values is evident on a personal level in the tug-of-war between the need for bourgeois material security and the need to be free to become what one wants to. The American will to become something spiritually while maintaining material status is both deep-seated and difficult to explain.

Many hypotheses have been advanced to explain how Americans came to have dual spiritual and material longings. The germ theorists stress the importance of the germination of European ideas and values in early American development. Historian Vernon Parrington, for example, has traced the contributions to American thought of English ideas of social and political independence, French romantic theory, and European theories of *laissez faire* and collectivism (born of the Industrial Revolution).[2] The founders of this country were much impressed by the English philosophers Thomas Hobbes and John Locke, for instance. Hobbes saw humans as egotistic individualists who try to ward off death by an endless acquisition of things and whose pursuit of security through private property is protected by the sovereign government. Individuals, in short, give up their right to gain everything to a sovereign ruler, who, in turn, promises them security from the chaos of the natural war of all against all. An even more influential thinker, John Locke, sought to improve upon

Hobbes's plan for law and order and stability by extending the distrust of human nâture even further—to the sovereign himself. Put simply, Locke believed in the separation of executive and legislative power in government so that the executive could not become a tyrant and the democratic majority could not tyrannize the minority. By heeding Montesquieu's advice in adding a third branch, the judicial, Americans developed a system of checks and balances of power to prevent any one individual or group from becoming strong enough to abuse the rights of others. The seeds for conflict between executive elites and democratic representatives of the people were planted in the American political system at the beginning.

In contrast to the emphasis of the germ theorists upon our European heritage, environmental theorists argue that the key to explaining American development is the impact of frontier expansion. What really counts, according to these theorists, is what happened to our forebears in the western woods. Thus, historian Ralph Gabriel focuses on the example of Bill Williams, the lonely trapper, found dead on a winter day in the 1850s, his body reclining against a tree, his feet stretched out toward charred pine logs half buried in the snow. Folk tales had grown up about the successful triumphs of Williams over the hazards of mountains and Indians. Now he had died as he lived, the individualist who had never surrendered his independence and had kept only a faithful mustang for company.[3]

The most influential environmental interpretation of America was Frederick Jackson Turner's frontier thesis, expounded in 1893. Turner claimed that "the existence of an area of free land, its continuous recession, and the advance of American settlement westward explain American development."[4] He argued that America is one country, homogeneous in spite of diversity, and that its internal unity makes it unique. What makes Americans distinctive, he continued, is that they are democratic, individualistic, and unauthoritarian. This unique American character resulted from what *happened* to Americans on the frontier: the experience of interacting with the free land and strong environment in the West made Americans what they are. The frontier, in short, promoted democracy, first in America and then later in Europe, according to Turner.

Henry Nash Smith later showed that Turner's vision was based, in part, upon "the myth of the garden"—the vision of an agrarian utopia in the West. Free land, free expression, and a chance for self-sufficiency were combined to form a social model based upon agriculture and the noble pioneer. Thoreau's ideal of a private Walden became a mass belief, concretized in Turner's thesis and nineteenth-century literature. In *The Virgin Land*, Smith claimed that the frontier myth that motivated Americans was made up of three parts: (1) the belief in and search for the Northwest Passage, which was really the belief in finding good things at the other end of the rainbow; (2) hunter-trapper-expansion mythology, which glorified radical independence in the face of nature's elements; and (3) the search for the Garden of the World, that is, the quest for a second Eden.[5]

But the Americans ran out of western frontier: their garden ran into the sea. What was more natural than to look further westward, to seek new gardens, new candidates for utopia? Hawaii, the Philippines, Guam, and Puerto Rico were not that far away, and many American foreign policy makers at the turn of the last century thought the natives of these lands needed a touch of democratic cultivation. Americans now sought a global garden. The ascent of this country to world power soon brought into focus the tension between democratic liberalism and political and economic imperialism. The limits of America's political and economic growth in the world arena are now becoming apparent, and the threat of such constraints may make the typical American tension between democratic, liberal idealism and material, imperial conservatism even more acute.

Political philosopher H. Mark Roelofs has argued that this tension may be characterized as a conflict between bourgeois ideology and Protestant mythology. The middle-class European emigrants who settled here were Protestant in wanting to save souls through personal acts of faith and bourgeois in desiring to create material wealth through private forms of capitalism. Roelofs wrote:

> To some degree, the two aims complemented each other, at least in practice. The Protestant churches ennobled the private entrepreneur for his virtues of industry and plain living and gave a religious sanction to his thrift. He, in turn, gave generous financial support to their institutions. At the same time, the alliance between Protestant and bourgeois was not easy. Protestantism preached piety, asceticism, otherworldliness. The bourgeois capitalist was, as bourgeois, mostly interested in the competitive race for financial success and industrial power. The result was a tension, a spiritual agony that became a standard motif of novels and plays throughout the liberal world.[6]

The case of the popular support for Jimmy Carter in the 1976 presidential campaign illustrates the bourgeois-Protestant tension that characterizes American liberalism. Carter's visual, spoken, and written image is one of religious goodness and individual moral commitment—the Protestant myth through and through. But underneath this necessarily vague and all-embracing myth, aimed to restore Americans' belief in themselves is a bourgeois ideology of material gain and self-aggrandizement—represented by the tough, operational campaign organization, out to win, whatever that takes. The tension between ideological, bourgeois realism and mythical, Protestant (here evangelical) idealism frustrates many Americans who long for a synthesis, or for more specific stands on certain issues. But the conflict so epitomizes the American mind and mood that Carter easily gathers support from all segments of American society.

Indeed, Carter illustrates other typical American tensions growing out of the antagonistic, yet complementary, bourgeois and Protestant longings: democracy versus security, spiritual quest versus materialism, and the establishment versus counterculture revolution. He appealed in his 1976 campaign to the democratic egalitarian promise of the American dream even at the cost of a reduction of national security through a proposed cutting of the defense budget. Yet simultaneously he maintained that America's defense would remain strong, though lean. His spiritual quest is manifest in his advocacy of virtue, love, and goodness in his political speeches, not to mention a certain independent self-righteousness that smacks of Protestant individualism. But he is nevertheless a shrewd businessman, selling each group what it wants to hear most in terms of its concrete bourgeois interests, and he understates his own power and control by keeping his image linked to the folksy atmosphere of Plains, Georgia, his brother's gas station and his peanut farming boots. Simultaneously, he exploits the counterculture's dislike of Washington, D.C., and the elitist East by maintaining his small-town, Southern, off-beat intellectual image. But this does not deter him from drawing on the technocratic and political expertise that Washington and Eastern intellectuals have to offer. Carter saw the contradictions that made up America, and stitched together a quilted image to match. He knows that power lies in symbolizing "the national mind," that good followership is the prerequisite to charismatic leadership.

It would appear that this Protestant-bourgeois tension will continue to be with us for the indefinite future. Most Americans can identify within themselves a spirit of independent, self-righteous virtue leading to good works which often comes into conflict with a selfish, materialistic desire to maximize their own profit. As times of economic scarcity and political polarization set in, the Protestant-bourgeois tensions that exist in the American populace seem likely to become even more self-evident.

In *People of Plenty*, historian David Potter has argued that material abundance and an unmatched degree of prosperity have always distinguished the American historical experience from that of other societies.[7] If that is so, then Americans are justly upset by recession, unemployment, and the real possibility that economic growth will be limited or even reversed in the future: restricted growth not only hurts the pocketbook but strikes at the very roots of the American promise of free opportunity and unlimited social mobility. Updating de Tocqueville, one could almost say that in the late twentieth century Americans are born free only to become unequal, and that having left a state of democracy, they are becoming increasingly class conscious.

In this sense, a major source of America's economic and social problems in the 1970s is the war in Vietnam. Although it is physically over (with rather disastrous consequences for the American image in the world), we are just beginning to pay its psychological and economic debts. The social burdens fell unequitably upon lower-class minority youth less capable of winning draft deferments. The economy of the 1960s promised prosperity and full employment on shaky grounds—the grounds of war. At war's end, recession struck the weapons industries, and the job market became flooded when the draft ended, soldiers came home, and others who no longer had to dodge the draft by staying in school sought employment.

Although at present some Americans (especially executive policy makers) may feel that something is missing from national life without war, historian David Kennedy has suggested that the absence of war is, in itself, *the* unique feature of American life over the long-term.[8] Kennedy argues that the wars and militarism that have dominated the American experience since 1941 are actually an anomaly in our tradition of pleasant geographic isolation. Moreover, he suggests that American individualism may have arisen in large part because of the traditional freedom of American men from compulsory military service. Whereas Turner argued that the frontier was the factor that stimulated "that buoyancy and exuberance which come with freedom," Kennedy traces this typical American optimism to freedom from conscription and from anxieties about national security. He even argues that the Jeffersonian principle of *laissez faire*, the ideal of small government and decentralized power in a federal system, became a reality more because of the absence of circumstances that made a strong central government necessary than because of extraordinary displays of will and virtue. Kennedy belongs to the same curious but profound school of historical explanation as de Tocqueville and Louis Hartz: what explains Americans most of all is that which they have *not* experienced.

The experiential school of American history is liberal insofar as it assumes that Americans could have become otherwise had they had other experiences. It avoids both the overly deterministic implications of the environmental school (Americans as simple reflections of the frontier) and the overly programed implications of the germ school (Americans as mere imitators of European culture). The classic work of the experiential school in the twentieth century is undoubtedly Louis Hartz's *The Liberal Tradition in America*. Hartz lucidly demonstrates that the success of American policy abroad and the fate of American freedom at home are tied together in an intricate knot:

> It is a principle applicable to all countries, of course, that the struggle for national survival leads to the constriction of internal freedoms. But the American problem is more subtle than this, for the psychic heritage of a nation "born equal" is . . . a colossal liberal absolutism, the death by atrophy of the philosophic impulse. And in a war of ideas this frame of mind has two automatic effects: it hampers creative action abroad by identifying the alien with the unintelligible, and it inspires hysteria at home by generating the anxiety that unintelligible things produce. The redscare, in other words, is not only our domestic problem: it is our international problem as well. When the nation rises to an irrational anticommunist frenzy, it replies to the same instinct which tends to alienate it from Western democratic governments that are "socialist." When it closes down on dissent, it answers the same impulse which inspires it to define dubious regimes elsewhere as "democratic." This is the peculiar link a liberal community forges between the world and domestic pictures: its absolute perspective, its "Americanism."[9]

According to Hartz, it is not just that Americans cannot understand socialist revolution or fascist reaction because they have not experienced them. There is also an absolutism to American liberalism, which prevents Americans from identifying with the social democratic regimes in Europe (supposedly our allies) or from effectively opposing authoritarian military or even fascist regimes throughout the world (in principle, our enemies). American liberalism has become such a rigid creed that it often prevents Americans from knowing who they are and, therefore, from knowing who their true friends abroad are. Ironically, American liberalism prevents Americans from being liberal. The self-defeating fight to preserve their ideological image prevents their living up to that image or modifying it to make it viable in a rapidly changing world.

America's liberal heritage is a paradox that will complicate the decision about the values Americans should hold in the future just as it has complicated American domestic and foreign policies in the past. The paradox, simply stated, is: the promise of the American Declaration of Independence of 1776 is liberal to the point of being revolutionary whereas the reality of the American Constitution of 1789 is conservative to the point of obstructing social change. In the Declaration Thomas Jefferson declared America's independence from Britain, justified by "self-evident truths": that all men are created equal, that they are endowed with unalienable rights (including life, liberty, and the pursuit of happiness), and that governments are instituted to protect these rights deriving their just powers from the consent of the governed. The purpose of the Constitution, on the other hand, was not so much to establish liberty and stimulate the creation of equal rights for all as to ensure stability and prevent any one group from seizing too much power. The Declaration advocated a liberal democratic ideology. The Constitution put constraints upon arbitrary power to prevent any person or group from upsetting the status quo.

Thus American democracy was never intended to be a "pure" democracy any more than American liberalism was intended to be purely liberal. The American Constitution was designed to check and balance the powers of the executive, the legislative, and the judicial branches by separating their functions. Professor Roelofs writes of the Constitution:

> This hard, conservative concern to maintain the status quo arises from a profoundly liberal view that what counts for society is to be understood solely in terms of transactional relationships between individuals, whether persons or corporations. It is also important to remember that in its almost compulsive anxiety to prevent any alterations in the existing balance of social factors, this outlook saw government in unusually negative and restricted terms. *It was to prevent things from happening.* Big states were to remain big, but not at the expense of small ones; that the rich might remain secure in their possessions, the poor were to remain in their poverty; that creditors would receive what was legally due to them, debtors were to remain in debt. *The first concern of politics was to ensure no change.*[10]

From the outset Americans were fated to become schizophrenic in their political liberalism: they would be torn between democracy and security, between the need to support government intervention in order to institute equal rights for all and the need to severely limit the role of government in order to preserve existing social forces and keep private transactions free from government control. No wonder that the political left and political right in America can both justifiably trace their legitimacy to the birth of the nation! No wonder that American foreign policy makers are often ambivalent in deciding whether to support a stable regime or a democratic one! America was born with a call for stability as well as a call for liberty. American liberalism was designed to preserve the power of certain social classes and groups as well as to protect the rights of individuals within them. Many marvel at the stability of the American

Constitution over the past two centuries. They should keep in mind that it was designed to ensure stability before all else.

Past theorists have indicated that the meaning of what it is to be an American today rests upon three interacting elements: our cultural heritage (the germ school), our environmental heritage (the environmental school), and our experiential heritage (the experiential school). To ask which of these elements is the primary one is like asking which is first, the chicken or the egg. Clearly all three elements are involved in the dynamic process of making Americans what they are. The more important question is how these three aspects of the American heritage have changed recently and how they are likely to change in the future. Only then can we perceive what the American image is today and predict what values Americans are apt to believe in tomorrow.

The way the majority of Americans interpret our cultural heritage is changing rapidly in the late twentieth century. The traditional American creed exalted property as the way to life, liberty, and happiness and celebrated competitive struggle as the way to independence and manhood. The Protestant-bourgeois tension was expressed in this "revolutionary" acquisitive creed of our founders, which had its roots in the revolt of English entrepreneurs against the feudal system. Today, however, most Americans believe they have achieved a comfortable middle-class status, and they want to hold on to what they have.[11] The revolutionary creed of making it has been subtly transformed into a conservative ideology of keeping what one has made.

But the majority of Americans no longer trust the government either to help them keep what they have or to intervene effectively for the disenchanted and disinherited. Opinion polls indicate the widespread alienation of the American people from both government and business. Thus, when pollsters asked if the government should take over and run the bankrupt Penn Central railroad, 61 percent opposed such a takeover. The main reason cited was, "As bad as the Penn Central has been run, the government would run it worse."[12] Moreover, the polls of the early 1970s indicated the odds of takeover by the federal government of almost anything in private industry were small and the threat of socialism weak not because of government unpopularity but because no large, low-income mass of people in the country favored such ideas. Indeed, the most conservative group in America was composed of those with incomes of $5,000 and under, since well over half of these were over fifty years old and were fearful and intolerant of change.[13] The effects of the deep recession of the mid-1970s are apt to be more widespread alienation from government and industry, deeper fears of change and insecurity, and perhaps a nostalgic longing for older American traditions and values whose revolutionary elements have been flattened out by time into conservative ritual and national pageantry.

The alienation of the 1960s, manifested in violent reactions to the Vietnam War, urban deterioration, and human inequality, has become more quiet and inward in the 1970s. Alienation today results not so much from the centralized repression of established institutions as from feelings of meaninglessness, powerlessness, normlessness, and isolation. The collective alienation of mass movements a decade ago has given way to the alienation and desperate loneliness of individuals and small groups, from the poor poet to the presidential assassin, from the nuclear family to Charles Manson's "family." Psychologist Rollo May has noted that violence springs from a feeling of powerlessness and is a revolt against meaninglessness.[14] But the violence today is more inward than outward, reflected by the fact that three out of four Americans use illegal drugs and that one family in three has someone with a chronic drinking problem.[15] It is a time when great American poets commit suicide, when students sell out their dreams to get degrees and jobs that pay.

Alienation is often a prerequisite for cultural development. Indeed the dominant psychic fashion among the young beat generation of the 1950s was existential alienation, expressed by Allen Ginsberg's poem "Howl." Protesting against the meaninglessness and powerlessness of Americans caught in a technocratic cage, this initial counterculture movement sought escape from the rational thought and efficiency demanded by modern American society in "feeling first" philosophies, Eastern religious thought, and an outright rejection of the predominant bourgeois life style. The subsequent hippy movement went against the mainstream more gently, espousing love and warmth as well as long hair and producing some of the best poetic folk music American culture has heard to date.

In many ways the moral perceptions of the hippies became the vanguard of a new moral awareness in the population at large: the leftist criticisms of the Vietnam War and Richard Nixon, considered extreme in the 1960s, became obvious moral certitudes after exposure of the Watergate scandal and the disastrous end of the Vietnam episode. Such truths were symbolically recognized among the entire American population when formerly conservative construction workers and businessmen began to wear their hair longer and to sport flowers and color in their dress. Counterculture poet Gregory Corso's poem "Hair" summed up the feelings of many:

I want to grow sideburns!
I want to wash you, comb you, sun you, love you!
as I ran from you wild before—[16]

But then, as art critic Hilton Kramer noted, a cultural backlash—a desire for normalcy and a reaction against the avant-garde experimentalism of the 1960s—set in. [17] Hair was trimmed and hair salons opened to a wave of new business. Counterculture trends were coopted by the theater, art, and entertainment establishment. A revival in classical ballet indicated that the American public was voting with its feet against the problematic, experimentalism of the stage and the emotional discomfort of the cinema—both more concerned with raising consciousness to social problems than with beauty, enjoyment, and technical competence.

Romantic escapism, well-plotted realism, and a reaction against artistic rip-offs characterize a growing conservative trend in the arts and entertainment worlds. That trend is also noticeable in politics, where even the harassed CIA is flooded with job applications from present college graduates. The one lesson that the American public appears to have learned from the counterculture is the pursuit of pleasure—a more refined enjoyment of the status quo while it lasts. The deeper, philosophical messages were lost in an almost decadent reaction and return to tradition, creating an upper-class snobbism uniquely American in its middle-class focus upon sentimentalism, romantic individualism, and the musical. Yet in politics, the more significant meaning of the counterculture was not totally lost—largely because of the evidence provided by the disastrous errors of government elites, particularly in foreign and security affairs.

The split between the truths of the head and the truths of the heart exposed by the counterculture became evident in the so called credibility gap that grew between the technocratic elites of government and big business and the everyday, middle-class working person. In 1973, after years of analyzing public opinion polls in America, Louis Harris summed it up: "Somehow, the leadership of the country has consistently underestimated the public's intelligence, its openness to change, its willingness to abide by a pluralistic set of values, and its growing affluence." [18] As large corporations and the federal government demanded greater and greater technological expertise from those they selected for powerful management positions, the very training required to gain that skill did not seem to allow either the time or sensitivity to develop humanistic values or even the most elementary knowledge of the true feelings, values, and objectives of the majority of Americans. Hard-headed, nonsentimental technocrats were sought to manage the nation's foreign and economic policies whereas ideally American democracy called for warm-hearted brotherhood, the toleration of difference and ignorance, and a certain sense of human sympathy. The counterculture served to make at least some Americans conscious of the contradiction between the values of America's conservative, material interests as an empire and of its tradition of individualism, humanism, and democracy as a republic.

Today the environmental and experiential aspects of American life have become almost inseparable. A century ago, Americans could isolate themselves physically and economically from international events with relative ease. But today economic and environmental problems combine and are felt on both the national and international levels. The heated controversy in the mid-1970s over allowing the English and French supersonic plane, the Concorde, to land in America's main cities is a characteristic example. The decision has implications not only for environmental limits on noise pollution, but also for British and French economic recovery, American-European relations, and even the economic health of poor New York City—not to mention the implications for business people of being able to travel twice as fast to Europe. A complex issue such as this tends to mobilize public concern largely on the basis of the region, industry, or class affected. As America has become more stratified socially, political and economic problems have become more intricate. And rather than striving to understand the complex interactions between domestic and foreign political and economic issues, many Americans seek some sort of personal escape—in home, job, pleasure, or simplistic ideological or religious beliefs. As social scientist Peter Marris has demonstrated, the sense of loss that accompanies the serious personal and social changes of our era leads many people to exercise a "conservative impulse," to feel a deep need to maintain continuity in goals and relationships.[19]

At one time, a great advantage of America's frontier was that it could serve as a safety valve for social problems and frustrations of those with the resources and skills to farm a homestead. Violence could be released in clearing land or in shootouts with Indians and outlaws. Just as Daniel Boone moved westward long ago for what he called "elbow-room," many Americans could seek the basis of their authentic individualism in virgin forests and on uncultivated land, where they could start over again in freedom from social encumbrances and the corruptions of urban life. As the frontiers shrank at home, Americans looked abroad for new opportunities and ways to escape domestic and personal problems: Hawaii, the Phillipines, Guam, Europe in World Wars I and II, Korea, and most recently, Vietnam. There were, of course, significant military, economic, and political reasons for American involvement in all of these instances. But the psychological need for an unending freedom of opportunity, a chance at total self-sufficiency and a restless longing for positive social change should not be underestimated in explaining American motivations. As the old frontier came to an end and the great, expanding American continent became the old, stodgy bureaucratic state, many Americans sought, in political programs such as the New Deal, the New Frontier, and the Great Society, a new chance to forget their losses and botched lives by finding a challenge for their rugged, individualistic spirit.

America's basic task in the future is to redirect this creative, restless energy and productivity, this aggressively rugged individualism, toward social purposes. The new social individualism that should emerge must accept boundaries—territorial, psychological, economic, and political limits. World ecological and economic conditions today make the rugged, independent philosophy of the American frontier impractical if not unethical. There is not enough food, energy, or living space to go around in the world (at least as resources are presently distributed). The ethic of independence must be replaced by an ethic of interdependence: freedom through sharing with others rather than freedom from others should be the primary value. New World idealism and individualistic energy must be nurtured but redirected toward the social needs of the disadvantaged at home and abroad. Americans can have a positive influence upon where the world is going by setting a humanistic example of solving social problems. Or they can retire prematurely as individuals and as a nation, isolating themselves in a fortress, stopping social mobility at home and foreign assistance abroad, throwing both social duty and world power to the winds in a final, selfish, imperial splurge of pleasure.

Many American idealists, having turned to domestic affairs after the Vietnam debacle, found that establishing social justice at home presents an even more intractable problem than dealing with foreign affairs and brings less immediate pleasure. And the trend threatens to turn back toward what may be termed foreign policy hedonism: the luster of grand policy, shiny weapons, exotic countries, and international finance make policy making for the elite in control seem like an individual's pleasure machine. It was Kissinger, after all, who noted that "power is the ultimate aphrodisiac." Meanwhile the real, painful problems of working out social reforms and a viable political economy at home continue to be ignored. Foreign policy has become a form of escapism.

The culture ethos of America today seems apparent. But what will it mean to be American tomorrow? How is the American culture apt to be transformed, and what American values will change in the process? These questions, once considered too philosophical to be taken seriously by scientists or policy makers, have now come to center stage in American development and planning.

In 1966 Professor Nicholas Rescher sent out questionnaires to fifty-eight scientists to find out how American values were likely to change by 2000 A.D.

These scientists were an optimistic group, no doubt buoyed by the economic boom of the mid-1960s as well as by their native American (and scientific) spirit. Nevertheless, their projections are intriguing. They did not believe Americans were losing their commitment to values or that American values were being degraded. They thought, instead, that American values were becoming more and more social and less and less individual, that social injustices worry Americans more than individual ones. Yet, at the same time they believed there would be a strengthening of "selfish" values—personal pleasure, physical comfort, economic security, leisure—an increased devotion to cultural and esthetic values, as well as an emphasis on man-oriented, as opposed to God-oriented, values such as social justice, peace, internationalism. And they believed that these value changes would be affected less by technological developments (except in biomedicine) than by social and political movements.[20]

A heated debate has broken out between optimistic and pessimistic forecasters of America's future. The optimists, or the postindustrial elitists, believe that new technologies and human flexibility make a more affluent world possible. They agree with Rescher's group of scientists that the world will be increasingly dominated by secular and humanistic values. The pessimists, the limited-growth fatalists, argue, on the other hand, that population growth and human needs will soon outstrip the earth's resources and human capacity to produce, threatening to lead to a world catastrophe in the near future.

The limited-growth fatalists belong to a modern branch of the environmental school of explaining America: Americans will become the fall-out of an environmental catastrophe, which will occur within the next 50 to 150 years unless the world system is drastically changed, an unlikely possibility in their view. This dour forecast, which the Club of Rome popularized in its first report, *The Limits to Growth*, can be called neo-Malthusian.[21] In his 1798 essay on population, Malthus noted that while population grows geometrically (more people each year producing more people exponentially), food supply can only grow arithmetically. Eventually the food supply will be totally used up by the growing population. Using a similar argument, the modern, computerized limited-growth fatalists (who have become most popular with well-to-do minorities in rich countries) argue that unlimited population growth rates will overwhelm fixed limits of resources. Moreover, they argue that as capital investment is increased to help alleviate problems by producing more in industry and agriculture, pollution will increase exponentially. The neo-Malthusians draw conservative and pessimistic conclusions from these projections. Human beings will soon use up most of their food and mineral resources, and the earth will not give them much in the future no matter how hard they try to delay crises with new technologies. The rich countries, in order to maintain their threatened standard of living in a no-growth situation, will exploit the poor countries; the rich-poor gap will increase hopelessly, leading inevitably to a world-wide class war. Neo-Malthusian economics can easily become the basis for Social Darwinism in politics: it is only just and proper that the strong survive and the weak be allowed to die off in order to bring human needs and global resources back into equilibrium. The rugged frontier is everywhere and might makes right.

The optimistic postindustrial elitists disagree with this view. Basically, they argue that population growth will not be unlimited in the future and that food supply will grow at a greater rate than population. Moreover, they point out that technology will not remain constant and that human beings with their infinite flexibility will find substitutes for resources that threaten to dry up. Anthony J. Wiener, a leading postindustrial elitist, criticizes the political and philosophical effects that limited-growth fatalism projects:

> The idea of the limits of growth is more a problem in the sociology of ideas than in economics and ecology. It is important to ask: why is this such a popular, appealing notion at this time? We have so many more real, pressing problems, such as: weapons of mass destruction, poverty, inequality of income, unintended consequences of technology and strains caused by rapid social change. Well-educated, intelligent and affluent groups within industrial, affluent countries—those who are best able to contribute to the solution of these problems, if they are willing to pay the price—currently regard themselves as limited and are least likely to act.[22]

The only alternative, argues Wiener (and other postindustrial elitists), is to accept the inevitability of social engineering, even given its possible dangerous abuses, and turn over our social problems to technological and educational experts, elites who will head off catastrophe with new discoveries and more effective social controls. Knowledge is power and the knowledgeable should be given the power to do human good.

Superficially, the main dispute between the limited-growth fatalists and post-industrial elitists seems to be merely over the question of whether America and the world have run out of frontier (and the resources it implies) or whether human intelligence and technology can create new artificial frontiers to solve our problems and feed the starving. But this debate on the ecological and technological limits and values of America's future has profound implications for social planning and the possibility of democracy's very existence.

By advocating a focus on growth and technological expertise above all else, the postindustrial elitists point toward a social policy of total, capitalistic elitism in which the rich become enormously richer, pulling up the poor to make them moderately better off on the way, increasing the GNP and economic pie even at the expense of equality, social justice, and democratic representation. The thrust is toward creating a strong, imperial America with an expanding economy and a "new mandarin" elite of technocrats who possess unlimited powers and will presumably solve the problems of America and the world.

In stark contrast, the limited-growth fatalists envision a future social policy that is more concerned with distribution of existing advantages than with growth, more mass-oriented than elite-oriented. If the possibilities of economic and technological growth are limited—or, even worse, approaching zero—then the main political question is how to redistribute the decreasing pie more equitably: the rich will not get richer, but the poor will become so poor as to become desperate, starving to death by the thousands or lashing out in ineffective spurts of violence against the rich elites. The concern for democratic controls by the masses of technological and political power will become dominant, even if that means sacrificing imperial power and growth on the way. Social justice, equality, and democracy will become the paramount issues as suspicions of elite abuses of economic and political power increase, undermining the existing social system.

Perhaps a more important issue than the extent to which economic growth will occur, in terms of American values, is the attitude of the public toward economic growth and business in general. Norman Macrae, deputy editor of *The Economist*, surveyed attitudes about America's prospects in the third century and noted ominously:

> It would be impertinent for a foreigner to object to America's creeping ethic of anti-dynamism if it had merely sprung from American selfishness. When you have a GNP per head over $7,000 a year, you naturally begin to regard growing much richer as a bit of a bore—although American Christians and humanists should be reminding zero-growth Americans that, by discontinuing their own industrial dynamism which has helped so much to drive world technology up through the bud, they could cruelly reduce the forward prospects of the 2 billion angry people on incomes under $200 a year with whom we share this rather small planet. But the real horror today is that America is not going slowly stagnationist out of selfishness. On campuses across the continent, a peculiarly innumerate anti-growth cult is being taught to a generation of idealistic kids as if it was high moral philosophy, or even a religion.[23]

Macrae concludes that just as the British Empire declined in the late nineteenth century because of growing disbelief in the importance of economic dynamism, entrepreneurship, and money making, the American empire is apt to decline in its third century because of increasing upper-class snobbism, which looks down upon the business culture, entrepreneurship, and economic growth. He projects that increasing bureaucracy, class stratification, and social and ecological pressures may slow American economic growth unnecessarily and lead to a shift of world power, with this country losing leadership to less sophisticated elites at a fateful moment of historical transition. Optimistic about the real potential for American economic and technological growth and the benefits it could bring the world, Macrae notes that "industrophobia" and antibusiness attitudes are apt to suffocate this potential. They have already led to a relatively lower rate of growth in manufacturing output in the United States as compared to other industrialized nations.[24]

The fate of American democracy and world power seems to depend increasingly upon political economy, upon how and why Americans are motivated to work and produce for themselves and for others. Democracy or elitism, growth or economic stagnation, freedom or social equality—these are the critical issues whose resolution will shape America's future. How America's values in the past will relate to American values in the future ultimately turns into a debate over capitalism and socialism.

Notes

[1]José Ortega y Gasset, *The Revolt of the Masses* (New York: W. W. Norton, 1932), p. 18.

[2]Vernon Louis Parrington, *Main Currents in American Thought* (New York: Harcourt Brace Jovanovich, 1927).

[3]Ralph Henry Gabriel, *The Course of American Democratic Thought* (New York: Ronald Press, 1940), p. 3.

[4]F. J. Turner, *The Early Writings of Frederick Jackson Turner*, compiled by Everett E. Edwards (Madison, Wisc.: University of Wisconsin Press, 1938), p. 186. I am indebted to Professor H. Mark Roelofs for this interpretation of Turner.

[5]Henry Nash Smith, *Virgin Land—The American West as Symbol and Myth* (Cambridge, Mass.: Harvard University Press, 1950).

[6]H. Mark Roelofs, *The Language of Modern Politics* (Homewood, Ill.: Dorsey Press, 1967), p. 255. See also H. M. Roelofs, *Ideology and Myth in American Politics* (Boston: Little, Brown, 1976).

[7]David Potter, *People of Plenty: Economic Abundance and the American Character* (Chicago: University of Chicago Press, 1968,).

[8]David M. Kennedy, "War and the American Character," *The Nation*, May 3, 1975, pp. 522-526.

[9]Louis Hartz, *The Liberal Tradition in America* (New York: Harcourt Brace Jovanovich, 1955), p. 285.

[10]Roelofs, *The Language of Modern Politics*, p. 230. My italics.

[11]Demonstrated in public opinion polls; see William Watts and Lloyd Free, *State of the Nation* (New York: Universe Books, 1973).

[12]Louis Harris, *The Anguish of Change* (New York: W. W. Norton, 1973), p. 11.

[13]*Ibid.*, p. 36.

[14]Rollo May, *Power and Innocence: A Search for the Sources of Violence* (New York: W. W. Norton, 1972).

[15]Harris, *The Anguish of Change*, pp. 4-5.

[16]Gregory Corso, "Hair," in *The Happy Birthday of Death* (New York: New Directions, 1960), p. 16.

[17]Hilton Kramer, "A Yearning for 'Normalcy'—The Current Backlash in the Arts," *The New York Times*, May 23, 1976.

[18]Harris, *The Anguish of Change*, p. x.

[19]Peter Marris, *Loss and Change* (New York: Random House, 1974).

[20]Nicholas Rescher, "A Questionnaire Study of American Values by 2000 A.D.," in *Values and the Future: The Impact of Technological Change on American Values* (New York: Free Press, 1969), pp. 133-147.

[21]The most notorious limited-growth fatalists are Donella H. Meadows, Dennis Meadows, Jorgen Randers, and William Behren III, authors of *The Limits to Growth,* a report for the Club of Rome's *The Prediction of Mankind* (New York: Universe Books, 1972). The Club of Rome has since changed its tune and has argued for selective growth in more recent reports—supposedly a calculated strategy of consciousness raising.

[22]Anthony Wiener, "The Future of Economic Activity," *The Future Society: Aspects of America in the Year 2000*, an issue of *The Annals of the American Academy of Political and Social Science*, 408 (July 1973) pp. 53-54. For other examples of the postindustrial elitist position, see Daniel Bell, *The Coming of Post-Industrial Society* (New York: Basic Books, 1973); Herman Kahn and Anthony Wiener, *The Year 2000* (New York: Macmillan, 1967); and Herman Kahn *et al.*, *The Next 200 Years* (New York: William Morrow, 1976).

[23]Norman Macrae, "America's Third Century," *The Economist*, October 25, 1975, p. 8, Survey.

[24]*Ibid.*, p. 11, Survey.

3 CAPITALISM, SOCIALISM, AND LIBERALISM

Socialism: You have two cows, and you give one to your neighbor.
Communism: You have two cows, the government takes both of them and gives you milk.
Fascism: You have two cows, the government takes both of them and sells you milk.
Nazism: You have two cows, the government takes both of them and shoots you.
Bureaucracy: You have two cows, the government takes both of them, shoots one of them, milks the other and pours the milk down the drain.
Capitalism: You have two cows, you sell one of them and buy a bull.
—The New York Times, *September 14, 1975*

Americans are caught between the shortcomings of capitalism and the supposed threats of socialism. On the one hand, many see capitalism as an obstacle to individual equality and social justice; on the other, socialism appears to threaten individual freedom and initiative. Capitalism is held up as the motor of American economic and military power, while socialism promises equal opportunity and social justice. Which is worse: the oppression of the state or the tyranny of the majority? Is meaningful individualism possible in modern America?

The social revolutions of the 1960s and the economic recession of the 1970s have helped to initiate a search in America for a new form of political economy that goes beyond traditional free-market capitalism and yet stops short of state socialism. But, when looking for a new path at home, it is difficult to export a coherent ideology abroad. It remains to be seen whether this emerging political economy will ultimately destroy American power in the world by splintering its base at home or will become an effective basis for democracy that can be used as a powerful political and economic tool abroad.

Recently a group of students in Indianapolis showed copies of the Declaration of Independence to several hundred people and asked them to sign it. Most refused. Some thought it sounded dangerous. The talk of equality and natural inalienable rights to life, liberty, and the pursuit of happiness—not to mention the right to revolt against a government suppressing these basic rights—sounded too radical to many Americans, especially those that were relatively well off. Rapid social change was bringing Americans enough future shock without stirring up more trouble.

The United States has become older, fatter, more sophisticated, and cynical. In an age when the American empire is threatened with decay, many Americans have replaced the revolutionary ideals of the Declaration with their own pragmatic, conservative creed: Live and let live. In times of recession, inflation, and unemployment, people want to know what equality and social justice will cost *them*. Those on the right calculate what they might lose by a certain change; those on the left determine which changes will bring them the most benefits the fastest. Whether on the right or the left, people are turning from ideals to costs.

The main questions today are: Which form of political economy—capitalism or socialism—costs more? And which kinds of cost—economic, social, political, or moral—are least tolerable? In supporting R. E. Herrmann's conclusion that "Capitalism appeals to those with a winner's instinct, and Socialism to the losers," Fritz Zorn of Koblenz, Germany, wrote:

> This is exactly what Karl Marx claimed. It is the basis of all his teachings. He only added that in capitalism the winners are few and the losers are many, and that at a certain point of development and polarization, quantity may change into quality; i.e., the many may reject a system in which they, as the absolute majority, are always bound to be the losers. Since this can and will be done only by the majority, the process will be a democratic one. This is the essence of democratic socialism as represented by Willy Brandt, Austrian Chancellor Kreisky, Swedish Prime Minister Palme, Portuguese leader Soares and others.[1]

Zorn's notion that only a few win and most lose is overdrawn in that millions of people live well, at least materially, under capitalism, which no other prior economic system could claim; if he is referring merely to inequality of income, "losers" is the wrong word. But sympathy for losers or underdogs in the socioeconomic sense is an important aspect of the social climate a political economy creates. In this regard capitalist societies do appear to be overly enthralled with their winners and superstars. Using Zorn's terminology, we might rephrase the initial question: Which economic system—capitalism or socialism—can provide a technological democracy like America with more winners and with least cost to the losers?

The modern debate between capitalism and socialism is not accidental.

The effectiveness of these two forms of political economy in the twentieth century has established them as competitive models of national development in the Western world, and, to a lesser extent, even in non-Western developing countries. They differ, however, in how they achieve their effectiveness and what consequences follow for individual equality and freedom.

The effectiveness of the capitalist system stems from its realistic emphasis upon self-interest and the profit motive as the major incentives for private, and therefore public, economic growth. Self-interest and accumulation are its means; individual freedom of choice with respect to jobs, means of production, and life styles are its ends.

In contrast, the effectiveness of the socialist system stems from the total collective control by elites of the state's economy. Centralization and collective control are its means; individual equality, social justice, and stability are its ends.

The dilemma of the twentieth century is that both the capitalist and socialist forms of political economy have been shown to be inadequate. Modern corporate capitalism fans inflation and social injustice by encouraging a class disparity of wealth and income; state socialism stimulates repression and limits economic growth by permitting insensitive decisions by centralized authorities.

Capitalism naturally complemented the original American values of rugged individualism and continual self-improvement through the pursuit of self-interest and upward mobility. Indeed, if Adam Smith had not published *The Wealth of Nations*, the bible of modern capitalism, in 1776, one of our Founding Fathers would most likely have invented it—or a similar theory of political economy. In *The Wealth of Nations* the Scottish philosopher argued for self-interest—the "uninterrupted effort of every man to better his condition"— as the great motivator of economic activity. Individuals are driven by this mechanism to produce the goods and services society needs. The butcher, baker, and brewer provide substance for our dinner table not out of benevolence but out of the rational pursuit of their own self-interest. If they became inefficient or unneeded they would justly go out of business. The free market and the money of consumers would thus lead to a self-regulating pattern of production and need satisfaction. And each businessman in seeking his own profit, would be "led by an invisible hand to promote an end which was no part of his intentions," the common good.[2]

Moreover, since the free market of Smith's system was presumably self-regulating, he advocated *laissez faire*, or government restraint from intervening in the free market or regulating trade. He thought that unfair monopolistic conspiracies among businesses usually take place with government assistance. But we have since learned that monopolies can develop either with government help or without it—with detrimental effects for the free market and the common good.

The Wealth of Nations became so popular that it went through five editions in Smith's lifetime (at about $65 a copy), and thousands of copies are still sold each year. Initially, it stimulated one of the greatest eras of economic growth and accumulation of private wealth in history, culminating in the flowering of the Industrial Revolution in the nineteenth century. But, of course, not everyone got rich. Thousands, including small children, worked intolerably long hours in sweatshops. Small cottage workshops were destroyed and replaced with large industrial plants and dehumanizing working conditions. Charles Dickens's novel *Hard Times* lucidly describes the terrible conditions the Industrial Revolution produced in English cities. Rugged individualism became very rugged indeed for many. Some, such as Thomas Hill Green in England, began to worry about the human consequences of a public philosophy that rewarded individuals more for individual selfishness than for service to the community. In his *Principles of Political Obligation*, Green expressed moral outrage at a society that withheld from many of its members the goods, partly material but chiefly spiritual, which the culture of that society created.

Others were much more outspoken and specific. In 1848 Karl Marx and Frederick Engels protested, in *The Communist Manifesto*, that although capitalism had created more massive productive forces than all preceding generations put together, it led to dehumanization and worker exploitation. Marx believed that capitalism would eventually destroy itself as more goods were produced than the small wages of the workers could buy. One of his theses was that capitalism tends inevitably to crisis because capitalistic planning is anarchic and there is nothing to prevent an overconcentration of production in certain areas to the detriment of others. Furthermore, he suggested that the workers' standard and condition of living would worsen relative to that of the capitalist managing class. History has since contradicted this prediction: the condition of workers greatly improved with the wealth of capitalism. This error is critical, for Marx projected that the condition of workers would become so miserable that a revolution of the working class would overthrow the capitalists and establish a utopian socialist system. However, Marx did perceptively predict both the rise of large, oligopolistic corporations that would consolidate wealth and markets and the coming of cyclical depressions that would violently disrupt smooth capitalist growth patterns (like the depressions of the 1870s and 1930s and the recession of the 1970s). Despite his errors, it could well be that dogmatic

American liberalism has caused capitalist managers to ignore Marx at their own expense, forgetting the old adage that to defeat an enemy it is best to know him well first.[3]

The American political economy began to shift away from *laissez-faire* capitalism with Theodore Roosevelt's New Nationalism program and in the first administration of Woodrow Wilson. Reacting against the domination of large corporations and banks, after his election in 1912, Wilson created the Federal Reserve Act to supplant the so called dictatorship of private banks with a public board. He also convinced Congress to pass the Clayton Antitrust Act, which prohibited injunctions in labor disputes unless needed to stave off irreparable damage, thus affirming that labor strikes and boycotts were not violations of the law. The principle of free competition was modified by the principle of fair competition. Wilson tried to translate the American liberal creed into an economic liberalism adapted to the social changes of the modern industrial world. In foreign policy, he translated the conflict between bourgeois and Protestant beliefs within American liberalism into the agony between America's manifest economic destiny, or the right to intervene in foreign markets, and American messianism, or the right to make the world safe for democracy. Wilson changed his foreign policy from one of ascetic isolationism prior to World War I to one of violent American interventionism to save the world for democracy.[4]

American principles of capitalism underwent further modifications with the coming of the Great Depression, which inspired the ideas of John Maynard Keynes. This British economist argued that economic slumps could be reversed through government interventions to increase purchasing power. By cutting taxes, increasing government spending, and producing more money (creating a certain amount of controllable inflation), governments could stimulate free economies to produce at normal levels. Although Keynes's theories of government stimulus helped to bring the country out of the Depression (mainly by means of the government's wartime military spending), when things were moving again, everyone forgot the other side of Keynes: when an economic boom sets in, the government must increase taxes, cut federal spending, and initiate a tight money policy to keep inflation under control. These depressive measures are politically unpopular, and during the boom of the 1960s politicians did not institute them. Keynes thus modified original American capitalism by showing that without considerable government intervention, capitalist incentives alone do not seem to be able to pull a national economy out of depressions and recessions or to deflate economic booms to control inflation. In modern industrial societies, individual freedom of choice does not appear to lead automatically to economic and social harmony. To many Americans, such thinking resembles socialism in the worst sense of that term. They perceive threats to traditional, free-market capitalism by governmental controls, eventually even economic and political anarchy. They read the change from liberal capitalism to democratic socialism in terms of loss, not positive purpose and planning; they believe the fabric of national morale and tradition is being torn apart.

In *Between Capitalism and Socialism* economist Robert Heilbroner predicts that regardless of the strains to which the capitalist system is subjected, it will remain the dominant form of political economy in America and Western Europe during our lifetimes, whereas some form of socialism will be the predominant economic system in most of the rest of the world. Furthermore, he suggests that any large-scale attempts to project social trends should be based on these assumptions. At the core of all capitalist societies, Heilbroner sees a business system, characterized by a basically uncontrolled market system and private ownership of the means of production. He notes, "Whatever their incompatibilities in culture or lifestyles, Buddenbrooks and Babbitt were both businessmen, and as such they understood and shared important common activities and values and goals."[5] Heilbroner characterizes socialist societies, on the other hand, as dominated by some form of planning, guided by a socialist ideology that corresponds to the business ideology in capitalism. The difference between the two ideologies, he claims, is that capitalism is conservative, concerned mainly with justifying the existing economic order: "No capitalist nation or philosopher or economist has any grand designs for the fundamental reshaping of society through capitalism."[6] To the extent Heilbroner is right (to a large extent, I believe), capitalism may be in very deep trouble. For if it cannot become an instrument of change and social development in a time of economic crisis and social demands, it may soon be thrown upon the rubbish pile of history.

Even the strongest proponents of the capitalist system are now aware of the critical need for philosophers of capitalism to help solve the problems of this individualistic political economy. Many had their capitalist consciousnesses raised by the lucid pen of Peter Drucker, the management specialist. As early as 1946 Drucker argued, in his *Concept of the Corporation*, that the best friends of American capitalism were its best critics—those bent on showing the system's imperfections in order to make capitalism and corporations effective instruments of social change. Indeed, in noting that the ability of the Soviet Union to realize a stable "socialism in one country" was a precondition for Russian collaboration in the maintenance of world peace, Drucker wrote:

We will now have to learn that similarly the ability of the United States to participate in the maintenance of peace in a world of Great Powers, based upon competing principles of political and social order, depends on our ability to create a successful, stable and confident "capitalism in one country." . . . To make our free-enterprise system function—as the basis of domestic strength and unity and as a model for others—is the most important and the most immediate contribution Americans can make to international peace.[7]

If capitalism is the basis of American individualism and world power, its adaptability to rapid change will be one critical measure of America's capacity to be a healthy democracy and effective world power at the same time. From Wilson's era through the Cold War of the 1950s to the present, Americans have defined themselves in contrast to Soviet and other kinds of socialism. They have perceived socialism as anathema and taken free-market capitalism for granted as the basis of their domestic liberty and foreign policy rhetoric. But Americans can no longer afford to take capitalism for granted. Purists would argue that we have already left capitalism behind and now have a mixed form of economy, best described as state or welfare capitalism in which the state controls much of the liquid capital and therefore most public policy decisions. Critics would argue that classical capitalism has revealed hopeless contradictions between freedom, productivity, and equality in the crisis of the 1970s and that, since no one has forwarded solutions to these contradictions or viable alternatives, capitalism will drift inevitably into some type of socialism because of domestic political pressures: the age of equality has replaced the age of profit. No matter which side one is on ideologically, it is obvious that to have a healthy democratic society at home and a strong, clear-cut foreign policy abroad one must have an effective political economy consistent with the needs and values of the majority of people in the nation.

With their heritage of rugged individualism, antiauthoritarian distrust of the state, and individual freedom of choice, Americans seem fated to base their future planning on the assumption of individual freedom. But the reform of capitalism requires mitigation of the unjust extremes that often emerge from rugged individualism and the profit motive. Some form of social capitalism is needed that would permit certain kinds of social planning for the future consistent with the humanistic promises of the American creed. And this new form of political economy is apt to be more viable as an ideology at home and abroad in the future if it is not called capitalism. The socialists, after all, originated the term "capitalism" to describe Adam Smith's "system of natural freedom"; today, the word has become as much of a hated relic of the past as "colonialism." To cling to such old rhetoric and the rigid ideology it suggests is self-defeating politically both at home and abroad. Alternative visions of political economy more appropriate for our times must be developed.

Once upon a time there were three utopias: Rawlsville, Nozickland, and Randia. Each was based on a different idea of individualism, each subscribed to a different kind of political economy, each wanted to become *the* utopia that would drive the others out of competition.

Rawlsville, otherwise known as the Land of Ignorance or the Land of the Virtuous Veil, was the most well known of these utopias. It was visited by the most sophisticated intellectuals of the time who praised its elegant simplicity, gothic complexity, and monumental achievement. Many thought it to be the golden land of equality, the fairest land of all. For the people of Rawlsville never transcended their original position of ignorance, and everyone knows that ignorance is bliss.

Each person in Rawlsville was totally unaware of his or her own abilities, talents, or social and economic background. In short, no one knew of anyone else's natural or social advantages, and so no one was more gifted or favored than another. It was a land of perfect justice and of absolute equality of income. Then one day visitors began to drift into Rawlsville. They took rooms, stayed on, and grew to like the place. They wanted to become permanent residents, absolute Rawlsians through and through.

This posed a grave problem for the natives of Rawlsville. For unlike themselves, the visitors knew what they represented, what natural gifts they possessed, what social and economic background they had come from. The absolute equality was threatened by the entrance of inequality, by the unveiling of knowledge.

However, as an extremely intelligent and absolutely rational group, the Rawlsians soon came to a unanimous decision: each of the foreigners would be rank-ordered in Rawlsville in such a way as to maximize the prospects of the least advantaged. The dumb, the blind, the poor, and the weird were quickly installed as leading elites in Rawlsian society. The bright, the beautiful, the rich, and the healthy were given the lowest possible clean-up positions at the bottom of the social ladder. Furthermore, to maintain this state of equality, the foreigners were forbidden to change their places in society or to speak to anyone about their former knowledge of their unequal gifts or backgrounds. As time passed, equal incomes reduced productivity until none could be distinguished in his poverty from any other. In Rawlsville to be unequal was not to be free, to be knowledgeable of one's personal differences was to be unhappy. Happiness began and ended behind the veil of ignorance.[8]

Next door to Rawlsville was Nozickland, an anti-Rawlsian utopia established by an angry young group of conservatives who believed more in individual freedom than collective equality. Each of these tall blonde individualists was an entrepreneur who strode throughout the countryside selling protection policies to fearful inhabitants. Thus the state of Nozickland arose as if created by an invisible hand, each entrepreneur helping to create the state unintentionally in pursuit of his or her own self-interest. The laws of the land provided that this state's power be limited to providing protection against force, theft, and fraud, and to enforcing contracts. As long as no one invaded the rights of others, each person was to be secure in his or her person or liberty or property. Of course many fearful little people sold themselves into voluntary slavery to large, rugged individualists who were strong enough to hold their own. Justice in the society was by entitlement, which meant that all had a right to keep what they had under the present distribution of goods and holdings, but no one—especially not the state—could take entitlements (or property) away from others. This was a land of possessive individualism where each got what he or she could earn, protected by the state. Happiness went to the strong, the beautiful, the rich, and the gifted.[9]

Beyond both Rawlsville and Nozickland, in an agricultural belt, was Randia. Here one hundred hungry people gathered and discovered agriculture. They obeyed two absolutes of nature: to save enough of their harvest to feed themselves until the next harvest and to save enough seeds—stock seeds—to plant during the next season. They learned that the two basic concepts that distinguished them from the hunters and made their lives more stable were time and savings, and that savings can buy time when one is hungry or unlucky.

One day these self-sufficient, productive farmers had saved more grain than they could store without spoiling. So they invented a commodity which would keep longer and which they could trade for grain when necessary: money. Money, the tool of saving that permits delayed consumption and buys time for future production, must be imperishable, rare, homogeneous, easily stored, not subject to wide shifts of value, and always in demand. The Randian farmers used gold coins for their money. Their system worked perfectly: each person lived by his or her own competence at farming and knowing the value of time, savings, money, and the will to produce.

One year an apparently rich man with a long white beard and a red-white-and-blue top hat came to Randia and promised to buy the community's excess grain if he could trade on their market with paper promissory notes backed by future production instead of gold coins. In fact, this man did not produce at all.

He merely took the grain and consumed it or gave it away to others in other communities. He kept paying the Randians higher and higher prices, paying in promissory notes, arguing always that he was their best customer.

A short while later a young farmer, who had been wiped out by a flood, asked to borrow grain from others in the community, but their prices had gone up and they did not have enough grain to spare. So the young farmer went bankrupt. A dairy farmer to whom he owed money raised her prices to make up for the loss; a trucker who needed milk gave up his chickens that he could no longer afford because of the rise in milk prices; an alfafa grower who couldn't afford the higher egg prices, sold some of her stock seed, cut down her planting and canceled her order for a plow with a blacksmith, who went bankrupt. And all of these Randians then presented their promissory notes at the same time to the white-bearded best customer, who told them that they were no longer worth anything since they were promissory notes not on *his* future production but *theirs*. But the Randians could produce nothing further and were left with only their land, empty equipment, no stock seed to plant, and an even diminishing food supply.

Suddenly the Randians realized they had been wiped out by inflation: they had naïvely allowed the white-bearded customer—the government—to give them rubber checks. The government had mortgaged their future without their consent, for the promissory notes were based on the future tax receipts of the farmers—their future production. They had been duped into thinking that it was the number or wealth of consumers that made their production possible rather than the natural laws limiting their production or the quality of their products. By extending too much credit they had extended their own savings, bringing on inflation and bankruptcy. The law of supply and demand had been violated by allowing artificial credits and by creating artificial demands. Disguised as altruism, the government had subverted their economic system, bit by bit, appealing to their greed and their longing for a false security. Moreover, the government had slowly consumed all of the country's stock seed, the savings needed to keep production going. All that was left for future generations was nonedible paper, trucks full of paper, paper that spread from Randia to other communities until inflation and recession plagued them all. [10]

The sad fables illustrating these three utopian possibilities focus attention on a classical dilemma in political thinking: the inverse relationship between individual freedom and social equality. Many political thinkers argue that the more equality that exists in a state, the less freedom a citizen has, and vice versa. Thus, Rawlsville advocates the maximum of social equality, but destroys the opportunity and freedom of citizens to choose their way of life. It is based upon an influential book by John Rawls, a Harvard philosophy professor, called *A Theory of Justice*. The critical thesis is Rawls's "difference principle" by which he means that the only justifiable basis for any inequality is that it maximize the prospects of the least advantaged.

Novickland, on the other hand, begins with the assumption of maximum individual freedom, allowing "equal justice" only for those who are presently entitled to it—the advantaged. It is based on another influential book by a Harvard philosophy professor, Robert Nozick's *Anarchy, State and Utopia*. In contrast to the distributive theory of justice behind the difference principle of Rawls, Nozick posits an entitlement theory of justice, which holds that the state is justifiable only to the extent that it enforces what people are already legally entitled to.

The dystopia of Randia illustrates what supposedly happens if a government aims for Rawlsville rather than Novickland: government intervention, disguised as altruism for the disadvantaged, mortgages the future of the productive people in society, leading to inflation, recession, and bankruptcy. It is based on the capitalist libertarian philosophy of Ayn Rand, who has extolled the virtues of individual selfishness in her novels *The Fountainhead* and *Atlas Shrugged*, as well as in her nonfiction works, such as *The Ayn Rand Letter*. Originally a Russian immigrant (with some similarities to Solzhenitsyn in her devotion to individual freedom, expressed beautifully in her novel *Anthem*), Rand takes the extreme capitalist stance of arguing that each person deserves the total reward for his or her competence and productivity and that any other principle of society works to enslave creative producers to immoral incompetents and mindless bureaucrats of the state. The relevance of Ayn Rand's views to America's future was made clear when President Gerald Ford appointed Alan Greenspan, a fervent believer in Randianism, as his main economic advisor.

Utopian (and dystopian) thinking has the advantage of flushing out one's values, pinning down one's starting points and ultimate aims. By oversimplifying reality it stimulates people to identify their values and put them in order. But the problem with America's future is that most Americans want both freedom *and* equality and are not willing, as abstract philosophers are, to clearly stand for one over the other. They find themselves in the dilemma of Buridan's ass, the donkey who stood between two tempting bales of hay and starved to death because it could not choose. Must Americans arbitrarily choose either equality or freedom as a priority? Or is there some reasonable compromise, some criterion of choice that goes beyond the arbitrary?

In his book, *Equality and Efficiency: The Big Trade-off*, economist Arthur Okun argues that a free-market economy creates an undesirable degree of economic and social inequality and that government must intervene to trade off some efficiency for somewhat greater equality. Yet, he points out that a free market is superior in efficiency to all species of statist planning. In criticizing Okun (while admiring his moderation), Irving Kristol justly remarks that the more important trade-off is the one between equality and freedom, not equality and efficiency. Even more to the point, Kristol argues that like other versions of egalitarianism, Okun's is flawed by a misconception of the relation between the ideal and the real. Kristol quotes Okun:

> *Abstracting from the costs and the consequences*, I would prefer more equality of income to less and would like complete equality best of all." I have italicized that opening clause to emphasize what an extraordinary statement this is for an economist—of all people—to make. For once you abstract from costs and consequences, you are no longer living a mortal life on this earth. . . . There is no society without inequalities among people, just as there is no architecture without functional and ornamental inequalities among otherwise similar (or even identical) stones. The reason is that all societies represent equilibria of costs and benefits, however defined. To express a preference for "complete equality" is to talk poetry or theology, not economics or politics or sociology.[11]

Kristol's perceptive observation exposes the weaknesses of utopian thinking in dealing with the equality-freedom debate: utopia literally means nowhere, which is where Rawlsville, Novickland, Randsville, and many academic ideas are situated. Americans today have no choice but to begin "beyond the veil of ignorance" in the actual here and now of their daily needs and value choices as presented by an imperfect society. Their attachment to rugged individualism and freedom of choice as ideal, precludes the possibility of absolute equality as a viable political goal in America for the foreseeable future. Given freedom as a starting point, the critical question for America's future then becomes: What costs to their freedom are the majority of Americans willing to tolerate and for what ends? What kinds of inequality will they demand to keep as a fundamental right, and what social and economic inequalities are they willing to eliminate for the sake of fellow Americans who are less well-off? To ignore these present limitations in structuring a future for America is to ride roughshod over majoritarian democracy as a form of government (however mixed).

There are some obvious kinds of inequality most Americans are set on preserving. The basic one is the right to be an individual. This right is not to be taken for granted as the Soviet Union, the People's Republic of China, and America's own Watergate and CIA scandals have illustrated in the negative only too well. People born with unequal gifts and intelligence should have the right to cultivate them and not be discriminated against. Likewise, less gifted and handicapped people should be given *as equal an opportunity as possible* (weighed against costs) to develop their individual personalities to the limits of their capabilities.* Not to provide a reasonable amount of welfare and "affirmative action" programs for such disadvantaged people is paramount to replacing the ideology of liberal democracy with the ideology of Social Darwinism. Respect for the individual worth of each human being in the nation must be preserved at all costs. What financial and social forms this respect should take that Americans can afford is the question.

Another inequality most Americans want to preserve is the inequality of reward for unequal effort, or, more money and status for those who work harder and more skillfully. Equality of outcome regardless of input is looked upon suspiciously by Americans who are upset with a society which actually rewards many people for not producing (for example, by paying some people more in unemployment insurance than they could receive from a mediocre job). Unequal pay for unequal work is a proposition most Americans accept. The question is: How much inequality of income is fair? To what extent can incomes be equalized without incurring intolerable costs in the motivation to produce and in economic productivity and growth? These are the tough questions that ideologues of all persuasions must face squarely if their policies for America's future are to be realistic.

Income and tax inequities in America have become a major social concern of all groups—including the Rockefeller family. In his book *The Second American Revolution*, John D. Rockefeller 3rd argues for a "humanistic capitalism" that would restore the humanist values of America's democratic revolution as a guide for the free enterprise system. One of Rockefeller's concerns is that according to a 1972 study by the Cambridge Institute, in the past twenty years lower-income groups have payed heavier tax burdens whereas upper-income people are paying roughly the same as before. Also, personal ownership of capital (in stock and bond holdings) is still concentrated among a very small percentage of the population.[12]

The real problems in humanizing the present system of American capitalism are intricate and difficult. Although welfare expenditures have now overtaken defense expenditures as a larger proportion of the federal budget, the national economic outcome is no better: huge government deficits accumulate

---

*The view of "intelligence" taken here is not that all forms of "intelligence" are genetically determined, but that each person is born with a range of capabilities in certain tasks (i.e. unequal "I.Q.'s" measured by upper-middle class culture and biases) which can be greatly affected, positively or negatively, by one's environment and educational opportunities.

that are alleviated only somewhat by the heavier tax burden on the people. If such large governmental expenditures continue to lead to deficits in the future, lower-income brackets in America will feel the effects most seriously both in terms of tax burdens and inflation. The poor appear to pay most for the empty rhetoric of conservative politicians pushing soon-to-be obsolete defense systems and of liberal politicians promising the people that they can have their welfare cake and eat it too. And the truly poor people in the Third and Fourth Worlds starve and suffer from malnutrition while American politicians waste American wealth that might, theoretically, be transferred eventually to them. Some unpleasant changes in the habits of American affluence and miserly foreign aid bills appear to be in order. In all probability belt-tightening will be necessary whether or not Americans choose to transfer wealth, goods, and know-how outside the United States. The age of affluence may be replaced by an age of austerity whether Americans choose a future of selfish or social capitalism.

If, indeed, an age of scarcity and austerity is upon us for the indefinite future, the criterion for deciding between equality and freedom, social justice and economic growth is no longer one of arbitrary value choice but of objective human needs that are much greater than existing resources at home and abroad can satisfy. Only the superrich can choose merely between values (what one wants) as opposed to basic human needs (bodily, psychic, and social prerequisites for healthy human existence). When needs overwhelm values for most of humankind, freedom itself becomes a question of self-discipline and restraint rather than of abandon and unharnessed spontaneity. The political and economic trends of our times appear to give Americans only one basic choice: self-restraint or government-restraint, private enforcement of social discipline (limiting wants to actual needs) or increasing state interventions to keep law, order, and economic stability. This unpopular choice is repressed in political campaigns and the public media which depend upon the masses for support and dollars. But the choice is there and points towards an unavoidable ethic if capitalistic democracy in any recognizable form whatsoever is to survive: freedom must be socially redefined in America through the eyes of social justice to make equal opportunity possible; and, social justice, in turn, must be sought with sufficient restraint to make individual incentive and economic growth feasible.

In *Politics for Human Beings* I argue with Ralph Hummel that politics should be viewed as social action that attempts to solve the tension between social facts and human needs.[13] Freedom then becomes the individual's ability to satisfy personal needs in a restrictive environment of social facts (such as existing institutions, powerful personalities, values, and the rules of the game of the political culture). But such individual freedom is attained only with and through the actions of others: social cooperation alone makes individual freedom to satisfy one's needs possible in a modern technological society such as America. The argument of this book carries the social dimensions of individual freedom even further. The greater the economic scarcity and the greater the number of human beings in need, the more individual freedom depends upon social cooperation. The crucial political question is whether such social cooperation for the satisfaction of collective needs should be left to private initiatives and organizations (as in extreme *laissez-faire* capitalism) or whether the state should take over the enforcement and organization of social cooperation and basic need satisfaction (extreme socialism). In 1929 John Dewey wrote in *Individualism Old and New*:

> We are in for some kind of socialism, call it by whatever name we please, and no matter what it will be called when it is realized. Economic determinism is now a fact, not a theory. But there is a difference and a choice between a blind, chaotic and unplanned determinism, issuing from business conducted for pecuniary profit, and the determination of a socially planned and ordered development. It is the difference between a socialism that is public and one that is capitalistic.[14]

In a technological society planning is inevitable, whether there is abundance or not. But in an era of increasing resource and energy shortages and endemic economic crises domestically and internationally, planning becomes even more critical if the basic needs of even the richest society are to be satisfied. Private planning and local control are attractive but insufficient, as the near bankruptcy of New York City in 1975 symbolized all too well. Private planning and local self-determination within communities will exist in the future only to the extent that individual self-restraint and voluntary social cooperation make them possible: the future of America will be dominated not so much by the American Bill of Individual Rights as the unofficial Social Bill of Individual Duties. Individuals will be free in a political and economic sense to the extent that they exercise the responsibilities that make it possible. If capitalism is to survive in the future, it must become a social capitalism based upon not merely the inequality of greater reward for greater individual effort, but greater power and freedom for those most socially responsible who work to make equal opportunity a reality for all citizens throughout the society. America, in short, must create a new political economy, a social liberalism in which the positive freedom of individual development is contingent upon social duty for community development. (See chapter 11 spelling out in detail the key concepts and assumptions of social liberalism.) Freedom of opportunity must be understood as the freedom to become more socially responsible in individual undertakings. And the right to become an elite in America, in addition to being open to all, must be earned by all. There must be no free rides to political power without social responsibility for either the rich or the poor.

Notes

[1]Fritz Zorn, "Losers into Winners," letter to *Time* magazine, September 1, 1975, p. 1.

[2]Adam Smith, *An Inquirey into the Nature and Causes of the Wealth of Nations* (New York: Random House, 1937).

[3]See William A. Williams, *The Great Evasion—An Essay on the Contemporary Relevance of Karl Marx and on the Wisdom of Admitting the Heretic into the Dialogue about America's Future* (Chicago: Quadrangle Books, 1964).

[4]For the development of Wilson's American values and personality as related to this foreign policy, see R. Isaak, *Individuals and World Politics* (North Scituate, Mass.: Duxbury Press, 1975), chap. 4.

[5]Robert Heilbroner, *Between Capitalism and Socialism: Essays in Political Economics* (New York: Random House, 1970), p. 80.

[6]*Ibid.*, p. 81.

[7]Peter F. Drucker, *Concept of the Corporation* Chapter One: "Capitalism in One Country," (New York: John Day, 1972), p. 2.

[8]Rawlsville is a fictitious utopia created from the principles of the influential book by John Rawls, a philosophy professor at Harvard, called *A Theory of Justice* (Cambridge, Mass.: Harvard University Press, 1971). For a series of articles on Rawls's theory of justice, see *The American Political Science Review*, 69 (June 1975), 588-674.

[9]Nozickland is a fictitious utopia created from the principles of the National Book Award-winning work of Robert Nozick, a philosophy professor at Harvard, called *Anarchy, State and Utopia* (New York: Basic Books, 1974). For an article comparing Rawls and Nozick critically, see Marc F. Plattner, "The New Political Theory," in *The Public Interest*, 40 (Summer 1975).

[10]Randia is a fictitious utopia—actually a dystopia epitomizing America's future—based on the ideas of Ayn Rand, the novelist and popular capitalistic individualist; adapted from "Egalitarianism and Inflation," in *The Ayn Rand Letter*, 3, 19 (June 17, 1974), part 2; and 3, 20, (July 1, 1974), part 3.

[11]Irving Kristol, "The High Cost of Equality," *Fortune*, November 1975, p. 199.

[12]John D. Rockefeller, *The Second American Revolution* (New York: Harper & Row, 1973), p. 81.

[13]Robert Isaak and Ralph Hummel, *Politics for Human Beings* (North Scituate, Mass.: Duxbury Press, 1975). This book uses Abraham Maslow's empirically grounded need hierarchy, which beginning with the most basic needs, recognizes the following categories: (1) physiological needs, (2) security needs, (3) love needs, (4) self-esteem needs, and (5) self-actualization needs.

[14]John Dewey, *Individualism Old and New* (New York: Capricorn Books, 1929), pp. 119-120.

4 DEMOCRACY AND ELITISM

> Liberal democracy on the American model increasingly tends to the condition of
> monarchy in the 19th century: a holdover form of government, one which
> persists in isolated or peculiar places here and there, and may even serve well
> enough for special circumstances, but which has simply no relevance to the
> future. It is where the world was, not where it is going.
> —*Daniel P. Moynihan,*
> *"The American Experiment,"*
> The Public Interest, *1975*

> The decline in governmental authority resulting from the "democratic dis-
> temper" in America reduces the capacity of the government to deal with complex
> problems. While public expectations rise, problems become more intractable.
> Economic nationalism is encouraged. Foreign burdens are resisted. The decline
> in the governability of American democracy at home means a decline in the
> influence of America abroad.
> —*"The Governability of Democracies,"*
> Trilateral Commission Report,
> *1975*

The future of capitalistic democracy has rarely been more in doubt than it
is today. The threats to American democracy stem not so much from outside
aggressors as from critical social, economic, and energy issues. American
governmental and academic elites have solemnly announced that liberal democracy as Americans have known it may be obsolete. By passing off their personal
pessimism as public policy, they have begun to transform their dark "democratic distemper" into a self-fulfilling prophecy. Although their perceptions of
the many complex problems that democracies face in the late twentieth century
are often acute, these influential spokesmen misinterpret what American democracy means. Their basic mistake is that they begin with an unreal, utopian
vision of democracy.

Absolute or pure democracy has never existed, yet it is from the perspective of this utopian form of democracy that academic elites and power-hungry
politicans criticize existing political arrangements in the United States and
abroad; indeed, generations of Americans have been taught that pure democracy

should exist—here and now. Pure democracy means direct government by the people—total equality. But total equality has never existed, nor would most Americans be likely to tolerate it. Rather, Americans, like the Greeks long ago, have settled for indirect government by the people—representative democracy. Elites, in other words, are inevitable (representing democratically elected inequality, if you will). Americans do not dislike equality, but they prefer order and stability, and history has yet to reveal a case of long political stability without some form or other of elite leadership.

Indeed, the misunderstanding about the meaning of democracy in America is the key to the American predicament, which, simply stated, involves a conflict between the need for democratic, mass participation and the need for educated, elite control of diplomacy and world power. Striving for absolute, pure democracy without compromise can lead only to self-defeating domestic factionalism and the eventual disintegration of America's power to influence world political events. Aiming, on the other hand, for an effective, open system of representative democracy in America can provide a stable basis for a balance of freedom, equality, and productivity at home and for a coherent ideology of democratic social capitalism to be exported abroad. Paradoxically, never to think in terms of pure democracy is to give up the essential American idealism which makes a laudatory system of representative democracy possible; but to think only in terms of pure democracy is an ideological blindness, a pathological idealism that defeats its own purpose by demanding too much always to receive too little.

"Democracy," said Plato, "is a charming form of government, full of variety and disorder, and dispensing a sort of equality to equals and unequals alike." Aristotle agreed: "If liberty and equality, as is thought by some, are chiefly to be found in democracy, they will be best attained when all persons alike share in the government to the utmost." But Aristotle by no means believed in pure democracy, which in the days of ancient Greece meant "mobocracy," or rule by the poor unenlightened masses who would too easily be tempted into corruption by demagogues. To prevent such a development, Aristotle (and America's founders) supported a mixed form of government, based upon a balance between rule by the many (the democratic masses) and the few (the oligarchic or aristocratic elite).

Aristotle was just one of many Greek thinkers to argue for a mixed government of some kind to solve the famous "cycle of government" problem. The Greeks thought that different types of government, classified by the number and kinds of governors involved, rose and fell in a regular cycle. This pessimistic cycle began with government by the one—a good monarch, who over time became a bad tyrant, corrupted by power. Eventually this monarch would be overthrown by the few, a group of influential aristocrats who set up their own government only to become a selfish oligarchy, themselves corrupted by money and power. In time, the few would be overthrown by the many, the outraged poor masses. Although they would try to bring all power to the people, aiming for a pure democracy, they would eventually come to worship demagogues, the strongest of whom would become a tyrant starting the dark cycle all over again. Accepting this gloomy view of corruptible human nature, tending toward envy and class conflict, Aristotle believed that a stable government could be achieved only by circumventing the cycle. He advocated mixing the many with the few so that neither would be able to get the upper hand to corrupt the political system.

Aristotle's concern for the corruption of power and the instability resulting from factionalism was echoed 2,000 years later in James Madison's *Federalist Papers* (Nos. 10 and 51). The American founders drew up a constitution in 1789 that was brilliant but conservative in its desire to preserve stability over everything else. The document gave the federal government enough power to prevent the divisiveness of factionalism and yet checked and balanced that power within the federal government and between federal, state, and local governments to make any total domination of government by any one group or individual difficult. It thus protected all individual citizens from potential governmental abuses. As H. Mark Roelofs has noted, the trick was to capture the whole of the Greek cycle of government within the framework of a single constitutional structure that would preserve stability and government legitimacy:

> All that was needed to achieve this objective was to include within the constitution each of the various social economic classes: Give, in one constitution, the hero-leader a monarchical office, the upper classes a small council, and the people a large assembly. Through these, each class could voice its particular interest. . . . No class, simply because of the institutionalized presence of the others, would be able to get all that it inevitably desired. But, it was hoped, each would be sure of enough of something for itself that none would ever choose to desert what it had for the terrible risks of total revolution.[1]

Even the idea of basing the stability of the American political system upon a large middle class had its origins in Aristotle, who wrote:

> Thus it is manifest that the best political community is formed by citizens of the middle class, and that those states are likely to be well administered,

in which the middle class is large. . . . Great then is the good fortune of a
state in which the citizens have a moderate and sufficient property; for
where some possess much, and the others nothing, there may arise an
extreme democracy, or a pure oligarchy; or a tyranny may develop out of
either extreme—either out of the most rampant democracy, or out of an
oligarchy; but it is not so likely to arise out of the middle constitutions and
those akin to them. . . . And democracies are safer and more permanent
than oligarchies, because they have a middle class which is more numerous
and has a greater share in government; for when there is no middle class,
and the poor greatly exceed in number, troubles arise, and the state soon
comes to an end.[2]

Americans came from Old World Europe to create a New World Europe in
the United States which would be better able to satisfy their bourgeois, material
desires by providing the space and resources necessary for a large measure of
individual freedom, equality, and upward mobility. The founding fathers drew
inspiration from Aristotle and the Greeks to create a relatively stable and
permanent system of middle-class politics, in which individuals were given the
opportunity to make it and the legal right to protect what they had made. The
bourgeois, middle-class nature of stable democracy cannot be overstressed—
especially in an affluent society like our own. Americans take their relative
affluence and middle-class stability for granted and therefore have the time and
energy to go on to more radical things and higher-level need satisfactions (in
politics, art, or leisure).

Sociologist Max Weber suggested that modern democracy in its clearest
form can occur only under capitalist industrialization.[3] The absence of an
enduring political tradition of democracy in the Third World confirms Weber's
observation. Seymour Martin Lipset has demonstrated empirically that stable
political democracies have large middle classes. Using the empirical indices of
wealth, industrialization, urbanization, and education, Lipset demonstrates, in
Political Man, that such middle-class prerequisites are necessary (though not
sufficient) for stable democracy in Europe, Latin America, and English-
speaking countries.[4] And his findings have been substantiated by a similar
survey of Middle Eastern states conducted by Daniel Lerner and the Bureau of
Applied Social Research.[5] As Lipset notes:

From Aristotle down to the present, men have argued that only in a
wealthy society in which relatively few citizens lived at the level of real
poverty could there be a situation in which the mass of the population

intelligently participate in politics and develop the self-restraint necessary to avoid succumbing to the appeals of irresponsible demagogues.[6]

If capitalist industrialization, wealth, urbanization and widespread education were critical prerequisites for a stable democracy in America and have been shown to be vital elsewhere as well, it seems reasonable to build into American foreign policy encouragement for the cultivation of these prerequisites elsewhere. But foreign policy to date has lacked any consistent foreign aid support for the development of stable democracies on these bases. Rather, the focus has been upon America's strategic and economic interests: policy makers have preferred stable fascisms to democratic socialisms. As will be argued in detail later, although such strategic and economic interests *are* critically important, there is no reason that they cannot be coupled with an altruistic interest in the economic development of the Third World. The alternative is a prolongation of the so called nonideological and noninterference foreign policy of the present, whereby American policy makers often bend over backwards to respect the domestic sovereignty of foreign governments—particularly in stable, powerful states, even if they are fascist in nature. A nonideological foreign policy of this sort rests, presumably, upon mere balance of power considerations. But when America's world power is based upon democratic consensus at home, where the ideological stakes are very high indeed, a nonideological American foreign policy is a contradiction in terms and is built upon a foundation of sand. S. M. Eisenstadt, the sociologist, has even made the extreme claim that "The United States is the most ideological society that has existed in the world."[7]

America can be viewed as one of the most ideological of societies because, in the process of democratization, it has become a completely liberal state. Americans, and other citizens of stable liberal democracies as well, take individual liberty and the market economy as their basic assumptions. And this is not surprising. For as political philosopher C. B. Macpherson pointed out in the Massey Lectures of 1965, the liberal state and the competitive market economy preceded the development of democracy in all Western liberal democracies:

> Democracy came as a late addition to the competitive market society and the liberal state. . . . It is not simply that democracy came later. It is also that democracy in these societies was demanded, and was admitted, on competitive liberal grounds. Democracy was demanded, and admitted, on the ground that it was unfair not to have it in a competitive society. It was something the competitive society logically needed.[8]

That a belief in dogmatic liberalism is widespread throughout American society is an observation easier for most of us to accept than another, more profound one: a liberal state need not be democratic. If democracy is considered in terms of its original meaning—rule by the common people, the plebians— we can easily imagine a state run by representatively elected elites who operate to maximize the interests of the upper class and upper-middle class more than the interests of the common people. For democracy in the original sense of the word implies absolute equality, and, as has been pointed out before, Americans believe primarily in individual freedom and only secondarily in equality or social justice. Americans tend to be rugged, competitive, possessive individuals through and through, products more of their market economy and liberal state than democratic idealism or the right to one vote per person. Indeed, Americans do not regard one man-one vote highly, as is indicated by the fact that even after the Watergate affair and corporate campaign funding scandals they seem to be reluctant to attach rigid legal limits to campaign spending. The freedom to buy votes and influence people is still regarded by many as more important than the absolute equality of each person's voice in the political decision-making process.

If America was primarily democratic and secondarily liberal and market-economy oriented, the lower class and lower-middle class would revolt against the liberal state and competitive market economy. But this is not the case. The lower classes in America want more upward mobility *within* the existing liberal state and market economy: they want more of the same pie, not a new one. They want politicians and economists and business people who can continue to produce goods efficiently, and elites who get most of the goods are willing to share them. They don't want just any man for President, but the *best* man. And they would rather have a free society in which some are more free than others than a thoroughgoing democratic society in which the state takes from their individual freedom to allocate more equality. Political scientist Philip Converse has shown that the American mass public is interested in simple, concrete values like higher wages and better living conditions, in contrast to elites who are more interested in abstract values like stability or democracy.[9] The experience of being lower class stimulates the desire to become middle class or upper class and to live accordingly—the "new rich syndrome." It is no accident that most of the leaders of the student movement of the 1960s against the existing liberal state and market economy were from upper-middle-class backgrounds, rich enough not to have to worry about basic material necessities, well-heeled enough to afford radical chic.

Thus although most Americans are brought up to believe they are living in a basically democratic society that aims ultimately to become a pure democracy and that just happens to be hooked up to a liberal state and a market economy, they in fact live in a liberal state and market economy that just happens to have become increasingly democratic with the extension of suffrage and civil rights. And if one grows up believing that one's society *is* democratic, the need to make it more so may not always be apparent. The fact that the American political system is based upon a conservative ideology of *laissez-faire* liberalism and a belief in the competitive market economy helps to explain why a supposedly liberal, American democracy supports nonliberal, nondemocratic governments abroad today. But most Americans are unaware of how conservative their ideological liberalism is, just as they were once unaware of how elitist their democracy was (before the democratic revolt of the 1960s and the debacle of the "best and the brightest" in the Vietnam War). The stability of America's liberal democracy is largely based upon its impurity (in the Aristotelean sense) and the commonsense, pragmatic materialism of Americans that keeps them from going against their own concrete interests for the sake of any abstract ideology—democratic or otherwise.

Democracy is fundamentally an ideal. Since democracy in a pure form has never existed in an historical nation-state, people who think it should are optimists who are bound to be disappointed with political reality. But properly used, the idealistic belief in democracy is a noble one, demanding that institutions be responsive to people's needs, lambasting corruption in public power, and pressing for legislative reform. The experience of political participation by the many, or the majority, is a good in itself. And democracy as a mind set that demands more participation for the many is a healthy sentiment that reinvigorates aging bureaucratic institutions.

There is a human tendency not to let an ideal rest in peace: it must be realized, pinned down, made concrete once and for all. Powerful conservative elites in prestigious institutions perceive the democratic state of mind as a danger to their interests, a concrete threat to their attempts at social control and law and order. They are dedicated to the social norms outside themselves which define meaning in their lives and legitimize their power and status. Liberals, on the other hand, perceive the democratic ideal as a concrete ideology that promises them self-fulfillment through social participation, a means of social mobility for either themselves or the less advantaged, a ticket to freedom. They are dedicated to human beings as ends in themselves, to be cultivated like plants by bettering the conditions of life.

America's future is clouded by the dilemma that the American creed embraces both conservativism, as the preservation of law and order and self-discipline, and liberalism, as the fulfillment of value through individual improvement and liberation. This dilemma is made more complex by the fact that liberalism, the American creed, is the legitimate calling card of both the law-and-order conservatives and the self-liberating liberals. Conservatives define liberalism as individual (or corporate) freedom *from* the state, whereas liberals define it as freedom *for* the people or the freedom *of* civil liberties. Liberalism for conservatives is defensive: its purpose is to protect existing individuals, rights, and institutions from abuses of power or revolutionary change. (Nozickland symbolizes their utopia.) Liberalism for liberals is offensive: it exists to proliferate freedom of opportunity, the freedom to become equal and to change society to make this possible. (Rawlsville is their utopia.) Rather than to say that Americans were born equal without having to become so, it may be more accurate to say they were born liberal without knowing what that meant to anybody else. Indeed, Americans may be the most private liberals in the world, each letting others define themselves as they will and, for the most part, trying to stay out of others' way.

The conservative interpretation of liberalism, which dates back to the banker's view of democracy held by Alexander Hamilton and the balance-the-budget *laissez-faire* liberalism of nineteenth-century economics, is supported today by economic and political elites who are keen on the need for highly qualified experts and who stress the priority of social control and efficient management over social justice and democratic participation. In contrast, the liberal interpretation of liberalism, which can be traced to Jefferson's idealistic views of democracy in the Declaration of Independence and to Keynes's advocacy of deficit spending, is supported by those who focus upon the need for increasing equality of opportunity for minorities and greater democratic participation. Both views of liberalism are as American as apple pie and any claim by either to be the only legitimate interpretation of the American creed is fallacious.

In 1975 the conservative view of American liberalism was epitomized by the Report of the Trilateral Commission's Task Force, "The Governability of Democracies," written by Michel Crozier of France, Samuel Huntington of the United States, and Joji Watanuki of Japan. The Trilateral Commission is an organization of influential academic, economic, and political elites from North America, Western Europe, and Japan. It was established in the 1970s to encourage closer cooperation among these three advanced democratic areas, to develop practical policy proposals in areas of mutual interest, and to lobby for these ideas. Its philosophy, according to its former director, Zbigniew Brzezinski, is "reformist and internationalist." But Brzezinski initially saw the Trilateral Commission as a way of stabilizing government structures in the advanced countries, and only recently has it become concerned with the problems between the advanced and lesser-developed countries. [10]

The commission's 1975 report on democracies argues that current demands on democratic governments have grown, while the capacity to meet them has shrunk. Based on studies of the situation in each of the three trilateral regions, the report concludes that democracies in Western industrialized societies are becoming increasingly ungovernable because of an "overload" of demands on government, increasingly fragmented political interests and political parties, and a general delegitimization of authority brought about by the pursuit of individualism and equality. While lack of confidence in the functioning of democracies has grown, no alternative image of political organization or social control with significant public support has emerged. The report claims that the current situation is one of "anomic" democracy: democratic politics has become more an arena for the assertion of conflicting interests than a process for building common purposes. [11]

Painting a gloomy future for democratic government, particularly in Europe and the United States, the report focuses upon the breakdown of traditional authority patterns, modes of social control, and a basic value consensus. European democracies, according to the report, will become increasingly ungovernable because they will not be able to master the complexities of economic growth and political development and because the bureaucratic means they use to maintain social control foster irresponsibility and consensual breakdown. Social control, in many European states, is imposed by a state apparatus that is isolated from the population, making breakdowns in the democratic consensus endemic. Ironically, European integration has only served to reinforce national bureaucratic structures. Vast cultural and economic changes are creating an "explosion of social interaction" characterized by the rejection of traditional hierarchical values and social control. The media presumably aid in this breakdown of traditional patterns and help to promote a sweeping cultural revolution in the intellectual world, which weakens Europe's sense of purpose and capacity to lead and govern itself. The report maintains that rationality itself is under attack and a political "regression" to the left in the future is possible as communist parties emerge as the parties of order and efficient organization.

The United States is viewed to be under most of the same pressures that affect Europe: increasing delegitimization of authority at all levels, fragmentations of traditional parties and forms of political control, and declining confidence in government and institutions at a time of rising popular demands upon government. The dramatic renewal of the democratic spirit in the 1960s in America has supposedly brought about a substantial increase in governmental activity, matched by a decrease in governmental authority. As a result, the governability of American democracy at home and the maintenance of American power and influence abroad are in question.

Professor Samuel Huntington, author of the American section of the report, measures the increase in American government activity in terms of governmental expenditures:

> In response to the internal democratic surge of the 1960 s, we find a massive "Welfare Shift" in government expenditures. This is the second marked shift and increase in government expenditures in the postwar period, the first being the "Defense Shift" of the early postwar years, in reponse to the external Soviet threat.[12]

Huntington points out that the defense shift was primarily the product of elite leadership (by Truman, Acheson, Forrestal, Marshall, Harriman, and Lovett and their perceptions of the Soviet threat), whereas the welfare shift was primarily the result of popular expectations and group demands. Thus the report continues:

> Between 1950 and 1960, total governmental expenditures rose by $81.0 billion, of which $29.1 billion or roughly 36% was for defense and international relations. Between 1960 and 1971, governmental expenditures increased by $218.1 billion, of which, however, only $33.4 billion or roughly 15% were accounted for by defense and international relations while expenditures for domestic programs grew by $184.7 billion. . . . Non-defense expenditures which had been 20% of GNP in 1965 were 25% of GNP in 1971 and 27% of GNP in 1974. Defense spending went down to 7% of GNP in 1971 and 6% in 1974.[13]

It is perhaps no accident that Huntington, an international authority on international defense problems, interprets this undeniable shift from defense to welfare spending as a loss of control by elites resulting from an increase in government activity without a corresponding increase in government authority. Increased democratization and government activity could, for example, be interpreted as healthy political signs—the way America's democratic liberals would see it. But the conservatives of the Trilateral Commission's report emphasize that democracies are going out of control, a condition for which elites (including academic elites) see no remedy. Indeed, they have become so pessimistic that they fear democracy has an intrinsic tendency to do itself in: "Democratic government does not necessarily function in a self-sustaining or self-correcting equilibrium fashion. It may instead function so as to give rise to forces and tendencies which, if unchecked by some outside agency, will eventually lead to the undermining of democracy."[14] The report does not specify what kind of outside agency should intervene to keep the status quo in equilibrium—but the idea has an ominous authoritarian ring to it. Conservative elites seem to be interested in projecting the future of American liberalism more for the sake of controlling rapid change than for anticipating change in order to humanize American society. The voice of Hamilton drowns out the voice of Jefferson.

In arguing that the more democratic a system is, the more likely it is to be endangered by intrinsic threats, the authors of the report have in mind the warnings of Alexis de Tocqueville, Walter Lippmann, and Joseph Schumpeter, all of whom perceived a danger of tyranny by the majority. For example, in his classic *Democracy in America*, de Tocqueville argues that the essence of democratic government is the absolute sovereignty of the majority, and nothing in democratic states is capable of resisting it. This influential argument is important enough to consider in some detail, for recent historical experience in America appears to indicate, contrary to de Tocqueville's thesis, that this country has more to fear from tyranny by the few than by the many. No doubt, the Trilateral Commission authors would argue that their intent was to prevent a pendulum-like reaction against "the best and the brightest" who kept America in Vietnam or against a corrupt and too powerful executive branch. The critical question seems to be whether to have faith in the few or the many; Americans often fail to get as far as Aristotle, who would have asked, "Which few?" or "What kind of many?"

De Tocqueville begins by arguing that in America the many control political power through the legislature, both houses of which come from the same class and tend to be heavily dependent upon their constituents' interests, depriving the executive of all stability and independence by making it dependent upon the caprices of the legislature. Furthermore, he notes that the moral authority of the majority is partly based on the notion that there is more intelligence and wisdom in a great number of men collected together than in a single individual, "that the quantity of legislators is more important than their quality."[15] This has contributed to a widespread belief that the majority can do no wrong and that if it does, the blame rests upon advisors. The interests of the many are preferred to those of the few, and those who constitute a minority can never hope to bring the majority over to their side, for to do so would require the majority to concede that wisdom does not always reside in numbers:

> The majority therefore in that country exercises a prodigious actual authority, and a moral influence which is scarcely less preponderant; no obstacles exist which can impede, or so much as retard its progress, or which can induce it to heed the complaints of those whom it crushes upon

its path. This state of things is fatal in itself and dangerous for the future.[16]

So far de Tocqueville is persuasive in cataloguing the possible weaknesses of democracy in America. But then, at the end of his argument, he falters. In a section called "Tyranny of the Majority," de Tocqueville surprisingly announces the hopeless weakness of his position: "I hold it to be an impious and an execrable maxim that, politically speaking, a people has a right to do whatsoever it pleases; and yet I have asserted that all authority originates in the will of the majority. Am I, then, in contradiction with myself?"[17] Exactly. For as de Tocqueville argues, the majority of humankind sanctions a general law, called justice, which limits the right of every people; and yet when an individual violates an unjust law, he or she does not have recourse to humanity but only to the sovereign majority of a particular state. This according to de Tocqueville, is the language of a slave. And since an individual possessing absolute power may misuse that power and wrong adversaries, a majority may be liable to the same reproach. But rather than moving, as Aristotle did, toward a mixed system of government that would prevent corruption and make some modified system of democratic stability possible, de Tocqueville rejects mixed forms of democracy outright:

> I do not think that it is possible to combine several principles in the same government, so as at the same time to maintain freedom, and really to oppose them to one another. The form of government which is usually termed *mixed* has always appeared to me to be a mere chimera. Accurately speaking, there is no such thing as a mixed government (with the meaning usually given to that word), because in all communities some one principle of action may be discovered, which preponderates over the others. . . . When a community really has a mixed government, that is to say, when it is equally divided between two adverse principles, it must either pass through a revolution, or fall into complete dissolution.[18]

Yet, America *does* have a mixed form of democratic government which has been basically stable for 200 years and has not yet ended in revolution or dissolution. Although he is often cited by academic elites as perceptive in predicting America's future in the nineteenth-century, de Tocqueville has proven to be wrong on his most crucial claim. Mixed government has prevented a tyranny of the majority from destroying American democracy as we now know it, and it is apt to continue to do so in the future. The destruction of America's mixed form of democracy in the future seems much more likely to come from a tyranny of powerful technocrats than from a tyranny of the masses. Indeed, a tyranny of the masses is a contradiction in terms. Where masses seize control, there are always demagogues in charge who either create their own private tyrannies or are swept away by chaos, as the Greeks noted long ago.

The corporate revolution has overwhelmed democracy in America, making the democratic ideal appear to be old-fashioned. Technocratic elites and bureaucratic hierarchies predominate; individual freedom has rarely been in greater jeopardy.

In his famous work *The Democratic Way of Life*, T. V. Smith wrote in 1926: "Democracy itself is, in truth, 'a state of mind.' It is a state of mind, first, of and toward the majority. It is a state of mind, second, toward and of the minority. It is a state of mind, finally and fundamentally, by and for the individual."[19] This noble statement of America's democratic creed sounds old-fashioned today because the democratic state of mind has been increasingly replaced by an apolitical, technocratic state of mind. Indeed, the ideology of modernity has become *apolitics* itself—the belief that all social problems should be handed over to technological experts rather than left for everyday people who seek to satisfy their own needs by commonsense solutions. And heavy-handed bureaucracies have consolidated this ideology of apolitics into a working life style that has largely replaced the democratic way of life. Constrained on all sides by government, corporate, and union bureaucracies, the individual citizen feels powerless.

The displacement of the democratic state of mind by apolitics is subtle, and perhaps inevitable, as a nation develops into an industrial society. Social scientist Jürgen Habermas argues that as a nation-state becomes modernized through technology, its amount of technologically exploitable knowledge increases without a similar development of democratic controls over such technology.[20] Never has Francis Bacon's observation that knowledge is power been more true than today. Modern societies increasingly depend upon technological developments and the knowledge of specialized elites for economic growth and military power, while everyday citizens feel their own knowledge and political power decreasing. Psychologist Rollo May has noted that feelings of powerlessness give rise to individual aggression and collective violence.[21] Thus the perceived political powerlessness of Russian revolutionaries in the nineteenth century led them to use assassination as a political tool, just as frustrated American individuals and revolutionary extremists have turned to presidential assassination as a symbol of protest against the dehumanization they feel in the political system of the United States. It appears to be the absence rather than the presence of meaningful democratic participation in politics that stimulates blind violence and lashing out against all elites and figures of authority.

This desperate antiauthoritarian individualism focuses upon large bureaucracies as well as individual elites, and a central target for the future appears to be the corporation. As social critic Irving Kristol wrote:

> Both the Founding Fathers and Adam Smith would have been perplexed by the kind of capitalism we have in 1976. They could not have interpreted the domination of economic activity by large corporate bureaucracies as representing, in any sense, the working of a "system of natural liberty." Entrepreneurial capitalism, as they understood it, was mainly an individual—or at most, a family—affair. . . . The large, publicly-owned corporation of today which strives for immortality, which is committed to no line of business but rather (like an investment banker) seeks the best return on investment, which is governed by an anonymous oligarchy—such an institution would have troubled and puzzled them, just as it troubles and puzzles us. And they would have asked themselves the same questions we have been asking ourselves for almost a century now: Who "owns" this new leviathan? Who governs it and by what right and according to what principles?[22]

The unpopularity of large corporations today is rooted historically in the healthy populist mistrust of large concentrations of American power that threatened individual freedom in the past. Following World War II corporations enjoyed a temporary popularity. Americans looked to these flexible, efficient organizations to help them out of the Depression and bring them the high standard of living and material economic growth they had waited for during the war years. But as soon as Americans were affluent enough to have time to concern themselves with the negative aspects of corporate capitalism, they became increasingly critical of big business, its concentration of power, its pollution of the environment, and its unfair hiring practices. European New Left social democratic parties also began to influence the old liberal progressive reformists in America, some of whom became new liberal advocates of trust-busting (instead of mere regulation of corporations, which the old liberals desired).

But Irving Kristol argues that the probability that big business will be broken up in the future is small because the economic and social costs would be too high. The adverse effects on productivity, capital investment, and the American balance of payments are fairly obvious. But the social and political costs Kristol perceives are more subtle:

Our major trade unions, having after many years succeeded in establishing collective bargaining on a national level with the large corporation, are not about to sit back and watch their power disintegrate for the sake of an ideal such as "decentralization." And the nation's pension funds are not about to permit the assets of the corporations in which they have invested to be dispersed, and the security of their pension payments correspondingly threatened.[23]

Although undoubtedly correct about the vested stakes of unions and pension funds in large corporations, Kristol misleadingly identifies the break-up of big business with the more moderate concept of decentralization (revealing his own form of conservative populist paranoia about change). Kristol and others argue that in advanced industrial societies which require knowledgeable elites and centralized management for critical functions, only decentralization offers the possibility of restoring a mixed democracy responsible to the needs of people in their local communities. But decentralization can be a conservative move. Indeed, one reason decentralization has become a slogan of populist politicians on both the left and right is because of its basic moderation as they understand it, that is, its inability to do anything that would fundamentally change the socioeconomic status quo and their power position in it. It was through centralization, not decentralization, that the New Deal and later Democratic legislation greatly increased opportunities for the disadvantaged by federal welfare, employment, education, social security, and tax reform programs. Dividing the existing hierarchy into smaller pieces and calling it decentralization *can* just become another clever smokescreen by elitist politicians who seek to stabilize the status quo and make no basic changes for the sake of the disadvantaged.

But if carefully defined, decentralization can provide, paradoxically, an even stronger core of centralized social welfare services in Washington while allowing greater grassroots participation at the regional and local levels in the country. Hence, in his popular textbook, *Management*, corporate management expert Peter Drucker strongly supports decentralization as an efficient and creative concept at the federal, corporate, and public institutional levels. He notes:

Decentralization must not create a weak center. On the contrary, one of the main purposes of federal organization is to *strengthen* top management and to make it capable of doing its own work rather than be forced to supervise, coordinate, and prop up operating work. Federal decentralization will work only if the top management job is clearly defined and thought through.[24]

In short, decentralization can make centralized authority more powerful and effective by limiting its tasks and can increase its legitimacy by letting local managers in the field have more decision-making power in areas where they know the people's needs.

The New York City Fire Department, for example, which adopted Drucker's *Management* as an "official text," has effectively used the theory of decentralization. It has made the central authority at the top more efficient at functions which must remain centralized (such as receiving calls that report fires and preparing the payroll), while simultaneously boosting the morale and efficiency of smaller units by delegating more authority to field captains who are most familiar with local needs and problems (in the area of personal discipline, for example). If carefully watched, decentralization can work to open up the elite structure of a technological society by passing down more authority to where it can do people the most good.

All societies come into being through the imposition of a social contract, constitution, or vision of social equilibrium imposed by some group of elites— whether elected or self-selected. The stability of Western democratic societies depends upon a balance between freedom and order. In this context, centralization represents the necessary federal order required to meet general public needs—defense, social welfare, educational standards, and so forth—whereas decentralization symbolizes the freedom necessary for meaningful democratic participation at the grassroots level. America's technological development brought with it a massive centralized bureaucracy at the federal level, epitomized by the executive branch. The democratic reaction against Vietnam policy making and the Watergate and CIA-FBI scandals was an overdue call for decentralization of federal power to restore a sense of democracy in the country.

In 1975 the American representative to the United Nations, Daniel Moynihan, announced to the world that democracy as Americans have known it was not the wave of the future but a holdover form of government from the past with few adherents in the world today. Indeed, Freedom House, a New York organization that views itself as an international watchdog of liberty, identified only 59 of the world's 209 nations and colonies as free. Freedom, in this case, meant an uncensored press, free elections, at least two political parties, and a working system of laws guaranteeing individual rights.[25] Will democracy flicker out in the future, or are these despairing warnings an overreaction?

The problem of the viability of democracy ultimately rests upon the meaning one attaches to the word. Academic and political elites, although well aware that there are many different democratic forms, often criticize democracy's problems as though they are predicting the doom of all democratic forms or the hopelessness of restoring a healthy democratic society. Journalists and speech makers habitually pull out only the most simplistic parts of complicated arguments, unwittingly making propaganda for antidemocratic forces by failing to note that the main intention of democracy's sharpest critics is to reform and revitalize it. Of course, the critics themselves share the blame for joining, nay, even leading, the pessimistic intellectual bandwagon of doom sayers. Too many people today seem bent upon making Spengler's *Decline of the West* into a self-fulfilling prophecy.

Some of the many forms democracy can take include the American capitalist-liberal version, the Marxist socialist version, and the Third World humanist, anticolonial version. American democracy, as has been shown, begins with individual freedom as a first premise and builds upon an ideology of *laissez-faire* liberalism in politics and economics, institutionalized in forms of mixed government. Socialist democracy begins with class consciousness as its first assumption and aims to achieve equality through elimination of class privilege and individual differences. Democracies in the developing countries take equality and community for basic assumptions and seek to establish rule by and for the oppressed people, often through single-party mass movements that call for the establishment of a new humanism to replace the old remnants of colonialism.

The role of elites is also defined differently in each of these visions of democracy. American elites are supposed to be elected representatives of the people who are granted only limited powers. This institutionalized distrust of the few protects the individual freedom of the many. Marxist-Leninist democracy is officially introduced through elite vanguards of class-conscious citizens, who are given total power to transform the society for the good of working-class people. Third World democracies are theoretically led by nationalist leaders who bring about the general will of the people and affirm the dignity and worth of the human being by seeking to eliminate capitalist colonialism and inequality. As C. B. Macpherson has observed:

> The underdeveloped countries have on the whole rejected the most characteristic features of liberal-democracy. . . . The competitive market society, which is the soil in which liberal ideas and the liberal state flourish, was not natural to them. Insofar as they knew the market society, it was something imposed on them from outside and from above. Their traditional culture was generally not attuned to competition. They generally saw no intrinsic value in wealth-getting and gave no respect to the motive of individual gain. Equality and community, equality within a community, were traditionally rated more highly than individual freedom.[26]

American democracy at home and abroad does risk the possibility of becoming obsolete if it remains conservatively defensive in clinging to outdated beliefs in *laissez-faire* capitalism as a political ideal. The rise of corporation, union, and government bureaucracies have made *laissez-faire* capitalism in its nineteenth-century form extinct. But by focusing upon their liberal, humanist creed and their ideal of individual freedom and opportunity, Americans can revitalize democracy at home and create a positive image for other countries abroad. Such a humanization of America's technological society will require a transformation, however, of America's tradition of rugged individualism. Rugged individualism must be replaced by voluntary social individualism, encouraged by credible state incentives. And just as individuals must become more socially responsible and self-disciplined in time of scarcity or face the consequences of the law, so must large corporations lead in social reform or face increasing popular hostility and government intervention. For individual freedom means individual responsibility; rights mean duties; equality means voluntary self-sacrifice to give opportunities to those who are less advantaged. These are the humanistic principles upon which the New World was founded. They must be restored to recover the spirit of the New World in America and to imbue Americans once again with pride in their nation at home and abroad.

Notes

[1]H. Mark Roelofs, *The Language of Modern Politics* (Homewood, Ill.: Dorsey Press, 1967), p. 235.

[2]Aristotle, *Politica*, trans. by Benjamin Jowett, in *The Basic Works of Aristotle*, ed. by Richard McKeon (New York: Random House, 1941), pp. 1221-1222.

[3]Max Weber, "Zur Lage der bürgerlichen Demokratie in Russland," *Archiv für Sozialwissenschaft und Sozialpolitik*, 22 (1906), 346ff.

[4]Seymour Martin Lipset, *Political Man: The Social Bases of Politics* (Garden City, N.Y.: Doubleday-Anchor, 1963).

[5]Daniel Lerner, *The Passing of Traditional Society* (New York: Free Press, 1958).

[6]Lipset, *Political Man*, p. 31.

[7]S. M. Eisenstadt, "Civilization and Modernization," Lecture at Columbia University, November 25, 1975.

[8]C. B. Macpherson, *The Real World of Democracy* (London: Oxford University Press, 1966), pp. 9-10.

[9]Philip E. Converse, "The Nature of Belief Systems in Mass Publics," in *Ideology and Discontent*, ed. by David E. Apter, (New York: Free Press, 1964), pp. 206-261.

[10]"The Trilateral Commission," a presentation by Zbigniew Brzezinski at Columbia's Faculty Seminar in International Political Economy, September 30, 1975.

[11]Michel Crozier, Samuel Huntington, Joji Watanuki, "The Governability of Democracies, Report to the Trilateral Commission, May 1975. Published as *The Crisis of Democracies* (New York: New York University Press, 1975).

[12]*Ibid.*, "Summary," p. 3.

[13]*Ibid.*, "USA," pp. 9-10.

[14] *Ibid.*, "Introduction," p. 8.

[15] Alexis de Tocqueville, *Democracy in America*, vol. 1 (New York: J. and H. G. Langley, 1841), pp. 275-277.

[16] *Ibid.*, p. 277.

[17] *Ibid.*, p. 280.

[18] *Ibid.*, p. 281.

[19] T. V. Smith and Édvard C. Lindeman, *The Democratic Way of Life—An American Interpretation* (New York: The New American Library, 1951), p. 10.

[20] Jürgen Habermas, *Toward a Rational Society* (Boston: Beacon Press, 1970).

[21] Rollo May, *Power and Innocence* (New York: W. W. Norton, 1972).

[22] Irving Kristol, "On Corporate Capitalism in America," *The Public Interest*, bicentennial issue, 41 (Fall 1975), 125.

[23] *Ibid.*, 130.

[24] Peter F. Drucker, *Management* (New York: Harper & Row, 1973), p. 577.

[25] Paul Weaver, "Making the U.N. Safe for Democracy," *Fortune*, November 1975, p. 117.

[26] Macpherson, *The Real World of Democracy*, pp. 24-25.

Part II

HOW AMERICA STANDS WITH OTHERS

Don't sell America short.

—Popular American saying, *1925-1929*

5 THE NEW RICH, THE OLD RICH, AND THE POOR

If the world were a global village of 100 people, 70 of them would be unable to read, and only one would have a college education. Over 50 would be suffering from malnutrition, and over 80 would live in what we call substandard housing.

If the world were a global village of 100 residents 6 of them would be Americans. These 6 would have half the village's entire income; and the other 94 would exist on the other half.

—*Fellowship magazine, February 1974*

The global corporation is the most powerful human organization yet devised for colonizing the future. By scanning the entire planet for opportunities, by shifting its resources from industry to industry and country to country, and by keeping its overriding goal simple—worldwide profit maximization—it has become an institution of unique power. The World Managers are the first to have developed a plausible model of the future that is global.

—*Richard Barnet and Ronald Müller, Global Reach, 1974*

The poor nations are not criticizing the rich nations because they are rich and because three-quarters of the world's income, investment, and services, and most of the world's research, are in the hands of one-quarter of its population. Nor are the poor nations asking for a massive redistribution of existing income and wealth. What they are really arguing for is a greater equality of opportunity in the future, which is impossible to achieve within the present economic imbalances and the existing world structures which favor the rich nations.

—*Mahbub ul Haq, Director of World Bank Policy Planning Department, "Rich and Poor Nations," 1975*

Not since World War II has the world economic system been in such flux. The breakdown of the old Bretton Woods world monetary system, the rise of the OPEC oil cartel and autonomous multinational corporations, the shortages of food and resources, and the world-wide plague of inflation, recession, and joblessness have deepened the normal pessimism of thinking people in the nuclear age. Not since World War II have the stakes in creating a new world economic order been higher for rich and poor alike. As the richest and most powerful country in the world, America has the most to lose from a violent revolutionary change in the global status quo; but with privilege comes responsibility, and the heavy moral and political obligations which fall upon this nation today are unequaled in world history.

Domestic economic and social problems have disguised this country's world power from Americans: they do not often think of themselves as an economic and political elite. But as a small portion of the world's population that spends almost half of the world's income, Americans cannot deny their elite status in socioeconomic terms. Moreover, not only is America one of the world's two full-fledged superpowers but, along with Canada and Australia, it is the breadbasket of the world: America's grain stocks constitute nearly half the world's supply. But the pressures exerted by Third World oil producers and opponents of America's political power throughout the world have created a defensive feeling of irritation among even the American elites who know their privileged status. For example, one high-level State Department official recently stated: "We have the food, and the hell with the rest of the world."[1] America is fast moving into the uncomfortable moral and political position of having the power to decide who starves and who lives in much of the Third World.

Even if America's world power declines compared to that of other nations in the future, its moral and political responsibility will remain great because of what it has had. For not only has this country represented the promise of a new world for other peoples, but within a short 200 year history, it has actually become the New World for many. In terms of abundance and opportunity, the American experience has never been equaled in history, and this existential fact will become increasingly clear as the world's economic difficulties and scarcities multiply. The question of America's future—which therefore becomes a question of the world's future—is if Americans can recover their individual discipline, New World idealism, and bravado to help lead the world out of its difficulties or if, instead, Americans will turn inward to a private and selfish hedonism, creating a rich conservative fortress and giving up their humanist ideals.

Moral arguments alone are unlikely to persuade national leaders to help reduce the increasing gap between the world's rich and poor nations or to completely restructure the international economic system. World economic instability has grown to such proportions that moral arguments seem academic. Third World nations are forming cartels on natural resources such as bauxite, copper, and iron ore, needed by the Old Rich nations, and are organizing politically so that they can disrupt world economic stability if the trend continues to go against them. Violence, blackmail, kidnapping, strategic terrorism, and other means are coming into vogue and are apt to become more widespread and serious with the proliferation of conventional and nuclear weapons. Without a major restructuring of the world economy, the rich may never find peace and could even lose their wealth, while the poor face malnutrition and starvation.

The policy changes forced upon Secretary of State Henry Kissinger may indicate the direction in which world politics could head. Kissinger's success in international diplomacy largely depended upon his national security expertise and his deft tactical abilities in one-to-one negotiations. These skills made him a perfect candidate to solve the Cold War problems that lingered long after a normalization of relations with the Russians and Chinese seemed necessary. By creating a blueprint for the preservation of *détente* with the Soviet Union and China at all costs, Kissinger fulfilled his national security mission with surprising successes during the Nixon administration.[2] But Kissinger perceived problems in world politics basically in terms of potential superpower conflict and avoided involvement with the world's poor countries as well as with economic problems. Initially his reaction to the demands of the Third World oil cartel was a refusal to negotiate seriously with poor nations that were demanding a new world economic order. From the conventional Old Rich viewpoint, it seemed natural enough to organize the wealthy oil consumers of the Western world into a bargaining unit to get the best deal with the New Rich oil producers. But even though the disruptions in the world economic system because of the oil price hike were not as disastrous as some economists projected, they did serve to give Third World countries a new sense of pride and power, and they suggested a means for organizing economically in order to gain more concessions from the Old Rich. Conventional Old Rich reasoning broke down when confronted with this emotional surge for influence and change on the part of the Third World. World public opinion shifted quickly to the Third World underdogs, particularly since the poorest nations were suffering most from the impact of high energy costs and the inflation and recession of the mid-1970s.

So in 1975, Kissinger was forced to reverse his position, realizing that world politics had shifted from strategic to economic priorities and that the United States had much more to lose through a policy of confrontation than through a policy of accommodation with the Third World. In his September 2, 1975, message to the United Nations Special Session on Economic Development and Cooperation, Kissinger recognized the interdependence of the rich and poor—a message which representative Ivor Richards of Britain called "the meatiest speech made on economic development since the Marshall Plan." In it, Kissinger noted:

Our first task is to ensure basic economic security. The swings and shocks
of economic adversity are a global concern, tearing the fabric of developed
and developing nations alike. The cycle of good times and bad, abundance
and famine, does vast damage to lives and economies. . . . Developing
countries are by far the most vulnerable to natural and man-made disasters—the vagaries of weather and of the business cycle, sharp increases in
the prices of oil and food have a devastating effect on their livelihood.
Recession in the industrial countries depresses their export earnings. Thus
economic security is the minimum requirement of an effective strategy for
development. Without this foundation, sound development programs
cannot proceed and the great efforts that development requires from rich
and poor alike cannot be sustained.[5]

But, alas, practical proposals by Congress and the executive branch to follow-up
on this hopeful message were not forthcoming.

Kissinger's Old World strategy of power balances may work for stabilizing
superpower relationships but it is apt to become increasingly self-defeating if
applied to New World problems of restructuring the world's economic system.
For Kissinger was ultimately a conservative maintenance man whose proposals
for economic reform were more symbolic than real. He sought more to establish
effective bargaining postures in order to preserve a pro-American status quo
than to solve the deeper problems of world economic production and distribution and the creation of equal opportunity in the evolving new economic order.
Even Kissinger's African initiatives seemed aimed more at countering Soviet
and Chinese influence in the area by stabilizing it than at transforming the
status quo for the sake of black Africans. Both China and the Soviet Union are
better off than the United States in the critical economic dialogue with the
world for several reasons. First, the two countries have coherent ideologies and
plans for modernization that promise greater power and wealth if adopted by
lesser-developed countries (regardless of whether or not these plans can actually
be fulfilled.) And second, the United States is in the scapegoat position of
representing the old imperial and economic order, since this country has
dominated the political and economic agreements and international institutions
created since World War II.

How did the world economic crisis originate? What does it mean for the
New Rich, the Old Rich, and the Poor? As an Old Rich nation, what policy
alternatives does America have, and what are their consequences for the poorest

nations in the world? These questions are critical to developing a new American foreign policy.

The origins of the late twentieth-century world economic crisis can be found in the nineteenth century. At that time industrial capitalism flourished in the developed countries of Europe, as well as in the United States, because of a liberal system of world trade which allowed goods and labor to cross national boundaries more easily and because of policies of colonial expansion which brought new resources for these developing Old Rich countries. Old World European industrial countries dominated the international scene politically and economically until they were replaced in this century by the United States, which instituted an economic system of American "paternalism." As paternalisms go, the world may well have been better off with an American variety; but paternalism must be seen for what it is—a sophisticated form of imperial domination.

Although many of the seeds for the American global economy of liberal paternalism were planted in the administration of Woodrow Wilson, American domination did not become explicit in institutional terms until after World War II. The nations in Europe which won the war militarily lost it economically and were heavily dependent upon American capital for their economic recoveries. Thus, in terms of both military and economic power, the Americans dominated the diplomatic bargaining tables when a new world economic order was established in the wake of the war. The Bretton Woods conferences of 1944 established a new financial system for the world and created the International Monetary Fund (IMF). Both were based on compromises heavily loaded toward the American position. Similarly, the United Nations and the World Bank, subsequently created, were also dominated by the policies of the Old Rich industrial countries, particularly of the United States.

American paternalism abroad was symbolized by the Marshall Plan for European recovery and American defense spending, aid, and tourism, which literally flooded the world with dollars—the international liquidity that stimulated much of the recovery of the developed nations of the world after the war. As political economists David Calleo and Benjamin Rowland noted:

> In spite of a constantly favorable American balance of trade, we continued to spend overseas substantially more than we earned. As a result, the United States eventually passed from being the world's major short-term creditor to being its principal short-term debtor. The dollar soon became the world's chief "reserve currency," meaning that foreign governments and individuals proved willing to hold dollars rather than cash them in for gold from our reserves. Hence our dollar deficits were unredeemed.

Instead, expatriate dollars came to constitute a large part of the monetary reserves of most foreign countries and were the principal currency in world trade and the international short-term capital market.[4]

Ultimately, however, America's inability to carry a large balance-of-payments deficit caused the breakdown of the Bretton Woods international monetary system in the 1970s. For the American paternal economic system was rooted on the assumption that the dollar, as the liquidity-creating reserve currency, was convertible into gold. But increasing this liquidity meant increasing America's payment deficit and, inevitably, this country's short-term debt eventually exceeded its gold supply. This assured the breakdown of the system since either the United States would have to bring its payments into balance, ceasing to create liquidity, or foreign dollar holders would refuse to hold dollars any more, knowing they were no longer backed sufficiently by gold—which was what actually happened in Europe.

On August 15, 1971, the Nixon administration shocked the world by unilaterally suspending the convertibility of the dollar into gold, thus ignoring the rules of an international economic system of fixed exchange rates. The devaluation of the dollar and the revaluation of Japanese and West European currencies that followed were basically half-hearted measures to restore the old system of fixed exchange rates.[5] Cut off from gold, both gold and the dollar became the objects of financial speculation. A new system of floating currencies, whereby all currencies were allowed to find their worth on the open market, was instituted. Few trusted the dollar anymore as the basic international reserve currency, though no one had a credible replacement for it. This was the moment when the total uncertainty of the world economic system which we feel so much today first became official.

Naturally, the breakdown of the world monetary system was not the only cause of uncertainty and world economic crisis in the 1970s. The food and energy crises contributed to a rampant world inflation, leading to a recession on all fronts and threatening a depression and international economic warfare. Bad weather and crop failures increased the demand for grain, causing spiraling food prices. And the cartel of the Third World oil-producing countries quadrupled oil prices and set the stage for other Third World attempts to create resource cartels to squeeze the Old Rich. When it was discovered that the oil-producing nations had more liquid assets than their own countries could absorb and that the poorest Third World countries were hardest hit by the oil price hikes, Kissinger tried to split the New Rich oil producers from the poor nations of the Third and Fourth Worlds. He argued that the burden of the $30 billion deficit of the poorest nations must be shared by Old Rich and New Rich alike and suggested that since the OPEC oil producers had more liquid money than they knew how to spend, they should help bail out their poorer Third World brethren. The New Rich and Poor viewed Kissinger's strategy as an attempt to maintain Old Rich wealth and power by passing on responsibility to others, although the OPEC countries did establish a token fund to help out the poorest oil-consuming nations.

The Third World reaction to the world economic crisis was to call for the creation of a new international economic order. Although some spoke more radically than others, most of the New Rich and Poor nations have united in a demand for replacing the American-dominated paternal system of welfare capitalism with an economic order that would give the Third World a greater voice in international economic decision making, that would provide capital and technology for modernization in developing countries, and that would be based upon a principle of equal economic opportunity for all to satisfy basic human needs.

One of the most effective, moderate advocates of the Third World position is Dr. Mahbub ul Haq, Director of Policy Planning and Program Review at the World Bank and previously a member of the planning commission of Pakistan. Having applied Western techniques of modernization and economic planning to Pakistan for several years, Haq slowly came to the conclusion that Third World countries must develop their own non-Western methods of development that begin with the particular needs of the people in the country at hand. And internationally he came to a conclusion with which almost every other Third World partisan would agree: the present world order discriminates systematically against undeveloped regions and must be radically restructured to make equal opportunity for poor peoples possible.

Dr. Haq points out that the world economic opportunities have changed drastically since the nineteenth century. No longer can goods and labor move as freely over borders as they did for Europeans and Americans a century ago. Strict immigration quotas and protective tariff barriers prevent Third World goods and labor from flowing into Old Rich or First World countries, thereby hindering the modernization of undeveloped nations. The poor, he suggests, are not asking for a massive redistribution of wealth, even though three quarters of the world's income, investment, and services and most of the world's research facilities are in the hands of one quarter of its population. Rather, the poor nations want greater equality of opportunity, which is impossible to achieve given the present economic imbalances and existing international structures which favor the rich nations.[6]

There are many ways, according to Haq that the present world order discriminates against the poor nations. First, the international credit system, which is critical for changing the condition of a poor nation, gave less than 4 percent of the $126 billion of international credit to poor nations in the last two decades, though those nations account for 70 percent of the world population. This occurred because the rich controlled the creation and distribution of international credit through the expansion of their own national reserve currencies (the dollar and the pound especially) and through their domination of the International Monetary Fund. In world trading patterns, developing countries got only a 10 percent return on the final price that consumers in the world market paid for their produce. Most of the rest went to middle men who control the processing, shipping, and marketing of the primary exports of poor countries. Furthermore, developed countries have much better access to world markets than do lesser-developed countries. Finally, the Third World has not had much of a voice in large, powerful international decision-making bodies like the World Bank. As Haq ruefully notes, "In Bretton Woods we have finance without democracy, in the United Nations we have democracy without finance."[7]

In suggesting changes to implement a new economic order, Haq points out that international institutions always lag behind national development by fifty to one hundred years and that just as it took many years for nations like the United States to arrive at a New Deal philosophy and a commitment to equal opportunity for disadvantaged minorities, likewise it has taken the international system a long time to develop such a philosophy. The job, he argues, is to improve the productivity of the poor peoples of the world, not to have them live on charity. These undeveloped nations went through nationalistic movements for political independence in the 1950s and 1960s, and their present demand for economic independence is a natural historical development that could have been anticipated long ago.

To create equality of opportunity for poor nations, for all nations, Haq argues there must be a fundamental restructuring of the economic system that promotes economic growth in nations both rich and poor. He suggests four steps toward changing the world economic order: (1) creating an international central bank to estimate credit needs and make loans to the poorest countries (replacing the United States which, by default, became the international bank just as the dollar was the world reserve currency); (2) establishing a plan for international taxation in the long run, whereby the rich would help the poor out of their poverty, by transferring resources (for example, by paying taxes for international commodities, offshore oil, and seabed development); (3) increasing the access of the poor to the markets of rich nations by permitting developing countries greater control over the processing of their own commodities and shipping and by encouraging rich nations to lower restrictive barriers set up against goods and labor from poor nations; and (4) restructuring some of the Bretton Woods institutions to give Third World countries a greater voice and greater access to international credit. Although Haq admits that in the short term the poor nations will not have the bargaining power to restructure the world economic system, in the long term he believes they will. The poor, after all, have the power to disrupt the world system through revolution, guerrilla tactics, and strikes which would force the rich to consider the cost of destruction versus the cost of accommodation.[8]

Although Haq's view is a moderate version of the Third World perspective, Old Rich governmental and academic elites tend to perceive it as unrealistic and unacceptable to those in power in the developed world.[9] Old Rich elites, after all, are used to thinking in terms of maintaining the existing status quo, investing in areas which will turn a profit and risk few losses, and making international business agreements favorable to their own company's or country's strategic and financial interest rather than those of the poor. The postindustrial Old Rich perspective and the Third World call for radical world economic reform appear to be in absolute conflict.

The philosophical and political opposite of the Third World perspective is the world view of the global multinational corporation. A multinational corporation is a business firm so large that it is global in scope with manufacturing activities in many countries. Although often the loyalties and interests of multinationals go beyond attachments to any particular nation-state, national governmental elites are hesitant to regulate them for fear of lowering the nation's growth rate or of causing corporations to leave the country and set up shop in a more favorable climate. Moreover, many of the governmental elites of the Old Rich countries come from a corporate background or at least share the same strong belief in the necessity for economic growth before all else as corporation. The ideology of profit and economic growth maximization for the company gives these large organizations a simple criterion for measuring progress, planning for the future, and selecting target host countries for new investments. And the poorest of the poor nations in the world are not apt to be high on the list of possible areas for investment according to such criteria.

The rise in power of the multinational corporation is occurring simultaneously with the decline in effectiveness of the nation-state—particularly in Old Rich industrial societies. The effect of this trend is to split private economic power from public political power, making multinational businesses into organizations for the self-aggrandizement of a minority with little social accountability and few democratic political controls. There is no guarantee that a multinational company's economic growth will stimulate the dominant home country's economy, much less aid the poor in that country or the poor of other countries. Moreover, the present popular movement to control multinational corporations seems aimed more at bringing the wealth of jobs of multinationals under national regulation by elected government officials in Old Rich countries than at reducing the widening gap between the rich and poor nations of the world.

For example, in their popular and provocative book, *Global Reach: The Power of the Multinational Corporations*, Richard Barnet and Ronald Müller argue that the individuals who manage a few hundred corporations, which are bigger and more powerful than most nations, will dominate not only the world economy in the future, but the technology and power of world management as well. They write:

> The rise of the planetary enterprise is producing an organizational revolution as profound in its implications for modern man as the Industrial Revolution and the rise of the nation-state itself. The growth rate of global corporations in recent years is so spectacular that it is now easy to assemble an array of dazzling statistics. If we compare the annual sales of corporations with the gross national product of countries for 1973, we discover that GM is bigger than Switzerland, Pakistan, and South Africa; that Royal Dutch Shell is bigger than Iran, Venezuela, and Turkey; and that Goodyear Tire is bigger than Saudi Arabia. The average growth rate of the most successful global corporations is two to three times that of most advanced industrial countries, including the United States. [10]

But after justly pointing out that corporations must be made more accountable to the societies from which they derive their initial wealth, Barnet and Müller end by advocating regulation not so much to better the poor nations of the world as to further nationalistic control by the people in rich nations:

> The bias in our laws favoring foreign investment should be systematically removed. Tax laws should not be used to encourage foreign investment. . . . A rational development program for the people of the United States would include a heavy investment in the public development of a variety of technologies to make the American people "self-sufficient"—independent not only of foreign governments but of a few oil companies too. . . . To encourage investment in job-creating technology in the United States, U.S. law should no longer subsidize corporate growth through foreign investment." [11]

Like President Nixon's Project Independence, Barnet and Müller's call for national self-sufficiency and the end of support for foreign investment caters to the rising mood of economic nationalism and trade protectionism that could ultimately lead to another world war growing out of trade conflicts, and that, in any case, will hit hardest the poorest nations who can least afford it. Americans in the future may unwittingly bottle up their own economic productivity without sharing any more with less fortunate nations. They will thus have less to share, making everyone worse off.

Barnet and Müller are well aware, however, that multinational corporations can actually injure developing countries by distorting their home labor markets, disrupting small indigenous businesses and creating unhealthy economic patterns based upon short-run public desires for products such as Coca Cola and white bread rather than for food and other products that would satisfy the real needs of the population. These corporations also tend to transfer their assets and funds to countries where taxes are lowest, but since their profits are often made in countries where taxes are highest, this undermines the tax base of those foreign governments. The challenge of the future is to create national legislation which encourages multinational corporations to become more socially responsible and to take the needs of the people of the host country into account yet which permits corporations to be productive and effective instruments of modernization and economic growth.

Since nearly half of the top 50 multinational corporations in the world are American, this country's citizens are again the elite in this sector of the world economy and must bear responsibility accordingly. The debate over multinational corporations in America today focuses upon their political role and economic efficiency in raising the American GNP more than upon whether or not they exacerbate the rich-poor gap.

Senator Frank Church and other members of Congress have been justly concerned about the role of multinational corporations in financially supporting authoritarian regimes more conducive to business stability than socialist regimes would be—even if democratically elected. Thus, for example, International Telephone and Telegraph (ITT) has admitted offering the Central Intelligence Agency (CIA) $1 million to prevent Allende from installing a socialist government in Chile through a democratic election. Although the CIA turned the money down, it played a heavy-handed role with Kissinger's approval using $11 million in public funds to help "destabilize" Allende's regime once it was in power. The CIA's efforts helped bring on a reactionary coup which installed one of the most repressive dictatorships in the world. Such an outcome is a clear-cut disaster for American foreign policy, which officially claims to be supporting democratic principles throughout the world, and Congress is certainly justified in its scalding criticisms. The political effect of such international scandals is similar to that of the Watergate affair domestically: the American people become increasingly disenchanted with their leaders and politics in general and support increasing restraints upon executive policy makers who may soon have less and less power to do good deeds (such as helping the poor) as well as nasty ones. To argue that this is just as well since the executive branch seems more predisposed toward nastiness than goodness merely reinforces the existing Old World spirit of cynicism in public affairs, epitomized by the Nixon White House and the apparent amorality of some of Kissinger's short-term foreign policy solutions.

Executives in both the American government and American corporations have one weakness in common: they consistently underestimate the need for legitimacy based upon comprehendible moral and political principles which the American public supports. There is a self-serving arrogance in the elite management of the country that stems from the inaccurate assumption that most Americans are basically stupid and that, therefore, the superintelligent elites should autonomously and secretly decide upon and execute the most important political and economic decisions for the country with little meaningful consultation with Congress or anyone else. The fact that such arrogant attitudes still prevail after the Watergate affair and Vietnam debacle is amazing: the popular reaction against executive power and Kissinger "mandarinism" is building to explosive proportions and is apt to cause a pendulum swing toward mobocracy. And such a development could easily lead to the next phase that the Greeks posited in their cycle: the takeover of American government by an anti-intellectual demagogue who initiates a 1984 technocratic tyranny "for the sake of the people."

In the future, arrogance on the part of corporate executives may result in severe regulations of multinational corporate activity that will cut American economic productivity markedly and usher in an era of selfish nationalistic protectionism that cuts back American help for poor nations even further. The corporations have drifted too long upon the subtle ideology of apolitics. They claim that the decisions by technocratic elites are apolitical because they are based upon specialized expertise and take place in the private sector free from the wrangling of many special interests. But without democratic controls such decision making can be dangerous. Thus Richard Nixon's claim of wanting to become an apolitical, efficient manager of the presidency was actually a sophisticated, technocratic cover for moral bankruptcy and political corruption which the American people supported all too easily in Nixon's landslide reelection in 1972. Recent congressional revelations of corruption in both government and corporate hierarchies should serve as a stimulus in the future for Americans to reject apolitics and its Old World elitist assumptions and to create a new American politics for human beings based upon real human needs and America's New World heritage of humanism and equal opportunity.[12]

The critical question for political economists to ponder is not whether capitalist acts among consenting adults should be permitted, but whether they hurt the life chances of the poor at home and abroad, and, if so, what can be done about it. In the last four years the per capita income of the one billion people in the thirty poorest countries, who already live at subsistence levels, has further declined while the income of those in industrial nations has remained constant. Presently, the richest billion people claim more of the world's scarce resources annually than the remaining 3 billion. Foreign aid, or "official development assistance," has fallen from .52 percent of the Gross National Products of industrialized countries in 1960 to .32 percent in 1975 and is expected to drop further.[13]

The picture in world trade is equally gloomy. The position of the developing nations in trade is declining relative to that of the developed nations, largely because the former relies heavily upon the exchange of primary products and resources as opposed to manufactured goods. In the past few years, four-fifths of the total resource flow to developing countries has been in trade (rather than aid or investment), and since the trade balance for the poor countries is constantly getting worse, there is little room for optimism in the future. Moreover, many of the developed countries—including the United States, Canada, and Australia—are becoming increasingly efficient and independent in agricultural production and are protecting their farming sectors when necessary. As a result, Third World producers find it difficult to penetrate these markets. A related problem is that subsidies in developed countries are generating inefficient crop surpluses, thus artificially depressing the international market.[14] Legislation in the industrial countries to authorize the elimination of import duties on products exported from developing nations can solve one aspect of the problem, but such legislation is unlikely to be forthcoming in an era of Third World oil and resource cartels and increasing protectionism in national economic policies.

In order to solve America's economic problems and to head off future balance-of-payments deficits, political pressure has been building for an American economic policy of neomercantilism. Advocates of this policy, which is based upon the concept of mercantilism, favor reducing imports, increasing home production and jobs, and increasing exports, though such steps are likely to have a negative effect upon other countries. Neomercantilism is thus a form of economic nationalism by which the costs of adjustment to a nation's decisions are borne by other countries, and problems inside one nation are exported to someone else. The most negative consequences of such mercantilist economic policies are apt to be felt by the poor nations.

Economic neomercantilism is similar to rugged individualism in that both advocate the self-sufficiency of the individual unit regardless of the consequences to those outside it. Ultimately neomercantilism glorifies the nation-state and implies a policy of international social Darwinism: nation-states should be allowed to exist only to the extent they can make it on their own, and weaklings, the "international basket cases" (as Kissinger referred to Bangladesh), must be allowed to wither away.

David Calleo and Benjamin Rowland advocate nationalistic neomercantilism in their book *America and the World Political Economy*. They see nation-states as organisms which have only limited tolerance for destabilizing intrusions from the outside and which survive only by mobilizing a self-preserving intolerance for all external instability. They argue that economic nationalism does not, in itself, lead to imperialism; rather, an imperial struggle for control over external markets arises from the inability of a nation-state to absorb its own economic products: "Rationally, the war for international markets becomes obsolete among developed nations."[15] And as for the Third World poor, they must shape up or be allowed to wither away:

> Third-World countries and regions must become their own markets. Like the West, they must learn not only how to increase production, but also how to absorb it. Poor countries should not expect, any more than [the] rich, to export their internal imbalances. New countries, like old, must face up to the problem of building viable national communities. The age of the minimal state should now be over.[16]

So the battle lines for the future political economic conflict among the rich and poor nations are clearly drawn. Third and Fourth World countries will argue (as did Haq) for a new economic order which allows the products and labor of developing nations into the markets of the First and Second Worlds and which restructures the existing economic and political system to give credit and equal opportunity to the poor. The First World, Old Rich countries, on the other hand, are most likely to continue to argue (like Kissinger, Calleo, and Rowland) that the problems of poor countries are basically just that and that Old Rich countries like the United States cannot, and indeed should not, do a great deal to help. Professor Nathaniel Leff of the Columbia School of Business even goes so far as to suggest that it is "illusory to think that any kind of large aid will reduce the rich-poor income gap in any short-term future," that any increase in wealth also increases the capacity for political repression, and that it "would be very good for all concerned if multinational corporations would not invest any more in developing countries."[17] The new international economic order, Leff suggests, is little more than rhetoric, which, if fulfilled, would not come close to bridging the rich-poor gap anyway. And his opinion seems to be spreading among the Old Rich.

In January 1976 a new monetary system was officially introduced at a conference of the International Monetary Fund at Kingston, Jamaica—appropriately a Third World setting. Although called a "radical departure from Bretton Woods," the new system was basically a reaffirmation of the status quo, legalizing the system of floating currency rates and the changed status of gold which had been operating informally (and illegally in Bretton Woods terms) since the United States had ended the convertibility of dollars into gold in 1971. The Jamaica agreement made significant progress in only one small way: it partially converted the IMF from a banking and exchange regulator into an aid agency by setting up a gold trust fund to make credit more easily available to the poor nations. And although the quotas of the IMF were enlarged by about $12 billion, primarily to make more money available for the poor, this agreement would probably provide only up to $3.5 billion the first year. Such an amount is clearly insufficient in terms of even beginning to meet the needs of the poor nations.[18]

Naturally the Old Rich and the Poor nations perceived the Jamaica agreement differently. A high American official called the agreement "a new Bretton Woods" and Hans Apel, Finance Minister of West Germany, said "All is solved."[19] But the poor nations and the oil-exporting countries were more skeptical, noting that the agreement depended upon ratification by national legislatures and accurately suggesting that the agreement did nothing radical to change the status quo in favor of Third and Fourth World nations. The notion of legalizing existing floating exchange rates was, after all, a main objective of American diplomacy in the negotiations and abolishing a fixed price of gold to let it seek market-level prices does nothing to change the rich-poor gap. But at least a serious dialogue between the rich and poor has been brought to the diplomatic table. A new monetary system may emerge over the long run from ideas of the four commissions established earlier in Paris to draw up proposals on the major issues affecting rich-poor relations: oil, raw materials, development aid and the financial and monetary problems it entails.[20]

America's role in the future creation of a meaningful new economic structure for the world will be as critical as it will be frustrating. As the wealthiest nation in the world with some of the most sophisticated economic and management expertise, America can contribute a great deal. But its contributions will necessarily be frustrated by attacks from New Rich and Poor nations upon its power and motives. These nations will argue that in leading the world toward a new system, this country is attempting to solidify a new variety of imperialism through multinational corporations, token changes in Bretton Woods international institutions (that safeguard American interest), and decreasing American activity in and support for the United Nations and other multilateral agencies. America's superpower and economic status in the world makes such attacks inevitable, and American policy makers must accept this existential fact and put less energy into defending the country and more into creating a positive role and image for it in the world.

Notes

[1]Cited in "U.S. Food Power: Ultimate Weapon in World Politics?" *Business Week*, December 15, 1975, p. 54.

[2]See R. Isaak, *Individuals and World Politics* (North Scituate, Mass.: Duxbury Press, 1975), especially chap. 8.

[3]"Excerpts From Kissinger's Address," *The New York Times*, September 2, 1975, p. 20.

[4]David P. Calleo and Benjamin M. Rowland, *America and the World Political Economy* (Bloomington, Ind.: Indiana University Press, 1973), p. 88.

[5]R. Isaak, "American Policy and the World Economic Crisis," *Journal of International Affairs*, 28, 1 (1974), 91.

[6]Mahbub ul Haq, "The New International Economic Order," a presentation at the faculty Seminar on International Political Economy at Columbia University, December 17, 1975. See also Haq's "Toward a New Framework for International Resource Transfers," in *Finance and Development*, 1975.

[7]Haq, "The New International Economic Order."

[8]Ibid.

[9]Ibid.

[10]Richard Barnet and Ronald E. Müller, *Global Reach: The Power of the Multinational Corporations* (New York: Simon & Schuster, 1974), p. 15.

[11]Ibid., pp. 376-377.

[12]See R. Isaak and R. Hummel, *Politics for Human Beings* (North Scituate, Mass.: Duxbury Press, 1975).

[13]Ann Crittenden, "Vital Dialogue Is Beginning Between the Rich and Poor," *The New York Times*, September 28, 1975.

[14]Harald B. Malmgren, *International Economic Peacekeeping in Phase II* (New York: Quadrangle Books, 1973), pp. 183-185.

[15]Calleo and Rowland, *America and the World Political Economy*, p. 256-257.

[16]Ibid., p. 259.

[17]Nathaniel Leff, "After the New Economic International Order," a presentation to the Faculty International Political Economy Seminar at Columbia University, November 25, 1975. See Leff's "The New Economic Order—Bad Economics, Worse Politics," in *Foreign Policy*, No. 24, Fall, 1976, pp. 202-217.

[18]Leonard Silk, "A Monetary Order Born in Jamaica: System Is No Longer a Dialogue of the Rich," *The New York Times*, January 11, 1976.

[19]*Ibid*.

[20]Hans Bartsch, "North-South Dialogue Begins in Paris," *The German Tribune*, December 21, 1975, p. 1.

6 PUBLIC OPINION, FOREIGN POLICY MAKING, AND FOREIGN AID

It is often assumed, but without warrant, that the opinions of The People as voters can be treated as the expression of the interests of *The People* as an historic community. The crucial problem of modern democracy arises from the fact that this assumption is false. The voters cannot be relied upon to represent *The People*. The opinions of voters in elections are not to be accepted unquestioningly as true judgments of the vital interests of the community.

—*Walter Lippmann*, The Public Philosophy, *1955*

To those who come to us with requests for aid one would like to say: "You tell us first how you propose to assure that if we give you this aid it will not be interpreted among your people as a sign of weakness or fear on our part, or of a desire to dominate you."

—*George F. Kennan, "Limitations of Economic Aid," 1958*

The political slant of Communist economic policies—whether of loans or technical assistance or barter or ordinary trade—is their great strength. *Equally, the lack of any political or ideological framework is the greatest single source of weakness in the aid program undertaken by the West.*

—*Barbara Ward, "For a New Foreign Aid Concept," 1956*

In *Democracy in America* Alexis de Tocqueville noted that since the public dislikes secrecy and loses patience quickly, democracies are inferior to other governments in conducting their foreign policy. And, indeed, the role that public opinion and congressional oversight should play in foreign policy making has become one of the most controversial issues of American politics in the late twentieth century. This issue is perhaps most critical for a new humanist foreign policy when it comes to American aid for poor nations in the world. Support for foreign aid among most Americans has traditionally been weak, and Congress has developed the slashing of proposed foreign aid bills into a fine art.

How many people should ideally make foreign policy to assure the maximization of America's national interest in the nuclear age? Who should be given foreign aid, on what basis, and who should decide? These questions provide dramatic focal points for the conflict Americans are now experiencing between the demands of democracy on the one hand and the prerequisites of world power on the other.

The Vietnam disaster, the Watergate affair, and the CIA scandals have all served to undermine the authority of the executive branch of government in the making of American foreign policy. After such abuses of the public trust, no one can blame Congress for its militant skepticism of all executive agreements and proposals in the area of foreign affairs, as illustrated by the passage of the War Powers Act. But whether the majority vote of 535 members of Congress provides sufficient flexibility, expertise, and wisdom in the making of foreign policy is another question. One could argue that some of the effectiveness of American foreign policy in the 1970s (as well as some "ineffective brilliance") has been due to the expertise of Henry Kissinger and his domination of the foreign policy-making process—whether or not one agrees with the values and policies he has epitomized. Effectiveness, after all, is necessary for the retention of world power, and conducting a national referendum on every major foreign policy issue of the day is one sure way to suffocate effectiveness. How much of its democratic soul, then, is America willing to sell for the sake of world power? And, can American democracy survive at home if it abrogates responsibility in the world to undemocratic states?

Political philosopher Walter Lippmann distinguished between The People—the majority of voters or poll respondents at a single, contemporary instant in time—and *The People*—a community of the entire living population of the past, present, and future. This distinction has certain vital implications for the creation of effective foreign policies in a democratic society. Lippmann wrote:

> The Gallup polls are reports of what people are thinking. But that a plurality of the people sampled in the poll think one way has no bearing upon whether it is sound public policy. For their opportunities of judging great issues are in the very nature of things limited, and the statistical sum of their opinions is not the final verdict on an issue. It is, rather, the beginnings of the argument. In that argument their opinions need to be confronted by the views of the executive, defending and promoting the public interest. In the accommodation reached between the two views lies practical public policy.[1]

As reasonable as Lippmann's interpretation sounds, it strikes one as being too simplistic and optimistic given the political corruption of the 1970s. But Lippmann covered himself by acknowledging the potential for abuse of power:

> A prevailing plurality of the voters are not *The People*. The claim that they are is a bogus title invoked to justify the usurpation of the executive power by representative assemblies and the intimidation of public men by demogogic politicians. In fact, demagoguery can be described as the sleight of hand by which a faction of The People as voters are invested with the authority of *The People*. That is why so many crimes are committed in the people's name.[2]

But Lippmann just does not go far enough in our age of nuclear technology and corporate power. Today, in addition to being on guard against the tyranny of populist demagogues running for President, Americans must be very wary of the subtle, apolitical demagoguery of technocratic experts in foreign, economic, and security affairs. This is the danger which the so called Kissinger factor holds for democracy, despite its attractive advantages of consolidating an effective foreign policy in extremely capable hands.

The classic dilemma of democratic nations in executing foreign policy is that to be effective, Presidents must have the power to act swiftly and sometimes secretly, but such power is easily abused to the point of subverting constitutional restraints on the executive and the democratic freedoms of citizens. This dilemma has become more accute because of the increasing number of experts in the executive branch and the incredible power exercised by Henry Kissinger, an appointed official who has often declined to submit to congressional cross-examination and who, to make matters worse, was reappointed by an appointed President of the United States, Gerald Ford. In the transition from the Nixon to the Ford administration, Kissinger appeared to be the most powerful individual in the nation, if not in the world, and yet he was carefully protected from democratic channels because of his appointed status and his dual roles as head of the National Security Council and Secretary of State. It is almost as if Kissinger read and took the motto of *The Whole Earth Catalogue* too seriously: "We are as gods, so we mgiht as well get good at it."

There seems to be only one solution to this classic dilemma in America's case: the return to the ideal of representative democracy which the drafters of the Constitution intended. The main political problem of the day is to assure that executive foreign policy decisions represent *The People*, that is, are consonant with the historical traditions of this nation. The Watergate affair was clearly a subversion of the American people viewed as a collective historical tradition. So were the miscalculations of presidential advisors in Vietnam and the support for the systematic subversion of a democratically elected regime in Chile afforded by ITT and Henry Kissinger. *The People*, the symbol of the long-range view of American interests and ideals in terms of its historical and ideological heritage, is a concept that has recently been underemployed by Presidents and their advisors who seek primarily to keep themselves in office and who too often treat each foreign policy problem as if it had no historical precedents and could be worked out like a new, technocratic jigsaw puzzle. Americans must devise means to assure that their executive representatives carry out their real interests and not merely the latest academic modes or corporate interests. *The People* must be brought back to The People.

There are, of course, many respectable thinkers in the nominalist tradition who reject the idea of *The People*. Some political philosophers, like utilitarian Jeremy Bentham argue that the interest of the community is merely the sum of all the interests of the individual members who compose it.[3] Superficially this approach appears to allow more individual freedom and to assure safeguards against blind, uncritical nationalism, for as individuals change, so does the community, supposedly in a positive direction. But the nominalist view easily slips into a rugged individualism which legitimizes a society of each out only for his or her own selfish gain, a Hobbesian state of war of all against all. The problem, in short, is to assure that individuals take others' interests or rights into account. As with required inoculations against serious diseases, if each person decides not to go to the trouble of being inoculated because the odds of a particular individual's getting the disease are very small, the whole society would be worse off and the odds of everyone getting it would go up enormously. The critical problem of democracy is how to inspire people to choose their own interest in such a way that, at minimum, their decision does not harm the rights of others.

The only effective inspiration of this kind over time is the traditional community and its norms—Freud's superego, if you will. Freud argued that in order for civilization to exist, the egos of individual citizens must give in to the superego or norms of society. Otherwise, chaos and anarchy would result and everyone would be worse off. He noted, however, that the tension between the individual and social norms was vital if culture was to be created.[4] The political question Freud's concepts raise is: Just what limits should this tension and its expression be held to for the sake of others in society and who should enforce these limits? Clearly the tradition of *The People* can be enforced through either democratic or authoritarian means. Democracy assumes that people will choose most of the time to act within the traditions of *The People*, whereas authoritarian rules assume people must be forced to go along with the ruling elite's view of the tradition. Americans, wisely suspecting that the ruling elite would often try to deceive citizens, set up a Lockean system of checks and balances to prevent any particular leader from having authoritarian power.

But with great diffusion of power and individual interest, what becomes of the community tradition, or the collective interest of all generations of *The People* over time? What is to prevent one generation from wasting away all the nation's resources at the expense of generations to come? The question becomes even more critical when one nation threatens to waste its resources while the people of other nations starve to death. These possibilities led critical thinkers like de Tocqueville and Lippmann to fear a tyranny of the majority, which may be defined as the suppression of all minority opposition and the imposition of laws that are ultimately in the interest of no one or of only a few demagogues at the long-term expense of the entire nation. The landslide victory of Richard Nixon in 1972 comes to mind here. Although the American people could not be blamed for not knowing what Nixon deliberately withheld from them in the Watergate affair, few wanted to hear the accusations of Nixon's opponents on this very point.

Ultimately, the question of who should decide will be resolved by a balancing of quantity and quality. Because elites appear to be inevitable in every political system and because of America's heritage of an Aristotelian mixed form of government, balancing the few with the many, Americans must work to make their elitist representative democracy one that is truly open and responsive in the future.

Elites, or people in higher positions in society's hierarchy, usually have different beliefs or value priorities than do the majority of ordinary people in lower social positions. Political scientist Philip Converse has demonstrated that in America elitist belief systems are marked by possession of information, ability to articulate thoughts, and interest in abstract values like freedom or stability. The belief systems of ordinary people, or mass publics, on the other hand, are marked by lack of information, difficulty in articulating thoughts, and interest in simple, concrete values like higher wages and better living conditions.[5]

This "elite-mass gap" in belief systems is a critical one in the making of foreign policy in a democratic society. A recent survey of elite and mass public opinion on foreign policy issues illustrates the elite-mass gap in attitudes. A large majority of the public were of the opinion that real American concerns should be at home, and 52 percent believed this country should build up its own defenses and let the rest of the world take care of itself. Only 26 percent of the elite (elected and appointed officials and opinion makers), on the other hand believed that real concerns should be at home, and only 10 percent favored letting the world take care of itself. Both the American public and the elite rated economic strength as the most important aspect of United States leadership in the world. But leaders placed moral values second, skill in negotiating settlements that avoid war third, and scientific progress fourth, whereas, in contrast, the public ranked skill at negotiations second, military strength third, moral values fourth, and technology fifth.[6]

The elite-mass gap can be seen with respect to the issue of foreign aid as well. Whereas 34 percent of the elite interviewed cited defense cuts as one of their first or second top priorities, only 17 percent of the public agreed; the public put greater emphasis on cutting foreign military aid (35 percent) and foreign economic aid (24 percent). The latter figures stand in contrast to those of the elite, only 30 percent of whom ranked cuts in foreign military aid first and only 5 percent of whom gave priority to cuts in economic aid.[7] Even more striking, whereas 62 percent of the elite thought it was very important to help improve the standard of living of less developed countries, only 39 percent of the public thought so. Yet 76 percent of the public thought it was very important to combat world hunger as compared to 61 percent of the elite. In summary, the elite thought that morality, development of poor nations, and international cooperation for solving energy problems were more important than did the public at large, whereas the public seemed to be slightly more concerned with the concrete issue of world hunger than did the elite.[8]

Both the elite and the general public in America believe that the preservation of world peace is the single most important objective of this country's foreign policy. And both would undoubtedly agree that a certain international expertise and ability at global abstract thinking are natural prerequisites for wise foreign policy decision making. The public at large is typically most concerned with concrete issues at home whereas the primary focus of foreign policy elites is upon international interactions abroad. Until the Vietnam War there was a tendency on the part of the public to accept this distinction passively, allowing the President, his advisors, and "his" State and Defense Departments to make and execute foreign policy with little public or congressional oversight. But the Vietnam debacle polarized public opinion and politicized foreign policy. And the international oil crisis made the public aware of the interdependence of domestic and foreign issues. Consequently, at a time when complex foreign policy issues require wise, elite expertise as never before, the breakdown of the distinction between foreign and domestic policy makes the selection and legitimacy of that leadership increasingly difficult. The right of the people to know what is going on cannot be denied, however. The creation of a wise and consistent American foreign policy in the future will therefore require both a more open and responsive elite and a more informed public, educated in critical foreign policy issues.

In support of Lippmann's distinction between *The People* and The People, sociologist Robert Nisbet contrasts *public opinion*, the product of an historical political community over time, with *popular opinion*, "an emanation of what is scarcely more than the crowd or mass, of a sandheap given quick and passing shape by whatever winds may be blowing through the marketplace at any given time."[9] Without such a sharp distinction between representative government proper and a regime that goes along with all eruptions whether true or false, of popular opinion, Nisbet believes the authority of democratic government would become hopelessly undermined, particularly "in areas where it is indispensable: foreign policy, the military, fiscal stability, and the preservation of law and order."[10] The paradox of the democratic form of government is that to be effective and stable it depends upon the voluntary delegation of authority by The People to a representative elite who presumably work for the long-term public interest of *The People*.

Perhaps nowhere are the distortions of the public interest in the name of public opinion more apparent than in the media—television, newspapers, books, and magazines. The media often select newsworthy events by their dramatic or popular impact with the audience, rather than by some objective criterion of what meets the real needs of the American people and those of other countries. Such distortions emphasize domestic parochial debates at the expense of foreign news coverage and foreign affairs educational specials. Historian Daniel Boorstin even suggests that pseudo-events created by the media for popular consumption often drive important, naturally occurring events out of circulation. Pseudo-events are media creations characterized by Boorstin as dramatic, repeatable happenings simplistically planned for widespread dissemination. They are often heavily financed social tidbits or exciting incidents that spawn other pseudo-events and overwhelm real news and any sense of proportion. Boorstin describes two focuses of pseudo-events:

> The rise in the power and prestige of the Presidency is due not only to the broadening powers of the office and the need for quick decisions, but also to the rise of centralized news gathering and broadcasting, and the increase of the Washington press corps. The President has an ever more ready, more frequent, and more centralized access to the world of pseudo-events. A similar explanation helps account for the rising prominence in recent years of the Congressional investigating committees. In many cases these committees have virtually no legislative impulse, and sometimes no

intelligible legislative assignment. But they do have an almost unprecedented power, possessed now by no one else in the federal government except the President, to make news.[11]

Dramatic news is too often created out of relatively insignificant events to attract a greater audience to the media or to gain more votes or popularity for politicians—sometimes in the name of the people. One of the most troubling policy questions Americans must face in the future is: How much should the media and its financing be regulated to assure that media coverage nation-wide is not just propaganda for class or interest groups who can afford it or who stage dramatic events to make themselves newsworthy? A related question worth pondering is: How should newscasters select the most important half-hour of events for evening news TV broadcasts—by international importance, national political significance, or mass popularity? The need to ask such questions becomes evident from a casual glance at many newspapers, which usually give scant coverage to international news of the day, or at weekend TV news programs, which bury international affairs in an avalanche of sports and feature stories. News broadcasters have a responsibility to help the public audience learn to distinguish the significant from the insignificant—a responsibility often shirked for the tempting pleasures of psychodrama, jokes, and feature pablum aimed at entertaining more than informing. Outside of the schools, the media provide almost the only outlet for education in foreign affairs.

Survey research indicates widespread public indifference and ignorance of foreign affairs.[12] If this fact, in turn, leads news media to de-emphasize the importance of foreign policy issues, public support for foreign aid and foreign policy commitments may wane as world problems wax, and a self-preoccupied isolationism may slowly replace a healthy, cosmopolitan view of international interdependence and American responsibilities as a world power. The media often appear to be engaged in replacing critical thought and enlightened responsibility with popular entertainment and artificial melodrama. The danger is that the American popular image of the world may soon approach novelist Max Frisch's definition of technology: the knack of so arranging the world that we don't have to experience it.

The expression of public opinion involves a classic problem: how best to articulate the general will of *The People* in concrete political terms. The mechanism which usually claims to do this is the party system. One-party systems, which are operative in the Soviet Union and the People's Republic of China, dictate *The People's* will, whereas multiparty systems, found in the United States and most of Western Europe, claim the sovereignty of *The People* through regular elections. In terms of foreign policy making and consistent uses of foreign aid, one-party systems have significant advantages over multiparty systems.

For example, in comparing American and Soviet foreign aid programs, the advantages of America's economic wealth appear to be offset by the factionalism, short-term planning, and absence of a clear-cut ideology that characterize the working out of its program—drawbacks which the one-party, one-ideology Soviet state avoids. Soviet administrators do not need to defend their aid programs in public, to concern themselves with rivalries or overlaps between different aid-granting agencies, or to worry about changes in the goals of or support for the programs because of election-year pressures. As political scientist Robert Walters notes:

> The lack of an equivalent to the role played by the U.S. Congress in the administration of Soviet aid has allowed the Soviet program to achieve an organizational cohesiveness and stability unknown to American economic assistance. Moreover, the centralized political system accounts for the conspicuous absence of candid criticism of aid from various political figures and interests within Soviet society.[13]

The Cyprus dispute between Greece and Turkey in the 1970s illustrates an American foreign aid disaster which the Soviet Union, with its one-party system, could have avoided easily. Secretary of State Kissinger promised Turkey military and economic aid from the United States, but Greek-Americans mobilized themselves and lobbied effectively in Congress against the aid package. When Congress blocked foreign aid to Turkey, Turkish leaders— understandably believing that the United States was no longer to be trusted as an ally—threatened to force all NATO bases and troops to leave Turkish soil. Eventually, the Turkish aid bill did go through, resulting in the alienation of Greece from the United States. When asked what he frankly thought about the Turkish aid episode in terms of American national interests in foreign policy, Kissinger responded, "It was a disaster."

In the future, domestic and party factionalism can be expected to make American foreign policy making even more difficult as members of Congress seek an increasing role. To complicate matters further, the American two-party system may well break down in the future as voters increasingly identify themselves as independents or lose confidence altogether in party leaders and political organizations. America is indeed passing through an era of "the twilight of authority," to use Robert Nisbet's phrase, in which established institutions, leaders, and moral and political principles are all thrown into question. In the immediate future a clear-cut American foreign policy based upon a widespread domestic consensus and ideological understanding may be extremely difficult to come by. The only hope is to redefine what America should stand for at home and abroad and then to try to mobilize the nation behind such a vision.

Since World War II American foreign aid has been given, with few exceptions, on the basis of a defensive and reactionary philosophy: give to unstable or poor countries in order to contain communism, and defend American interests against Soviet or Chinese intrusion. Such a negative philosophy is, understandably, not as attractive to many developing countries as the promises of modernization and world brotherhood made by communist ideology. As economist Barbara Ward has noted:

> In all this welter of Western insistence upon self-interest and self-defense, one looks in vain for any consistent exposition of a *positive* policy of foreign aid, some general political philosophy to match the Communist confidence in world brotherhood based on Socialist production, some framework of solidarity between givers and takers of aid, some aspect of human concern beyond the narrow limits of common fear. [14]

Since World War II, governments of countries like India, for example, have appeared to be more thankful to the Soviet Union, who decided to *sell* them steel, than to the United States, who *gave* them that commodity. India's recent pro-Soviet support indicates all too clearly that the Soviet philosophy of economic development and world brotherhood is more effective in the long run than the American philosophy of communist containment. American diplomats like Daniel Moynihan lament the increasingly overwhelming dominance of undemocratic regimes in the world without taking the next bitter step of analyzing which kinds of American policies helped the world into this sorry state. America's negative foreign aid philosophy linked with Old World balance-of-power rhetoric and heavy-weapons sales all contribute to a self-fulfilling prophecy of cynicism, Western retrenchment and decline, and a lack of hope for the Third and Fourth Worlds.

Moreover, the negative philosophy behind American foreign policy has had serious domestic consequences. The New Left has accurately demonstrated that American foreign aid has been used explicitly as a tool for an Old World vision of imperialism and social control that is not merely reactionary but also ineffective in a world of rapid social change. [15] Although it may well be that the United States, given its wealth and power, is fated to play some imperial role or other in the world in the last quarter of this century, it does not follow that American world power must be based on merely negative principles.

Imperialism, or the policy of seeking to extend a nation's or empire's political and economic control over less developed nations in an exploitative fashion, is repugnant from a moral and humanistic viewpoint—as Third World critics never fail to point out. But there are differences between kinds of imperialism. British imperialism in the nineteenth century, for example, recognized the need to prepare the colonized countries and their elites for eventual independence and home rule; the imperialism of Nazi Germany was much more thoroughly exploitative and dehumanizing in nature. America's present Old World imperialism, which seeks to preserve stability at any price (even at the cost of supporting authoritarian dictatorships), can, at minimum, be modified. It can be based upon explicitly humanistic and democratic principles which would more easily receive domestic support at home and Third and Fourth World support abroad. Nor need such a positive New World philosophy be naïve or weak—as the next two chapters will demonstrate.

Gunnar Myrdal, the economist, has argued persuasively that America's recent "aid," granted for purely selfish military or political reasons, may represent, in part, an overreaction to a naïve generosity in American aid to Europe following World War II, often with no strings attached. Myrdal feels that the dispensing of foreign aid as a gift (as opposed to a long-term loan at a low interest rate) is unnecessary, unnatural, and unwise, except when the beneficiary is an underdeveloped country with deep structural problems. As he also argues, "The whole international exchange situation would have been more wholesome now and in the past decade if the United States could have called for repayments of loans from West European governments—gradually and with due considerations."[16] Furthermore, the Marshall Plan and European reconstruction programs skewed American aid and generosity heavily toward potentially rich countries in Europe, and the resulting lack of gratitude and resources turned Americans sour on aid before their generosity could be spent on poorer nations that really needed it:

> Imagine that there had been no reconstruction task to be carried out in Europe, but that otherwise nothing was different. I feel rather certain that as the colonies were then becoming liberated—which on a deeper ideological level touched sympathetic cords in America—and as knowledge about the great difficulties encountered by newly emerging and other underdeveloped countries was disseminated, efforts to aid them would have been forthcoming earlier and more strongly from a United States coming out of the war with feelings for its responsibility in the world—feelings that had

then not yet hardened in the way they later would, partly under the influence of the experiences with the West Europeans during the Marshall era.[17]

American policy, in short, seemed to fly from naïve idealism in aid policy following World War II into Old World, cynical realism with the Cold War global politics of the 1950s and the disillusionments abroad in the 1960s and 1970s. As former ambassador George Kennan once pointed out, "There is the basic fact that any form of benevolence, if prolonged for any length of time (even in personal life this is true), comes to be taken for granted as a right and its withdrawal resented as an injury."[18] Americans were eager to shoulder world responsibilities after the war but were burned for their lack of experience and maturity. This led to a self-pitying, cynical reaction and withdrawal beginning with aid and carrying over to a threatening widespread inward nationalism, if not isolationism, in the post-Vietnam period. America's "loss" of Angola to the Russian and Cuban side of that civil war in 1976 was, in a real sense, a psychological loss that the Russians astutely anticipated in the post-Vietnam period. They picked up chips on the international gameboard where they could while the opportunity was open.

But the basic and most tragic transformation of American aid policy since World War II has been the increasing duplicity of the program—in both its advocacy and execution—to the point that citizens can no longer distinguish humanitarian aid from weapons and defense expenditures. Old World American policy makers—believing themselves realistic in pursuing short-term gains in aid packages as an end, no matter what means are needed to cover up their real intentions from the public or Congress—sometimes appear astoundingly surprised when suddenly neither the public nor Congress believes their rhetoric any longer and both resist aid requests of any kind. Old World, Machiavellian diplomacy may work for some empires, but not democratic empires if they are to remain democratic. Amoral balance-of-power calculations that use aid as just another tool cannot be expected to generate public support in a moralistic and humanistic culture such as America's. As Myrdal put it, "*Aid policies cannot be morally neutral*. And popular support as a response to a moral commitment will not be found for a neutral aid policy. Moral feelings are never neutral to social conditions." And he goes on to cite Sweden's governmental basis for giving aid: "We can reasonably try so to direct our assistance programs that they do, to the best of our judgment, tend to promote political democracy and social equality. It is not consistent with the motives or aims of Swedish assistance that it should help to preserve anti-progressive social structures."[19] American aid policy, with its defensive support of dictatorships in the name of stability, strays far from the Swedish criterion for aid—a criterion which is consistent with America's democratic and humanistic ethos and which would generate much more public support for aid programs.

Of course the Old World counterargument comes immediately to mind here, like a bad habit. The substance of the argument is that the United States is an oversized empire, not a small neutral country like Sweden, and to keep an empire strong requires a realistic aid policy that uses aid as one weapon against enemies who may want to undermine this country's national security and world peace. We have been so conditioned by this argument that it sounds like a campaign slogan that either party's candidate or even a President, could use. But this objection fails to take into account that an empire with a democratic and Christian heritage like America cannot afford to neglect the moral bases of political power and popular support or to use moral principles now and then only as clever covers for devious balance-of-power maneuverings supposedly too complex for the public to comprehend. And, indeed, many American citizens have been conditioned to accept the supposed need for amoral power politics out of apathy, disgust, or long experiences of powerlessness that have led to political indifference.

The problem with the Old World "realist" argument in terms of aid is, ironically, that it is short-sighted and not realistic enough. Typically, it underestimates the intelligence of the public and the need for an aid program over time that can gain their enthusiastic support. Moreover, its duplicity is bound to be exposed eventually in a democratic society with a free press, at which point Americans will withdraw support not only for all aid programs but for the legitimacy of any form of elite leadership whatsoever. The Watergate and CIA scandals are apt to be too soon forgotten by elites and too long remembered by citizens called on for support of aid programs and other foreign policy matters.

What, then, *is* the alternative that allows an aid program which is consistent with America's democratic, humanistic creed and yet which takes into account America's role as an empire with security needs and interests throughout the world? I think the alternative must begin with a principle that can never be taken for granted and which is rarely resorted to in cynical times like our own—honesty. Policy makers must be honest, first of all, about the level of intelligence of the people. After all, if the American government requires its citizens to work toward at least a high-school education and, at some future date, even a junior college level of learning, can it continue to behave in foreign policy matters as if these same citizens were all dunderheads? The so called Fourth Estate—the press and the media—can guarantee the new-found honesty of policy makers. The television news media alone can assure that the

truth about duplicity will out. And the properly "romantic" field of investiga-
tive reporting can keep newspapers full of stories of governmental elites who
once again tried to deceive the people. By beginning with honesty as a basic
principle, foreign aid policy becomes instantly credible and government efforts
can be put where they are most sorely needed: in persuading Americans of the
real needs of the people abroad in terms of American interests, humanism, and
world peace.

I believe that America can create an effective foreign aid program in the
future by separating and seeking public support for three distinct kinds of aid:
(1) *humanitarian aid*, to be restricted to basic food and the medical needs of
desperate people as assessed by international authorities and to be distributed by
international agencies on an automatic basis (for example, 1 percent of the
American Gross National Product each year, whether in food, medical supplies,
or dollars); (2) *modernization aid*, to be restricted to the economic and social
development of needy countries as assessed unilaterally by the United States on
an explicitly political basis (such as some movement toward a democratic form
of government as understood in the American tradition to be made in a certain
time period under penalty of loss of aid); and (3) *national security, defense, and
military assistance*, to be restricted only by the condition that the people and
Congress are willing to support such spending for what it is—military spending, whether for ourselves or for others, whether for our economy or others'
security. My thesis is that the American people are no longer naïve or unin-
formed enough to continue to support attempts by tricky government officials
to mix these three different kinds of aid programs, disguising negative kinds of
military spending with positive humanistic cover programs.

There is a tremendous practical advantage to be gained by separating
humanitarian from other types of aid, funding it, automatically, and adminis-
tering it through international or multilateral agencies. In a world where
increasing numbers of people will starve to death and in which the United States
is in the unfortunate position of being one of the global food monopolies, the
responsibility for identifying the first victims to be fed and for distributing the
food and medical help to them would be taken from American shoulders and
placed on the multilateral agency. This will work, however, only if Americans
take the initial responsibility by automatically transferring a generous percentage of this country's annual Gross National Product to international agencies
solely for humanitarian aid purposes. (One percent of the American GNP would
not be an unreasonable starting figure, and it would represent a significant
increase in aid now given officially in this catergory.) Such a clear-cut, automatic way of providing American humanitarian aid should generate popular
support since there would be no way for clever or corrupt politicians within the

United States to try to bend this particular category of aid to their own ends.

If the first category of humanitarian aid goes over well with the public, eventually modernization aid might also be made automatic and handled by international agencies, with a democratic qualification or two. Realistically, however, the American people should be expected to accept any automatic transfer of their earnings abroad only slowly. At the beginning modernization aid might be funded biannually, to coincide with congressional elections, and be run on an explicitly political basis to counter Soviet and Chinese modernization models and aid efforts. The assumption behind such aid is that it is not in America's national interest to support modernization efforts of nations that do not intend to make any provision for democracy or free elections at any time in the future. To support undemocratic regimes would be only to gain perhaps a short-term military ally at the cost of helping to strengthen a long-term ideological adversary. A modernization aid program would require that the United States develop a range of possible modernization plans, paying off those we favor most with the most funds. Democratically elected socialist or even communist regimes *might* be considered for aid, with payments scaled down to the extent that such regimes practice patently undemocratic principles. The basic concept is to encourage countries to open themselves to ideas and a choice of political forces as Americans understand these things. We would thus encourage needy countries to begin radical reforms upon themselves at home not only to increase productivity and economic stability and efficiency, but also to widen democratic political freedoms. No interest in democracy, no aid for modernization.

The category of national security, defense, and military aid would be used to cover all prior treaty and alliance commitments (including those made on amoral or undemocratic balance-of-power principles). Such aid would be renewable only as long as the American public could be persuaded that these allocations of support were in the national interest. It might be useful to draw a sharp distinction in the public mind between military or security *assistance* and aid proper—whether for humanitarian or modernization purposes. In a real sense, to "aid" a nation militarily may not, in the long run, aid it at all but merely lead to arms races, aggression, and violence. Security "aid" does not necessarily make nations more secure, since heavily arming a people to make peace possible is always a contradiction on some level or other. The argument here is not that the United States should deny other nations arms when superpower stakes are involved. Rather, the thesis is simply that it is best to be honest about requests for hard military assistance for Old World balancing acts, distinguishing such requests clearly from humanitarian and development aid. Moreover, military assistance budgets should be the least automatic of all since military situations change rapidly and in military matters the national elite is most likely to try to disguise its real intentions from the population at large.

As aid bills move more toward clear-cut criteria for modernization and humanitarian help for other human beings on the basis of obvious needs, funding should become more automatic, aid criteria should be depoliticized, and multilateral agencies should replace the United States as the administrator. Similarly, if assistance requests move away from clear humanitarian objectives into the more dubious category of security and military assistance, funding should become less automatic (subject to review at least annually) and the public should be made more alert to the possible dangers.

Notes

[1] Walter Lippmann, *The Public Philosophy* (1955), Chapter 4, in *The Essential Lippmann*, edited by Clinton Rossiter and James Lare (New York: Random House, 1963), p. 88.

[2] *Ibid.*, p. 86.

[3] The holist position—that the whole community is more than the sum of its parts or of the individuals who make it up—paradoxically appears to make the existence of individual freedoms possible in a large nation-state or empire like the United States. For in such a case to deny that individuals can ever represent more than themselves or their immediate living constituencies while in office would preclude the existence of a national historical heritage and long-term national interest in a democratic society. If Bentham were right, a simple majority vote through referendum on every foreign policy issue would be guaranteed to reflect the national interest—which history shows to be a dubious notion.

[4] Sigmund Freud, *Civilization and Its Discontents*, trans. by James Strachey (New York: W. W. Norton, 1961).

[5] Philip E. Converse, "The Nature of Belief Systems in Mass Publics," in *Ideology and Discontent*, ed. by David E. Apter, (New York: Free Press, 1964), pp. 206-261.

[6] "American Public Opinion and U.S. Foreign Policy 1975," a survey conducted by the Chicago Council on Foreign Relations and the Louis Harris Polling Organization, ed. by John E. Reilly, (Chicago: The Chicago Council on Foreign Relations, 1975), p. 5.

[7] *Ibid.*, p. 6.

[8] *Ibid.*, p. 13.

[9] Robert Nisbet, "Public Opinion Versus Popular Opinion," *The Public Interest*, 41 (Fall 1975), 168.

[10] *Ibid.*, p. 166.

[11] Daniel J. Boorstin, *The Image: A Guide to Pseudo-events in America* (New York: Harper Colophon Books, 1961), pp. 40-41.

[12] See Hadley Cantril and Lloyd Free, *The Political Beliefs of Americans* (New York: Clarion, 1968); and John Robinson, *Public Information about World Affairs* (Ann Arbor: Survey Research Center, 1967).

[13] Robert S. Walters, *American and Soviet Aid: A Comparative Analysis* (Pittsburgh: University of Pittsburgh Press, 1970), p. 240.

[14] Barbara Ward, "For a New Foreign Aid Concept," in *Readings in American Foreign Policy*, ed. by Robert A. Goldwin and Harry M. Clor (New York: Oxford University Press, 1971), p. 582.

[15]See *The Trojan Horse: A Radical Look at Foreign Aid*, ed. by Steven Weisman (San Francisco: Ramparts Press, 1974).

[16]Gunnar Myrdal, *The Challenge of World Poverty: A World Anti-Poverty Program in Outline* (New York: Random House, 1970), p. 338.

[17]*Ibid.*, p. 342.

[18]George Kennan, "Limitations of Economic Aid," in *Readings in American Foreign Policy*, ed. by Robert A. Goldwin and Harry M. Clor (New York: Oxford University Press, 1971), p. 595.

[19]Myrdal, *The Challenge of World Poverty*, pp. 372-373.

7 SUPERPOWER STAKES WITH RUSSIA AND CHINA

Brezhnev asked his advisers what he should seek in America. "Ask them to sell us cars," suggested one. "Ask them to build us computer factories," said a second. "Ask them to build atomic-power stations," said a third. "No," replied Brezhnev thoughtfully. "I'll just ask them to build us Communism."

—*A "joke" that circulated within the Soviet establishment in 1973, from* Atlantic Monthly, December 1974

It is important to remember that the decade of the 1950's was the *only* period in the entire history of Chinese-Russian relations in which the two nations were closely allied. This ten-year aberration from a century-long pattern of national tension and territorial competition, and even tutelage, was in essence a response to a common enemy that, temporarily, was perceived as the greater threat: the United States. As this threat seems to recede in the wake of détente, the traditional animosities between China and Russia are resurfacing, and the relationship is reverting to the more familiar animosity. The end of the Vietnamese war has removed one of the major policy issues on which the two powers found themselves in agreement in the past.

—*John G. Stoessinger, "China and the Soviet Union: Retrospect and Prospect,"* 1974

Foreign aid is often viewed by foreign policy elites as merely a symbolic chip among many to be risked in an international poker game among the superpowers—the United States, the Soviet Union, and, to a lesser extent, the People's Republic of China. America's future as a world power clearly depends upon the astuteness of American diplomats at playing in the superpower contest for power and influence among the uncommitted nations of the world. Yet the trend is for Americans to worry more about restoring democracy at home than countering Soviet and Chinese moves abroad. Many want to put America's own house in order in the aftermath of government scandals and a disastrous war before concerning themselves with the rest of the world and America's stake in it. The American empire is being shaken down to its very foundation in order to reestablish a firm basis for a sound domestic and foreign policy.

But the shakedown of the American empire from within combined with its defeats abroad have provided the other two superpowers with a unique historical opportunity for imperial expansion. Secretary of State Henry Kissinger anticipated this development in his *détente* policy—a blueprint for a superbalance of power which would decrease tensions among the superpowers and preserve the basic structure of the status quo. The recent criticisms of *détente*—that the Soviet Union has gained the most economically and has violated military agreements with its arms build-up—are often accurate but somewhat irrelevant. What Kissinger seems to have anticipated is the inevitability of the decline of the American empire in the post-Vietnam period and the consequent necessity of demobilizing America's main antagonists, Russia and China, both militarily and psychologically. Through *détente*, Kissinger hoped to cut American losses stemming from the lack of domestic backing for an aggressive American foreign policy. Criticisms of *détente* are often irrelevant because they offer no positive alternative that makes as much global sense for American interests in the present historical circumstances. A new American isolationism is not a viable alternative since that would merely speed up American losses, with not just military and political consequences but economic consequences in international trade and investment as well. Kissinger's Old World blueprint cannot simply be rejected outright without a clear-cut New World policy alternative to replace it.

Kissinger himself came to represent the ultimate symbol of the tension between America's conservative imperial interests as a world power and America's ideology of democratic liberalism. The thrust of the criticism aimed at Kissinger was not so much that his blueprint would hurt the national interest, but that the Secretary himself had grown too powerful and that his use of secrecy and undemocratic means represented a threat to liberal American democracy. For example, in his introduction to the unauthorized publication of *The Pike Papers*, the congressional report on CIA intelligence failures, Aaron Latham concluded: "In many ways, the moral of *The Pike Papers* seems to be: controlling the intelligence community must begin with controlling Henry Kissinger."[1] This simplistic but popular conclusion spotlights the tension between imperial and democratic impulses in the working out of American public policy: a superpower cannot operate without secrecy and consistent executive behavior and controls, yet a democracy cannot operate with too much secrecy or an imperial executive power that undermines domestic freedoms (of the press, for example) and the ideological image of democratic liberalism abroad. In terms of effective foreign policy execution in America today, the

President, the secretaries of state and defense, and the director of the CIA are damned if they do and damned if they don't. And the American people are unlikely to be satisfied with a mature balance between democratic and imperial interests that results from a cynical "draw": they want a new, coherent philosophical basis for such a mature compromise, a clear-cut way of knowing what America should represent at home and abroad. While ambiguity may be one of the characteristics of greatness, many Americans are tired of the ambiguous. They seek a commonsense political philosophy and programs with which they can identify.

After many recent visits to America, Countess Marion Doenhoff, publisher of the prestigious West German newspaper, *Die Zeit*, concluded: "The visitor returns home with the impression that Watergate not only destroyed every leadership authority and led wide circles to masochism, skepticism and cynicism, but that Watergate, on foreign policy grounds, was also an incomparable tragedy for the Western world too—almost a Waterloo."[2] Dependent upon America for security and leadership in economic recovery, Europeans appear to be quicker than Americans in sensing the international implications of the undermining of authority in America by the Watergate episode.

History is rather clear, if somewhat cynical, when it comes to the question of the rise and fall of empires and civilizations: some imperial force or other always dominates certain regions or the world as a whole, and where the power of one empire or collective force declines, another becomes stronger to fill the vacuum. In world history, then, empires and civilizations are always expanding or declining; those that expand dominate the future, while those that decline cling to memories of the past. As an empire threatened with decay from within and a decline in military and political power abroad, the United States now faces a critical question: can it afford to allow the replacement of a *Pax Americana* with a *Pax Sovietica* or with a Third World revolutionary imperialism subtly directed by the Chinese communists? In all probability, either such development would spell the eventual end of Western civilization as Americans and Western Europeans understand it.

The United States can maintain or reassert its influence as an empire in world history at the moment, providing leadership for the Western world and its civilization, in at least three major ways: (1) a strategic superbalance of power to preserve the status quo in a dynamic equilibrium—an approach that focuses on the strategic American-Soviet-Chinese triangle and is most clearly represented by the policies of Secretary of State Kissinger;[3] (2) trilateral alliance among advanced industrial nations to preserve stability and increase economic growth through progressive and aggressive economic and political policies—an approach that focuses on the economic North American-West European-Japanese alliance and is most clearly represented by the policies of the Trilateral Commission and its first director, Zbigniew Brzezinski;[4] and (3) a New World democratic consensus and strategic modernization plan that seeks to restore Western strength and values by creating strong alliances with Third World countries—an approach that focuses on a north-south economic *détente* among democratic countries that are open to a political economy of social liberalism (in constrast to pure capitalism or socialism). The last position is the one developed by this book.

Kissinger's policy of building a strategic superbalance among the United States, the Soviet Union, and China as the foundation for peace has been based upon Old World balance-of-power assumptions. In the classical balance-of-power game of diplomacy, the members of the elitist club of great powers work to prevent any of the member states (or any coalition) from becoming strong enough to overwhelm the other states and disturb the status quo. As a brilliant student of the balance-of-power politics of Metternich and Bismarck in the nineteenth century, Kissinger saw both the strengths and weaknesses of this approach. His Ph.D. thesis, significantly entitled *A World Restored: The Politics of Conservatism in a Revolutionary Age*, demonstrates that he was not taken in by the Enlightenment assumptions of clockwork rationality underlying the classical balance-of-power framework. Rather, Kissinger preferred Bismark's notion of a dynamic equilibrium of great powers to Metternich's more static model, and he was also aware of the importance of secrecy, ambiguity, and surprise given the indeterminacy of world politics in the modern era. In creating a structure of peace for American foreign policy based on a deliberately ambiguous concept of *détente*, Kissinger hoped to salvage the stability and legitimacy of the classical balance-of-power model while simultaneously making it adaptable to revolutionary changes that threatened such a conservative order. In short, Kissinger sought to preserve America's national interests in fluid relations, with other major powers, to coopt change through his own vision of a stable world order.

Kissinger's strategic blueprint for a dynamic balance of power is conservative in that it assumes that America will lose most from any radical revolutionary upset of the international status quo. It rests on the idea that the best way to maintain the established order is to prevent the other great powers from upsetting it by making them legitimate members of a great power elite with vested stakes in the existing order.

When Kissinger first perceived a change in the global system of world power in the 1960s from a bipolar domination by the Soviet Union and the

United States to a multipolar decentralization of power, he envisioned a dynamic balance-of-power blueprint involving five major power units—the United States, the Soviet Union, the People's Republic of China, Japan, and Western Europe. But as it became increasingly clear that Western Europe was far from united and was, like Japan, heavily dependent upon the strategic military power of the United States, Kissinger shifted his focus to a superpower triangle of the United States, the Soviet Union, and China. Positively, the results of this realistic shift were the historic 1972 American-Soviet summit, the SALT I agreement on strategic arms limitation, and the opening of American diplomatic relations with mainland China. But negatively, the consequences were an inadvertent prior commitment to improving American relations with the Soviet Union before improving relations with Western Europe and Japan and an implicit recognition of China as a full-fledged superpower before that country had the required military and economic potential to merit such status. Indeed, China seemed to gain most from the new strategic triangle by formally entering the superpower club without having to relinquish its position of leadership in the Third World.

Kissinger's policy of superpower balance was appropriate when the Secretary came to power for it enabled him to incorporate the realistic consequences of the Soviet and Chinese revolutions into a blueprint of international stability that served American interests. Basing his national support on the fear of nuclear war and his reputation as a strategic security expert, Kissinger attempted to keep America's major adversaries at bay by promising a "nonideological" and economically tempting package of great power stability with respect to their world status and prestige. However, Kissinger's intention to create a stable structure of world peace that would preserve the basic power distributions in the world was, in fact, a hidden conservative ideology. As such, it was more consistent with American needs for stable international markets and security than with Russian and Chinese communist commitments to constant revolutionary struggle to change the status quo and substitute their own ideal socialist images. In short, Kissinger's policy of creating a *détente* with the Soviet Union and a *rapprochement* with the People's Republic of China did serve to head off the threat of military conflicts among the superpowers but has failed in its economic, social, and political objectives because of the great ideological and economic differences among them.

Détente is a loose, unofficial agreement on the part of elites of two or more nation-states to bring their nations into warmer relations by cooperating in certain limited areas such as trade, the exchange of technological information, and military security arrangements. But because of the undeniable American economic superiority over the Soviet Union, the American-Soviet *détente* holds more potential advantages for the Soviets than for Americans. Theodore Draper has even referred to *détente* as a new form of appeasement:

> Most of the debate on *détente* has made it appear that the only alternatives are *détente* and cold war. . . . That the cold war may not be the only alternative to *détente* seems to have escaped notice. It might also be asked: "Do you want to go back to 'appeasement'?" In fact, an even more incredible question to some might be: "Do you realize that appeasement was built into *détente*?"[5]

Professor Raymond Vernon has predicted that the United States could lose both economically and politically from *détente* if American policy makers attempt to use the same cooperative approach toward the Soviets that they use toward Western democracies like Canada, Italy, or Taiwan. The risk arises from the different rules of the game according to which Soviets and Americans play international politics. The main American rule of international transaction is that anything is allowed unless it has been restricted by the state. The Soviet rule, in contrast, is that nothing is permitted unless it is initiated by the state. Accordingly, Vernon has noted that if American policy makers use concepts like tariff protection, antidumping laws, most-favored nation treatment, currency convertibility, and patent licensing—expecting to play by American rules in bargaining—they are apt to find themselves further upsetting America's trade and monetary position, as well as undermining agreements with its normal allies in Europe.[6]

Vernon's warnings take on even more weight when the full extent of Soviet economic weakness is revealed. All the goals that the Soviet Union set in the past five years for its economy were never met, except in the area of foreign trade, which was forced to fill the gap. And living standards rose much more slowly than anticipated.[7] Moreover, both official Soviet data and Western recalculations indicate a striking decline in the rate of economic growth and productivity in the Soviet Union in the past quarter century.[8] By the mid-1960s, Prime Minister Aleksei Kosygin called for the abandonment of economic isolationism to keep the Soviet economy from slipping too far behind. The Brezhnev regime tried to overcome the failure of the Soviets to keep up technologically with the West, a central cause of economic weakness, through *détentes* with France and Germany. But this means was insufficient, and so by 1972 the American-Soviet *détente* became the main source of scientific-technological transfer.[9] The Soviets are therefore interested in *détente* basically for economic reasons, and, given the recent Soviet military arms build-up regardless of economic conditions, *détente* has become the means whereby the United States has eliminated the material weaknesses of its central adversary. Thus, not only was the price of *détente* too high, but the material and technological transfer appeared to go where it would most damage American stakes in the superpower competition—to the Soviet Union.

The Soviet Union's weakness has led columnist C. L. Sulzberger to call it a "supergiant with clay feet" and Otto von Hapsburg, a "paper tiger."[10] Such evaluations lead one to ask: "If the Soviet Union is so weak, why all the fuss about nuclear war and *détente*?" The evidence indicates that the creators of the policy pushed it on the American public in order to shore up executive power in the era of the Vietnam defeat and the Watergate scandal. Former American Ambassador to the Soviet Union, George Kennan, for example, has noted that the image of detente "was oversold—for different reasons in each case—by our government, by the Soviet government, and by the American press; and as a result of this overselling, many people came to address to the behavior of both countries expectations that were unreal and could not be met fully."[11] Kennan goes on to argue that both the Americans and Soviets have overreacted to the nuclear threat each represents to the other, stimulating a dehumanizing and deadly arms race that distorts the priorities of superpower politics in a potentially suicidal manner. *Détente*, then, must be kept but trimmed back to realistic dimensions and expectations, accepting the fact that it basically applies only to preventing situations from becoming potential grounds for direct military conflict between the United States and the Soviet Union.

Others, such as Soviet novelist Aleksandr Solzhenitsyn and the Chinese communists, have warned the West against *détente* on ideological and military grounds. The Chinese are all too aware that the Soviets, rather than themselves, gained most from the American defeat in Southeast Asia, and they are rather desperately encouraging the strengthening of NATO and the Southeast Asia Treaty Organization as counters to the spread of Soviet ideological and military influence throughout the world. Clearly, the Chinese fear the Soviets more than the Americans. It was they who pointed out the CIA's underestimation of the extent of the Soviet military build-up long before the presidential election campaign of 1976 exposed it as an issue. There is, in short, a power vacuum on the world stage caused by American defeat and withdrawal which only the Soviet Union seems to have the ability and willingness to fill.

For their part, the Soviets seem content with their traditional two-prong diplomacy of promising peaceful coexistence through the Helsinki agreements in order to gain economic and propaganda benefits, while simultaneously using subversive money, arms, and troops in "national wars of liberation" such as in Angola (and, to a lesser extent, in Portugal). Peaceful coexistence for the Soviet

Union means remaining at peace militarily with the United States while continuing class and ideological warfare throughout the world, supplemented with arms and the paid mercenary troops of allies (like Cuba) where appropriate. This is the meaning of the emerging *Pax Sovietica* which is rapidly replacing the moribund *Pax Americana*. And the Chinese don't like it one bit.

The most popular alternative to the strategic balance-of-power approach advocated by Kissinger is the trilateral approach advanced by the Trilateral Commission and Zbigniew Brzezinski of Columbia University. The idea of forming the Trilateral Commission was conceived by David Rockefeller and others at a time of severe strains between the United States and Western Europe and Japan (due, in part, to the Kissinger focus on relations with the superpowers). The role of the Trilateral Commission was, in Rockefeller's words, "to bring the best brains in the world to bear on the problems of the future."[12]

The thrust of the trilateral approach is to make cooperation on economic problems between advanced industrial countries the basic priority of American foreign policy. (This stands in contrast to Kissinger's approach of stressing the strategic problems of balancing the superpowers.) Director Brzezinski described the Trilateral Commission's philosophy as reformist and internationalist rather than conservative or apocalyptic. Although admitting that "We are a rich man's club," Brzezinski noted that the commission is significantly different from other such clubs in agreeing upon a need for action and using the commission as a framework for sustained effort in the three advanced industrial regions. Furthermore, Brzezinski argues that the commission's reformist, incremental approach is the only way to mobilize domestic support in an increasingly unmanageable international environment. Pessimistic, Brzezinski is convinced that "if we do not pursue the incremental approach, we will be pursuing a reactionary one. In this instance, we will probably win hands down in the short run but lose in the long run."[13]

Concretely, the Trilateral Commission has established a number of task forces to develop policy proposals, focusing upon topics such as monetary problems, energy, trade, less developed countries, internal political processes, the international management of resources, the renovation of international institutions, and ways of engaging constructively with communist countries. A final task force will pull together the results of all the other task forces and provide a long-range view less apocalyptic than the visions offered by other organizations like the Club of Rome. No communists are permitted membership on the commission, although rather unsuccessful attempts have been made to add some socialists to the roster. Nevertheless, the commission is presumably committed to reform of the international political system, not merely an analysis of it. As a private group, the Trilateral Commission has only advisory power, but its influence in priming, if not "designating," future secretaries of state in the countries involved may make it even more powerful in the long run.

Advocates of trilateralism suggest that the security focus of the balance-of-power approach is still "a high priority item" as a legacy of the past, but that future American foreign policy must stress economic interdependence among Western industrial states to give this security a solid foundation.[14] According to political scientist Stanley Hoffmann, trilateralism makes certain assumptions about the solution of world economic problems:

> [Trilateralism holds that] China's importance is purely marginal, and the Soviet Union remains outside the mainstream of the world economy. . . . Moreover, one finds, as another cold war legacy, the conviction that the Russians' interest in intense cooperation with the "advanced nations" is tactical at best, that their willingness to play by the same rules as these nations is dubious, and that a real change in their behavior will be obtained, not through early and direct efforts at accommodation, but at the end of a long process in which they will be confronted with a successful "trilateral" organization of the non-Communist world.[15]

Thus both the Kissinger approach and the Trilateral Commission's approach aim to preserve American primacy and see the security problem as basically an American-Soviet one. Both represent "exercises in nostalgia," to use Hoffmann's phrase, for neither adequately confronts the present and future dilemmas of nuclear proliferation and north-south relations (i.e., northern industrial nations' interests versus southern developing countries' interests). The rich and powerful want to stay that way, after all, and both the balance-of-power and trilateral strategies of American foreign policy represent ways for the well-to-do to maintain their interests and privileged positions. In this sense Kissinger epitomizes the most probable future trend in American foreign policy: the maintenance of the status quo in the name of international stability and peace.

Since trilateralism appears to be the only alternative to Kissinger's balance-of-power theory which has support among the foreign policy elite (neoisolationism being largely an antiestablishment alternative), the short-term future of American foreign policy is apt to be dominated by a strategic shift away from Kissinger's American-Soviet-Chinese triangle and toward the trilateral American-West European-Japanese model. However, the Kissinger legacy has been deeply enbedded enough in the popular mind and foreign agreements to commit Americans to many of his basic assumptions for some time to come. Consequently, America's future will be characterized by tensions between the trilateral and balance-of-power visions of American hegemony. These tensions have grown as a result of the American use of strategic balance-of-power policies not only to affect military security matters, where they were intially appropriate, but to influence economic and monetary policies with American allies, for which they were unfit, causing unnecessary antagonism and stimulating the creation of competing economic blocs.[16] From the trilateral viewpoint, it is imperative that the *détente* between the United States and the other superpowers created by Kissinger not go too far since trilateralism is based upon a Cold War logic of organizing an interdependent economic bloc of Western industrial democracies that keeps the influence of the Soviets down by outpacing them economically. In sum, the "strong man's club" and the "rich man's club" do not always see eye to eye even though all the members want to be both strong and rich and to assure their position of influence in the world.

In terms of the increasingly dangerous problems of nuclear proliferation and international terrorism, neither the strategic balance nor the trilateral approach offers anything but vague generalities. The advocates of superpower *détente* have not dealt with the issue that such a *détente* may stimulate nuclear proliferation among lesser powers. And the advocates of trilateral economic growth, who recommend the use of goods as a way of "buying off" nations from going nuclear offer no assurance that their trilateral honey will be effective. The ominous case of India even suggests that competition among the rich and powerful to win over developing "client" countries may actually stimulate nuclear armament as a desperate way to decrease dependence upon great power good will.

To the extent that the trilateral and strategic balance approaches fail to deal adequately with the problems of the Third World or the developing countries to the south, terrorism and nuclear armament can be expected to increase—as a means of blackmailing the rich and strong, if nothing else. Despite fine rhetoric to the contrary, neither the strong man's triangle nor the rich man's triangle has worked out a satisfactory plan for Third World development. Both view most poor countries (with the exception, of course, of the oil-producing countries) as marginal to the basic economic and security needs of the United States.

Thus, Kissinger paid attention to Third World countries only when they appeared to be chips in the superpower sweepstakes (as in Angola and Namibia), or when they threatened the stability of international political structures (as in the United Nations), or when they attempted to upset the world economic equilibrium (as with OPEC). And although the trilateral advocates of a "community of advanced nations" have noted that "the problem of the less-developed nations is the moral problem of our time,"[17] their strategy seems self-serving more than therapeutic. As Hoffmann has suggested:

> Their answer makes one wonder whether they do not subscribe to Acheson's nasty distinction between moral problems and real ones. For they clearly assume that the solution of the Third World's problems depends on the advanced nations "generating a major response" in concert: should the rich succeed in defining their common plan, the poor would have to accept their leadership. . . . Increased participation "by all of the advanced countries in institutions designed to improve the lot of the Third World" is a bizarre bait to the less advanced, and arguments about their interest in unimpeded development of their resources by "cosmo-corps" may also appear as somewhat less than disinterested to them.[18]

In short, America's foreign policy in the future is apt to be dominated by an emphasis upon the northern strategic and trilateral triangles (each representing a different north). The tensions between the two plans is likely to be resolved by a shift from the strategic balance to the trilateral blueprint. But this probable future seems oriented more toward consolidating the gains of the past than toward solving present and future problems. As such, these triangular attempts to preserve American hegemony may become increasingly ineffective when they are recognized for what they are: reactionary efforts by the strong and the rich to preserve the old rules of the game of nations and the present economic order. Ironically, the optimum way to maintain American power in world affairs may be to avoid this conservative image and to identify America with the inevitable forces of change.

Any alternative to the balance-of-power or trilateral triangles must avoid the errors of neglecting the importance of the present world dominance of northern countries and of underestimating the internal problems within the trilateral bloc of Western industrial states or the great differences between the First and Third Worlds. The old triangles may be taken as givens without necessarily taking them for granted. On this foundation, Americans may be able to construct a more positive foreign policy for the future, aimed more at improving north-south hemispheric relations, shoring up the declining image and power of democratic regimes throughout the world, and refurbishing America's New World image in a way that would benefit the nation in the superpower sweepstakes and in economic competition with its Western allies. This country's heritage, in short, provides the basis for the creation of a foreign policy that both represents progressive social change and enables the country to preserve past gains through conservative politics and whatever military threat and mobilization is necessary. Far from being mutually exclusive, a strong America and a progressive democratic America may be brought into a synthesis.

The major threat to America in the near future lies in the temptation to pursue a solipsistic neoisolationism that looks to the outside world only for the selfish goals of neomercantilism—increased exports, decreased imports, and full employment at home regardless of the consequences for other peoples abroad. This new, selfish inwardness stems not as much from self-love and national pride (as it does in France, for example) as from self-contempt and feelings of national shame and uncertainty over recent national experiences and guilt over the pursuit of material gain and pleasure. New counterculture life styles and ways of thinking may have overcome the guilt for some Americans but not the uncertainty concerning personal goals in life or future world trends and not the selfish bent of rugged individualism that puts the self above all else. Individuals, of course, have a right to develop and express themselves and defend their own interests; but without an effective counterbalancing of meaningful community norms and social obligations, such rugged individualism can tear the nation's social fabric apart and use up vital energies at home that may be desperately needed abroad. Americans must develop a commitment to positive community and international action in order to eliminate human suffering and promote individual life-chances. A golden opportunity exists to link America's "Third World at home" (the poor and discriminated against) with the Third and Fourth World peoples abroad, to help ourselves by helping others. The rich in America must be given incentives to spread their resources more widely, at home and abroad. And the problem of domestic unemployment must be viewed as an international economic problem, rather than merely a narrow national one. Such shifts require major changes in America's political economy and educational programs, as will be shown in later chapters.

In terms of America's superpower stakes in the world, by creating a plan for democratic modernization at home and abroad based on the humanistic tradition of Jefferson, Americans may be able to project a credible ideology in foreign policy which can effectively compete with Soviet and Chinese models in the developing world. Not to compete is to give up the ideological game of international politics and America's influence upon positive historical change. The extent of this country's economic and political need for continuing good relations with Third and Fourth World countries is not fully realized by many Americans. As Brzezinski has noted:

A . . . major historical change—one that has also transpired since World War II—involves the transformation of the resource-autarkic American economy into an increasingly resource-dependent economy. Some experts have estimated that the United States is already dependent on imports for 26 out of some 36 basic raw materials consumed by its industrial economy; and this dependence is growing most dramatically, but by no means exclusively, in the energy field. This shift is imposing a mounting fiscal drain on the U.S. economy (with mineral imports costing eight billion in 1970 and likely to cost about 31 billion dollars by 1985) and it also heightens the U.S. stake in a stable and uninterrupted flow of international trade. As a consequence, America finds herself so deeply involved in the world economy, a condition reinforced by its special monetary role, that on the economic plane the concept of isolationism becomes at worst a suicidal policy and at best an irrelevance.[19]

Brzezinski believes that the the recent dissolution of purpose in American foreign policy and the tendency toward neoisolationism, despite the obvious dependence of America on other countries, are not due merely to the Vietnam experience but are perhaps better explained by the Klingberg cycle. In the early 1950s, Frank Klingberg suggested that since 1776 America's foreign policy has been characterized by alternating cycles of extroversion and introversion. To support this claim, he systematically collected data—presidential messages, party platforms, election results, frequency of foreign treaties, naval expenditures, armed expeditions, wars, diplomatic warnings, and annexations—and he then derived the following historical phases of introversion and extroversion:

Introversion	Extroversion
1776-1798	1798-1824
1824-1844	1844-1871
1871-1891	1891-1919
1919-1940	1940-

Klingberg also accurately predicted that America was due to retreat from world involvement in the 1960s.[20]

Despite the undeniable utility of this theory in explaining change from an historical viewpoint, there is a danger of falling into a belief in historical determinism if individuals or national elites take such cycles too seriously. A dedicated Klingbergian might argue, for instance, that American leaders may as well resign themselves to waiting around for another twenty years or so until the next extroversion phase is due. Even if Klingberg's cycle continues to be accurate, foreign policy makers and advisors should at least be planning for a rational and effective program of national extroversion when the time comes. And the increasing dependence of America upon other nations for resources and economic and political cooperation may serve to mute the Klingberg cycle, to shorten the phases, or otherwise alter the regular pattern. Elsewhere, I have argued with Ralph Hummel that such cycle theories need not be perceived deterministically, but can become useful tools for analyzing historical facts and social change to make individual foreign policy making more effective.[21]

If the Soviets thought that American policy makers believed introversion or isolationism to be inevitable in American foreign affairs in the post-Vietnam period, they would be foolish not to capitalize upon such acquiescence by expanding their influence unchecked. That is why Kissinger was so worried that the victory of the Soviet-backed forces in Angola was an ominous precedent and why the Chinese have been concerned that the American-Soviet *détente* would lull the Americans into indifference to the Soviet arms build-up and subtle forms of Soviet imperialism which they perceive as threats to their own security and influence. The threat of indirect Soviet and Chinese intervention in southern Africa explains Kissinger's efforts there to preserve stability through *ad hoc* conservative tactics. Conceivably, by creating an activist American foreign policy based upon a new democratic consensus at home (in contrast to Kissinger's Old World conservatism) and aimed at competing effectively with the Soviet and Chinese models of modernization abroad, America could become a positive force for democratic and humanistic change in world politics once more.

Notes

[1]Aaron Latham, "Introduction to *The Pike Papers*," the House Select Committee on Intelligence Report, in *The Village Voice*, 21, 7 (February 16, 1976) 71.

[2]From the front-page commentary of *Die Zeit*, February 6, 1976, as translated in *The German Press Review*, 76-6, February 11, 1976, p. 3.

[3]This alternative is spelled out in R. Isaak, *Individuals and World Politics* (North Scituate, Mass.: Duxbury Press, 1975), chap. 8.

[4]See the Trilateral Commission reports and Zbigniew Brzezinski, "U.S. Foreign Policy: The Search for Focus," *Foreign Affairs*, 51, 4 (July 1973).

[5]Theodore Draper, "Appeasement and Détente," *Commentary*, 61, 2 (February 1976), 28.

[6]Raymond Vernon, "Apparatchics and Entrepreneurs: U.S.-Soviet Economic Relations," *Foreign Affairs*, 52, 2 (January 1974), 249-262.

7C. L. Sulzberger, "Supergiant with Clay Feet," *The New York Times*, February 29, 1976, Op-Ed page.

8Official Soviet data indicate that the rate of economic growth and productivity fell from 10.9 percent in the period 1950-1958, to 7.2 percent in 1958-1967, to 6.4 percent in 1967-1973; Western recalculations of the Soviet figures show the actual decline to be from 6.4 percent in 1950-1958, to 5.3 percent in 1958-1967, to 3.7 percent in 1967-1973. *Détente*: Hearings Before the Committee on Foreign Relations, U.S. Senate, August-September 1974, p. 32. See also Marshall I. Goldman, *Détente and Dollars* (New York: Basic Books, 1975).

9Draper, "Appeasement and Détente," p. 28.

10C. L. Sulzberger, "Supergiant with Clay Feet"; and Otto von Hapsburg, "U.S.S.R.: Superpower or Paper Tiger?" *Saturday Evening Post*, July-August 1973, p. 10.

11George Kennan, "Is Détente Worth Saving?" *Saturday Review*, March 6, 1976, p. 12.

12"The Trilateral Commission: A Private North American-European-Japanese Initiative on Matters of Common Concern," a bulletin with a statement of purpose and membership, November 1, 1974.

13Professor Zbigniew Brzezinski's presentation of "The Trilateral Commission and Its Implications for American Foreign Policy," at the Faculty Seminar on International Political Economy at Columbia University, September 30, 1975.

14See Brzezinski, "U.S. Foreign Policy: The Search for Focus," 720.

15Stanley Hoffmann, "Choices," *Foreign Policy*, 12, (Fall 1973), 13.

16See Stanley Hoffmann, "Weighing the Balance of Power," *Foreign Affairs*, 50, 4 (July 1972), 618-643.

17Brzezinski, "U.S. Foreign Policy," 717, 726.

18Hoffmann, "Choices," 19.

19Brzezinski, "U.S. Foreign Policy," 710.

20See Frank L. Klingberg, "The Historical Alternation of Moods in American Foreign Policy," *World Politics*, January 1952. Brzezinski adds: "It is to be noted that the phases of extroversion have lasted about 27-28 years, and hence the last phase of extroversion should have ended around 1968, according to Klingberg's analysis." Brzezinksi, "U.S. Foreign Policy," p. 709.

21For a theory of how to locate individual action and efficacy within historical cycles in order to use them for personal and national political goals, see R. Isaak and R. Hummel, *Politics for Human Beings* (North Scituate, Mass.: Duxbury Press, 1975) pp. 50-53, 174-188, and 205-206.

8 ISOLATIONISM OR INTERVENTIONISM?

Why did so many Americans rebel against the fact that their country had acquired superpower status, whereas most Russians regarded it as a matter for satisfaction and pride? Perhaps the future historian will explain this curious contrast with reference to the different historical traditions of the two countries; perhaps he will point to mistakes committed by American leaders and the superior tactical ability of the Russians. Very likely he will draw the conclusion, rightly or wrongly, that an American-style democracy was, in the long run, simply incapable of sustaining an active global policy; it lacked the sense of mission, the perseverence and the ruthlessness that globalism demanded.

—*Walter Laqueur*, Neo-Isolationism and the World of the Seventies, *1972*

As a nation we have what General de Gaulle uncharitably labeled "a taste for intervention." Applied intelligently and with restraint, as in Western Europe after the war, this taste has done credit to our nation and served its interests. But expanded indiscriminately and without measure, it has involved us in struggles we do not understand, in areas where we are unwanted, and in ambitions which are doomed to frustration. Intervention is neither a sin nor a panacea. It is a method, and like all methods it must be directly related to the end in view. Otherwise it is likely to become an end in itself, dragging the nation down a path it never intended to follow, toward a goal it may find repugnant.

—*Ronald Steel*, Pax Americana, *1970*

As a superpower in a century of revolutionary change, the American nation is constantly faced with the choice of whether to intervene in the affairs of other states to protect American interests, particularly when other great powers are potentially involved, or rather to risk isolation from such foreign action, with possible losses in political and ideological influence. Perhaps no other issue highlights the American predicament of being a conservative world empire with a liberal democratic ideology more clearly than does the isolationist-interventionist dilemma.

Until the French Revolution of 1789, the legitimacy of great power intervention in the domestic affairs of other states was not questioned. However, that profoundly democratic revolution, so close in spirit to (indeed, drawing inspiration from) the American Revolution, changed the rules of the game of nations in many ways: it polarized Europe into reactionary conservative and democratic liberal forces. Great power intervention would never have the same legitimacy again, particularly after international law "prohibited" such intervention in the early twentieth century. As a conservative superpower with a liberal, democratic soul, America was fated to feel guilt for any attempt at American intervention abroad and to feel weakness in any retreat from the world into isolationism. As President Park's foreign policy advisor in South Korea, Kyung-Won Kim, noted, we are still living the consequences of the French Revolution.

Kim, in fact, did a study of the French Revolution and international stability under Kissinger's mentorship at Harvard. In it he demonstrated that the differences in the ideologies of the conservative imperial powers and the French revolutionaries made each camp blind to the power of the others, misperception leading to violence and the breakdown of the international system.[1] In this sense the American predicament is much more complicated since the ideological heterogeneity that leads to misperception and overreaction exists *within* the United States itself. The advocates of strong, imperial American power and intervention are in constant conflict with liberal, democratic neoisolationists, making a consensus on American foreign policy appear to be extremely difficult.

The complex interdependence of the world in the late twentieth century makes the international situation radically different than that of the eighteenth century. Yet similar misperceptions stemming from ideological differences exist and, in fact, may actually be heightened by such interdependence, as the recent American controversy over American-Soviet *détente* illustrates. Without a homogeneous ideology at home, America can hardly be expected to have a consistent foreign policy abroad over a long period of time. Moreover, unless a domestic American consensus is worked out on foreign policy objectives, there will be no coherent American basis for either intervention or nonintervention in the affairs of other states—militarily, economically, or politically.

Imagine the world, for a moment, as a system in dynamic equilibrium: strong forces would replace weaker ones and yet struggle to control events by maintaining a sense of balance; revolutionary forces would seek to upset the system at every opportunity because it serves the strong rather than the weak. Communications or cybernetic theorists might add at this point that the world as a system in equilibrium would have a *negative* dynamism since all physical and human systems tend toward entropy and decay. Smart "information" elites, therefore, would try merely to stem the tide of decay as much as they could by effectively processing negative feedback from the environment into their information and decision-making systems. They would anticipate catastrophes in order to be less weakened by them, if not to avoid them altogether.

This simple "systems model" of the world, which is meant more as a metaphor than anything else, does allow us to derive some intriguing corollaries about intervention and isolation in international affairs. Four, in particular, come to mind:

1. If some great powers withdraw, others would expand to fill the vacuum and restore the balance in their favor.
2. Great powers would have to strive to keep the equilibrium of the system relatively stable or peaceful to preserve their advantages in the status quo, although this would not preclude attempts at tilting the balance in their favor.
3. Great powers would always be fighting an uphill fight and would inevitably lose to historical change and decay of their power in the long run.
4. Small revolutionary powers would have little to lose by undermining system stability.

The systems viewpoint, in short, is a rather gloomy one for everybody.

Now, imagine another vision of the world: all interaction between nation-states would be carefully regulated; each state would be equal before international law, sovereign, self-contained and independent; and all peoples of the world agree that it is immoral and illegal for any one state to interfere in the domestic affairs of any other state. Although still a blueprint which seeks to preserve the status quo as "peace," thereby giving those with the most the advantage, this "international law model" of the world does at least view all nations, great or small, as moral and legal equals. It grants them the dignity of a right to sovereignty and independence from heavy-handed influence or violent invasions from outsiders. The World Court would settle all disputes through an impartial body of international judges selected from various countries on a rotating basis, and the United Nations would seek to enforce international laws wherever it might be necessary.

This international law model is also meant as a metaphor, although many idealists would affirm it as more meaningful than that. It, too, suggests some intriguing corollaries about intervention and isolation in world politics:

1. Great powers would have to stay within their boundaries and refrain from intervening, particularly militarily, in the domestic affairs of other smaller states.

2. As equal, self-sufficient, independent societies, all nations would risk losing their own self-determination and equality if they disrupted the peace by interfering in the affairs of others.

3. Revolutionary powers would have more to lose by tempting great powers into aggression than they would by accepting the present, peaceful status quo, even though it represents a certain level of inequality for them in material wealth and power.

The model, in short, is a rather static, more optimistic one for everyone concerned, and of greatest benefit to those with the most to lose in the existing status quo.

Unfortunately, the second model is based on some untenable assumptions about the world today. Even the nations called superpowers are not totally independent, self-sufficient, and absolutely sovereign in today's world. All nations are interdependent in economic, military, and political ways; consequently, each nation-state is a sieve and a market that requires certain kinds of "intervention" in its domestic economy, polity, and security system if the needs of its people are to be met. Moreover, the model implies that someone will enforce international laws. Clearly the United Nations has not been given such powers by those with the power to grant them, and the Hammarskjöld peace-keeping military forces of the 1950s seem to be relics of the past. Only the great powers can enforce what they choose of international law, which means that they will often opt for the systems model rather than the international law model if their vital interests appear to be at stake. The power of public opinion to put force behind international law should not be underestimated; but public opinion represents primarily moral authority rather than enforceable legal authority. International law in the world is a very weak superego often overwhelmed by the egoistic expressions of self-interest by states, much as American social community norms are, collectively, a weak domestic superego which often fails to curb the rugged individualistic egoism of those seeking to maximize their own self-interests regardless of the effects upon others.[2]

As the apparently more progressive of two inherently conservative paradigms of world stabilization, the international law model must be well understood because it is apt to be the basis of American foreign policy (in theory and rhetoric) for the indefinite future. After duly noting that the assumption of the autonomous, independent nation-state is fundamental to the entire conceptual structure of traditional international law, international law expert Bayless Manning writes:

Both the word "intervention" and the word "foreign" presuppose a discrete self-contained political unit—the nation-state—into which something from the outside—another nation-state—intrudes. In an increasing number of situations, the effective moving forces of today's world operate *across* nation-state borders rather than working between nation-states. The world's pattern of hostilities, aggressions, and belligerence is becoming increasingly trans-national rather than international.[3]

*Inter*national law, in short, may have become hopelessly obsolete in a *trans*national era, rendering its taboo against "intervention" irrelevant.

Manning goes on to note that even the concept of national wars may have become obsolete, replaced by the notion of geographical conflicts or regions of violence:

> Under 19th century international law, a nation-state could legitimately enter upon a good, old-fashioned war with another nation-state at any time by going through a set of minimal rituals. Within the last generation, however, two developments of great importance have occurred in this respect. The first is that it is no longer clear that a nation-state may resort to force and wrap itself in an aura of legitimacy any time it wishes simply by declaration of war; it will not gain a position of accepted legitimacy without more of a demonstration. The other development—remarkably little noted—is that it seems that good old-fashioned wars pitting nation-state *A* against nation-state *B* have in fact disappeared from the face of the world in the last generation. . . . Today we are really talking about a geographic location when we give a nation's name to an outbreak of violence.[4]

If Manning is correct, then great powers enter into regional geographic conflicts where their interests are only indirectly involved partly in order to prevent brush fires from becoming forest fires, threatening to damage their cherished status quo.

In this light both international law and the United Nations are idealistic guises for great powers to use in order to protect their perceived national interests and to maintain a status quo structured in their favor. If widespread American reaction against heavy-handed military intervention to preserve the status quo, such as in Vietnam, should lead to a proclaimed idealism based on international law enforced by United Nations peace-keeping forces (as seems possible), such a shift must be seen for what it really is: a tactical change from a militant "realist" interventionism (that could rarely be effective because of American ideological restraints) to an apparent idealism that is, in fact, a more subtle and civilized form of realism by which the United States uses international organizations for its main foreign policy objective of stabilizing its world power. In short, in the future American foreign policy makers can be expected to use the rhetoric, if not the substance, of the international law model as a tool to build the systems model of stability that favors American interests. Third World countries can be expected to call this spade a spade.

However, few nations in the world would necessarily be better off, including the Third World countries, if the United States just gave up great power diplomacy and withdrew from the world stage. The existing interdependence of nation-states makes this alternative impossible; moreover, the interests of other great powers would probably not be served by American isolation. For example, total American withdrawal might tempt the Soviet Union to overextend its empire, which is already weak in social and economic terms at the center, bringing about its decline and fall sooner than might otherwise be the case. Third World countries would have little to gain from the small nuclear war that might result from the total breakdown of the existing international system. Even their future economic prospects are strongly enough tied to the Old Rich and New Rich countries to give the poor a certain stake in the existing international order, despite its inequity. American isolation would definitely stimulate instability in some parts of the international system, and for that reason alone its withdrawal is in the long-term interest of few nations.

Initially, the most likely consequence of a total American isolationism would be the replacement of a *Pax Americana* (which is inevitable) by a *Pax Sovietica* (which is not). Nevertheless, neoisolationism remains an extremely popular alternative, particularly among the young and a significant segment of the intellectual and academic community. Ronald Steel, for example, is a noninterventionist who admits the problems of the position: it would not only have precluded this country's invasion of the Dominican Republic in 1965, but also American intervention against Franco in the Spanish Civil War.[5] Moreover Steel perceptively observes, that we have not exploited our empire; our empire has exploited us.[6] The question, then, is whether the pursuit of neoisolationism would mitigate or increase this exploitation of ourselves (through a form of overreaction as bad as the excessive aggression of an earlier era). James A. Johnson has shown that the decade of the 1960s produced a new school of isolationism, and young Americans see no country for whose security they would fight.[7] Walter Laqueur even questions whether young Americans are really eager to help the underprivileged peoples of the Third World. And he notes: "The Soviet Union may ultimately become a status quo power, but American neo-isolationism will hardly hasten this process. On the contrary, it will create opportunities for the expansion of Soviet influence which did not exist in the past, and which the Russians would be foolish not to exploit."[8] Angolas wax as American power wanes.

Although the neo-isolationist atmosphere following the end of the Vietnam War caused American involvement to be postponed until it was too late, the main error of American foreign policy in the Angolan situation, a tediously typical error of American intervention, was to involve American influence officially in a half-hearted way on the reactionary side bound for defeat in a domestic conflict. Ironically, because of Kissinger's vocal protests to Congress and the media, America may have lost more in the Angolan case than the Soviets won by backing the victors. Soviet influence may exist in Angola in the short run only to be hated, as most colonial interventionism comes to be hated, in the long run. Kissinger was afraid that in terms of his superpower blueprint and balancing act, American acquiescence in Angola would set an ominous precedent for further Soviet attempts to tilt the balance its way. But by overdramatizing a situation in a country where immediate American interests seemed most remote to many Americans, Kissinger may have inadvertently alienated the American public even further from the possibility of American involvement in situations where the stakes are higher in the future. Recall the tale of the boy who cried "wolf" so often when no threat existed that when the wolf did finally appear on the scene, no one came to the boy's aid.

Kissinger's behavior in the Angolan situation may actually be an example of the great power mimicry effect which Thomas Frank and Edward Weisband discovered. Franck and Weisband demonstrated that great powers tend to mimic each other's rhetoric in justifying their actions, often setting precedents for each other without being aware of it at the time:

> When United States forces invaded the Dominican Republic, Washington arrogantly confronted the Organization of American States with a *fait accompli* more of the era of 1865 than 1965. But when the Warsaw Pact Powers brutally and stupidly suppressed Alexander Dubcek's attempt to impose a human face on socialism, the West was stunned and horrified. Few Western observers noted that the Russians were echoing the very words used by hardhead realists in Washington to defend America's Latin American policy. By failing to listen to themselves as if they were the enemy speaking, American policy makers had made it easy and cheap for Russia to reassert the darkest side of its nature. This cannot but be counted a failure of U.S. strategic planning.[9]

Kissinger's outspoken (and self-defeating) warnings to his domestic constituency may have had the ironic effect of helping the Soviets in their future strategic planning and of deterring further American enthusiasm for intervention, making the darkest possible outcomes a case of self-fulfilling prophecy. To listen to yourself as if you were the enemy speaking does not mean that you have to put words into the enemy's mouth.

The failure of American foreign policy in Angola was due not merely to the misuse (or overuse) of rhetoric but also to the bankruptcy of the Cold War containment doctrine upon which that rhetoric was based. The Cold War mentality has often made American foreign policy into a negative and reactive one, epitomized by the containment doctrine, which implies that some otherwise irrepressible positive force (communism) is spreading thoughout the world like a plague. Political scientist James Rosenau has noted that the long-standing consensus in support of containment policies shared by both policy makers and scholars has led America into "bad" and "immoral" policies and into a blindness to the domestic sources of those policies. The Cold War paradigm has, in effect, blocked those concerned with American foreign policy from inquiring into the dynamics of American life and identifying deeper social needs and attitudes and their impact upon public and private elites responsible for action abroad. [10]

Richard Barnet, director for the Institute for Policy Studies, has noted that the most fundamental foreign policy assumptions, which are beyond debate within the government because policy-making bureaucracies depend upon them for survival, grow out of the Cold War paradigm:

Basically the discussion of current American foreign policy since the debate in Indochina accepts uncritically the cold war model of reality. America's goal remains as President Johnson stated it: "We are the number one nation and we are going to stay the number one nation." Despite détente, the central threat to the peace is still the Soviet Union. Soviet power must be contained by maintaining superior nuclear forces and projecting conventional military might through alliances, military aid arrangements and foreign bases. The world must be made safe as possible for American economic growth by discouraging or aborting anti-capitalist revolutions wherever possible. American economic power must be employed to counter efforts of the nonindustrial countries to alter the present international economic system. [11]

Barnet goes on to argue that these assumptions have not been seriously debated in public for fear, by bureaucrats and politicians both in and out of power, that the result would be a diminution of their own political power and legitimacy, a cramp upon the political style of the executive branch of government.

In terms of the recent difficulties in shoring up the traditional American Cold War containment policy, Barnet is even more to the point:

> The fundamental purpose behind the anti-Communist policy was to contain the expansion of Soviet power. That purpose has failed not because of Soviet strength but because of America's growing weakness. It is not Soviet gains but American losses that have produced a shift in the balance of power. The United States has been forced to agree to the division of Germany and to Soviet control over Eastern Europe. (There is no other meaning to the Helsinki Conference.) The left is gaining strength in France and Italy, and will probably play an important role in Spain. . . . Although Stalin's massacres are over, the Soviet system remains essentially unchanged. (Indeed the cold war has probably produced more negative changes in American society than positive changes in Soviet society).[12]

The brutal truth is that in its stumbling retreat from world power, America has held up a splintered shield of Cold War containment policies to protect it and symbolize the power it once held. But to the extent that this country's foreign policy actions are controversial abroad (because of heavy-handed military and covert intelligence operations), the Cold War containment doctrine serves only to polarize domestic opinion at home to the point that no consensus on any active American foreign policy in the world can be assured.

One of the most poignant examples of the self-defeating, negativism inherent in Cold War thinking and amoral Old World balance of power tactics was exposed in the controversial Pike Papers, the House Congressional committee report of its investigation of the Central Intelligence Agency (CIA). This case involved the Kurdish minority in Iraq. The Kurdish mountain people had been struggling unsuccessfully for autonomy in Iraq for years. In 1972, the Shah of Iran (himself returned to power by the CIA in a 1953 coup), in constant rivalry and tension with Iraq next door, asked the United States to send secret military aid to the Kurds, hoping to inspire another Kurdish military offensive and make things hot for Iran.

Acting on the approval of President Nixon and Secretary of State Kissinger, Secretary of the Treasury John Connally informed the Shah the United States would support the plan, and a $16 million covert-action program was initiated. For two years the CIA sent arms and money to the Kurds, who began a military rebellion. The Kurdish leader was so grateful to the United States that he sent Kissinger a gold and pearl necklace for his new wife and suggested that the Kurds were ready to become the fifty-first state when their rebellion proved successful. But in March 1975, the Iraqi government made an agreement with the Shah to alleviate the growing Kurdish problem. The next day all aid from Iran and the United States was cut off to the Kurds, the Iraqi army moved in brutally on the mountain people. The Kurdish leader wrote desperate appeals to Kissinger in vain. About 5,000 Kurdish refugees died trying to escape the Iraqi forces. And the Shah, with an incredible consistency, forced 40,000 Kurdish refugees to repatriate to Iraq, where their unhappy fate is unknown. And the United States refused to send any relief aid to Kurdish refugees or to accept any Kurdish applications for asylum. When reporter Daniel Schorr of CBS helped to leak this information in the Pike Papers to *The Village Voice* (February 16, 1976), the American people learned how expensive Old World thinking can be. But the American principles behind such CIA debacles remain mysterious to many, alienating not a few. Why it was even revealed that the CIA had developed a plan to put chemicals in Fidel Castro's boots in Cuba which would cause his beard to fall out, thus depriving him of some of his charisma! (Not to mention the numerous CIA assassination plots planned for the all too successful Cuban leader.) No wonder that many Americans feel like withdrawing from foreign involvements over which they have little control and which tarnish the American image throughout the world.

Moreover, the isolationist tendencies in American public opinion have been reinforced by what sociologist Peter Berger refers to as a "new intellectual-industrial complex." Berger argues that of the two competing ideologies, capitalism and socialism, only socialism has a future among liberal intellectuals in the United States and Europe, and that this growing liberal constituency heavily supports more equality at home combined with less American power abroad. The economic elite used to oppose such isolationist tendencies, but the situation has changed:

> The maintenancy of American power in the world, previously perceived as an economic asset, is now coming to be seen as an economic liability. It is inflationary (Vietnam was *not* "good for Wall Street"); it is an insufficient guarantee for the safety of foreign investments; it unnecessarily antagonizes an important sector of the foreign market for American goods. [13]

The congruence of liberal intellectual and business elite opinion is furthered by another curious development: the tendency of the economic elite to seek increasing business with terribly stable communist countries, especially in Eastern Europe. These countries offer the advantages of being reliable trading partners and being secure from the risk of American intervention to protect economic, strategic, or political interests. A safe, stable communist country appears to be a better bet as a business investment than a formerly safe, stable authoritarian regime in a Third World country, where the domestic situation is apt to be more volatile and American foreign policy more uncertain. Arguing that despite the immoral aspects of American foreign policy in the past, it was *also* the only significant shield for free societies throughout the world, Berger concludes both that a contraction of American power would have ominous implications for the future of freedom everywhere, and that the only immediate beneficiary would be the Soviet Union.[14]

In sum, American foreign policy as it is now constituted promises in the future to help its former enemies as much as its friends and to seek stability for its own sake, even to the extent of supporting authoritarian and communist regimes regardless of the consequences for democratic principles. The probability that such an amoral American foreign policy, which pretends to be "beyond ideology" in the Kissingerian balance-of-power sense, will continue in the future has led many Americans to assume that it is better for this country to withdraw from the world than to continue to support the forces of evil and antidemocratic regimes. And the Soviet Union is likely to gain from this development not because it is a communist power that America has failed to contain, but because it is a great power with an inclination to expand its influence wherever it can, as successful empires have all done in the past.

Americans appear to have given up the goal of maintaining America as a successful empire. Perceiving no positive ideological consensus on which to justify such world power and having suffered through the traumas of power misused for negative ideologies, Americans seem inclined to retreat, at least for a while, and to figure out what there is to gain or lose before reentering the game of world politics vigorously. But simultaneously Americans are becoming increasingly dependent upon other countries for the satisfaction of their needs. Arab oil fills their gas pumps. International markets mean economic growth and jobs at home. American farmers welcome Soviet purchases of their grain. So while longing for withdrawal, Americans realize that they can't really go home again—at least not all the way. The distinction between domestic and foreign policy has broken down, leaving American citizens (as well as scholars) uncertain as to exactly what to do about it. Americans do not tend to think of their country as an empire that grows or declines in the incessant flux of history; they are now losing their empire almost without being aware of it.

Total uncertainty, however, does not prevent many Americans from quickly identifying what they *dislike*. This country's alliance with racist South Africa in Angola disturbed many Americans, particularly because the United States seemed bound to lose from the outset. Even Americans who appreciated South African benefits in the form of gold, diamonds, and profitable investments disliked this clumsy, last-minute intervention that only served to demonstrate to the Third World America's strong ties with a racially repressive regime. America's liberal stance against the principle of racial discrimination occasionally overflows its domestic boundaries into foreign affairs as when this country's United Nations Ambassador Daniel Moynihan denounced dictator Amin of Uganda as "a racist murderer" and received widespread popular support. Moynihan, however, went on to alienate almost all of the states in the Organization of African Unity by saying that it was no accident that Amin was their chief representative (a false accusation since the position is an automatically rotating one). Moynihan's use of rhetoric at the United Nations seemed to be a heavy-handed version of Kissinger's excesses, aimed at domestic consumption rather than effective diplomacy. Moynihan's oratorical ability and overkill reminds one of psychologist Abraham Maslow's observation: "I suppose it is tempting, if the only tool you have is a hammer, to treat everything as if it were a nail."[15]

But clearly Americans have more to worry about in their foreign policy than rhetorical overreaction. Their concrete material stakes are high in foreign affairs. For example, in the United States earnings on direct investment abroad, as a proportion of total domestic profits, rose from 9 percent in 1950 to 28 percent in 1969, and the percentage is apt to keep rising in the future.[16] Economist Fred Bergsten has shown that it is especially in America's self-interest to "renew U.S. cooperation in the Third World," if only for America's own protection.[17]

Specifically, in addition to oil, Third World commodity cartels have been set up for eight primary products needed or used by the First World—bananas, bauxite, coffee, copper, iron ore, mercury, phosphates, and tin.[18] The bauxite cartel is apt to be particularly effective and important in the future because very few countries control the mineral and the United States requires a large supply for aluminum. Furthermore, Third World countries are moving quickly to harness the productive potential of multinational corporations for the sake of their own national interests. Also many Third World countries are successfully beginning to penetrate American markets for manufactured goods through exchange rate depreciations and export subsidies and are organizing to block badly needed reforms of the international economic order through use of collective veto power in existing institutions. As Bergsten has noted:

> Unfortunately, the United States has continued to view developing countries primarily as pawns in its ongoing superpower competition with the Soviet Union (and, to a lesser extent, China)—as objects, rather than subjects, of world politics. The United States alone, or virtually alone, among the industrialized countries has failed to implement tariff preferences for the manufactured products of the Third World, reduced its foreign aid, opposed all commodity agreements, and opposed linking the creation of international monetary reserves to development assistance. The policies of the United States have thus contributed significantly to the radicalization of Third World policies, and even to its tilting against the United States in favor of industrial competitors in some instances.[19]

There is enough inherent antagonism between a First World superpower and Third World small powers without the former adopting explicitly antagonistic foreign policies that are apt to make confrontation (and the temptation or need to intervene) more likely. Indeed, I would argue that the most subtle and effective foreign policy stance for a First World superpower like the United States to take is an explicitly pro-Third World position, which at least makes America's tremendous power and wealth appear to be officially guided by good intentions. Such a "revolutionary" policy and image would not only improve America's relations with the Third World but could even mobilize idealistic domestic support at home for American foreign policy, making it more effective. The wise strong man can best afford to demonstrate empathy for the weak and unfortunate.

Egalitarianism has become for the twentieth century what liberalism was for the nineteenth—the political *summum bonum* of the age. Liberal intellectuals of the West not merely advocate more equality at home, but believe that this movement toward equality may be historically inevitable, spreading from domestic politics in advanced industrial democracies to the international system itself. The rich nations would thus reach out to help the poor nations, if not out of moral conscience, out of the necessity of increased international interdependence in economics.[20] But the critical political problem of our times is that the international goals of egalitarianism cannot be achieved by restricting America's power in the world to help achieve them. More equality at home through less American power abroad is ultimately a retreat into a selfish American nationalism and a parochial contradiction on the part of many liberal intellectuals.

As Robert Tucker has noted, a new political sensibility of egalitarianism and of developed nations' assuming responsibility for undeveloped nations has swept the liberal academies and media, but it may have stopped short of infiltrating the offices of business and government elites in Old Rich nations. As Tucker perceptively notes:

> The common root of the new sensibility in all its manifestations is of course the proposition of interdependence. But interdependence may still be seen to convey quite different lessons. To some, it conveys the lesson that though the methods of the old politics must be changed, the interests of the old politics remain essentially unchanged. In this sense, the politics of interdependence is a new way of having one's way and the new political sensibility is an ingenious—or artfully disingenuous—rationalization for what remains an imperial policy that makes such concessions as appear necessary to placate and, hopefully, to co-opt the disaffected.[21]

That the rhetoric of interdependence and international equality can be used by powerful elites to cover up their attempts to preserve their interests and position in a stable status quo is nothing new. But that these very elites may eventually undermine their own game by switching from Old World to New World words and methods of action is a new and intriguing prospect. Tucker continues:

> At the same time, there may be a substantial price to pay in abandoning methods to which one has become increasingly committed in act as well as in word. Those who have assumed that they could always "manage" interdependence in such a way as to serve their particular interests might find that in large measure they have instead become the managed. It would not be the first time this has happened.[22]

The egalitarian rhetoric of intellectuals like John Rawls may come home to roost in the international diplomacy of the Old Rich countries, subtly maneuvering them into new rules of the game which will eventually redistribute wealth and power more equitably.

Rawls's difference principle—the notion that the only justifiable basis for any inequality is that it maximize the prospects of the least advantaged—may become the international standard for morally justifying state intervention at home or abroad in the Era of Egalitarianism for the liberal intellectual elites of industrialized democracies like the United States.[23] But elites in less developed countries desire economic growth and prosperity first, as prerequisites to any meaningful equality for their peoples. And Third World economic growth depends upon First World investment and credit, indeed, upon First World *intervention* economically, regardless of the terminology used. In the future subtle New World forms of economic intervention on the part of Old Rich and New Rich governments and multinational corporations are apt to replace Old World military interventions. And Third World governments can be expected to complain publicly about this new intervention as a spreading form of imperialism in order to build up a stronger bargaining position in international negotiations while privately encouraging such outside investment, credit, and technological interventions as the only way to stimulate their home economies. Internationally speaking, Rawls's difference principle can only become materially real through an increase, not a decrease, of Old Rich and New Rich intervention in the affairs of Third and Fourth World countries.

But Americans may not be ready for the massive, positive kinds of First World intervention that are required to help the Third World. Disenchanted with the environmental and social effects of industrial capitalism and technological and economic growth at home, many Americans feel reluctant to impose Western forms of political economy upon non-Western countries. Modernization in the form of Westernization is thus becoming increasingly repugnant to both First World elites and representatives of the Third World, creating a value consensus that may ironically stimulate neoisolationism in American foreign policy. But underneath their official pronouncements, Third World governments do desire First World money and technological advice. Unfortunately, American businesses are not likely to invest heavily in Third World countries without guarantees from the American government, guarantees that usually go only to stable governments and those not openly hostile to Westernization. Americans, in short, may be tempted to apply Rawls's difference principle at home, only to apply an indifference principle abroad—the notion that the only justifiable basis for any American intervention or economic investment is that it maximize the prospects for economic stability and the American Gross National Product.

But another alternative form of American intervention abroad is possible in the future. By adopting a positive vision of America's influence in the world—based upon a clear-cut social philosophy that aims to stimulate economic growth, political freedom, and political equality (in contrast to the negative, reactionary communist containment vision)—Americans may find themselves in a unique position to help others while maintaining this country's own interests and ideals. Rather than thinking in terms of stopping the Russians and the Chinese, Americans would be better off discussing a model for world modernization which can counter the Soviet and Chinese models. Such a model would permit intervention in strategic locations in the Third World to encourage democracy more than capitalism, economic growth in the host country more than economic profit for the multinational corporation, a sense of independence and competence through American technological help more than a feeling of endless dependence upon the United States. Such objectives would have to be supported by federal government policies creating incentives for American businesses to expand in poor Third World countries and to grow economically in harmony with economic growth in those countries.

Once such a positive basis for American political and economic intervention is established, building upon domestic support and moral enthusiasm, the uglier forms of intervention—military and intelligence operations—also would take on a new purpose and legitimacy. Without such a positive program consistent with American democratic ideals, it seems inconceivable that the American people can be persuaded of the need for American military intervention abroad or covert intelligence operations—realities of superpower diplomacy, whether one likes it or not. Not only does the Vietnam experience bias the public against such activities from the start, but America's new friendships with the Soviet Union and China in the Kissinger era make such efforts at stopping the Russians and Chinese appear to be contradictions in terms of American foreign policy. Kissinger's concept of *détente*, which supports carefully controlled tension and American strength, may, indeed, accurately define America's role in the world in terms of existing international realities; but such a subtle program goes beyond the thinking of many Americans who understandably want to know what this country should represent abroad in a clear-cut, nonambigious, positive sense.[24] Reason alone will not suffice to mobilize Americans behind a new, positive consensus of American foreign policy objectives. There are emotional and moral needs and resources in America that can only be brought out by an explicit rejection of Old World diplomacy. The dangers of extreme idealism seem less likely to harm America or the world today than a continuance of the extreme cynicism of the recent past. And what is at stake may be no less than the future of Western culture and civilization as the world has known it for 2,000 years.

Notes

[1]Kyung-Won Kim *Revolution and International System* (New York: New York University Press, 1970). Kim's key hypothesis is: "A heterogeneous ideology tends to reduce international stability by sharply increasing the probability of distortion in perception." (p. 122) This hypothesis seems to apply as accurately to America's present role and ideology in world politics as it did to the role of France in the late eighteenth century.

[2]This interpretation of international law as the superego of the world is based on Sigmund Freud's brilliant work, *Civilization and Its Discontents* (New York: W. W. Norton, 1961). It is spelled out in R. Isaak, *Individuals and World Politics* (North Scituate, Mass.: Duxbury Press, 1975), chap. 7.

[3]Bayless Manning, "Foreign Intervention in Civil Strife: From Diplomacy to Politics," *Stanford Journal of International Studies*, 3 (June 1968), 1.

[4]*Ibid.*, 2.

[5]See Ronald Steel, "A Spheres of Influence Policy," *Foreign Policy*, 5 and 6 (1971-1972).

[6]See Steel, *Pax Americana* (New York: Viking Press, 1970).

[7]James A. Johnson, "The New Generation of Isolationists," *Foreign Affairs*, 5 (1971) 118. See also Graham Allison, "Cool It: The Foreign Policy of Young America," *Foreign Policy*, Winter 1970-1971.

[8]Walter Laqueur, *Neo-Isolationism and the World of the Seventies* (New York: Library Press, 1972), p. 6.

[9]Thomas Franck and Edward Weisband, *Word Politics: Verbal Strategy among the Superpowers* (New York: Oxford University Press, 1972), p. vii.

[10]James N. Rosenau, "Paradigm Lost: Five Actors in Search of Interactive Effects of Domestic and Foreign Affairs," *Policy Sciences*, 4, 4 (mber 1973), 415-436. See also S. J. Cimbala, "The Policy Sciences and Foreign Policy: An Introduction," *Policy Sciences*, 4, 4 (December 1973), 379-386; and Thomas Lairson, "Social Paradigms and American Foreign Policy: A Theoretical Analysis," a paper presented at the International Studies Association Convention, February 28, 1976, Toronto, Canada.

[11]Richard J. Barnet, "The Great Foreign Policy Debate We Ought to Be Having," *The New Republic*, January 17, 1976, p. 17.

[12]*Ibid.*, p. 19.

[13]Peter Berger, "The Greening of American Foreign Policy," *Commentary*, 61, 3 (March 1976), 25.

[14]*Ibid.*, 27

[15]Abraham Maslow, as cited by David Schuman in *A Preface to Politics* (Lexington, Mass.: D. C. Heath, 1973), p. 38.

[16]Richard Rosecrance, "International Interdependence," in *New Dimensions of World Politics*, ed. by Geoffrey L. Goodwin and Andrew Linklater (New York: John Wiley, 1975), p. 23.

[17]Fred Bergsten, "The Threat from the Third World," *Foreign Policy*, Summer 1973, pp. 102-124.

[18]See C. Fred Bergsten, "The New Era in World Commodity Markets," *Challenge*, September-October 1974.

[19]C. Fred Bergsten, "The Response to the Third World," *Foreign Policy*, 17 (Winter 1974-1975), 6.

[20]Economist Barbara Ward has expressed confidence that the rich countries, "having accepted the principle of the general welfare at home . . . were ready to apply it to the whole family of man." *The Widening Gap* (New York: Columbia University Press, 1971), p. 13. And a Brookings Institution report on world economics concluded, "The same motivation that leads the more advanced regions within a country to alleviate poverty in the less advanced may well be extended to the far deeper disparities that exist among different regions of the world." *Reshaping the International Economic Orders A Tripartite Report by Twelve Economists* (Washington: Brookings, 1972), p. 4.

[21]Robert W. Tucker, "Egalitarianism and International Politics," *Commentary*, 60, 3 (September 1975), 40.

[22]*Ibid.*

[23]See John Rawls, *A Theory of Justice* (Cambridge, Mass.: Harvard University Press, 1971), especially pp. 75-83; see also chap. 3 of this book.

[24]See Henry A. Kissinger, "Building an Enduring Foreign Policy: Creative Leadership in a Moment of Uncertainty," speech delivered before the Economic Club of Detroit, Michigan, November 24, 1975, reprinted in *Vital Speeches of the Day*, 42, 6 (January 1, 1976), 166-172.

Part III

WHAT AMERICA SHOULD STAND FOR

Liberal institutions straightway cease from being liberal the moment they are soundly established: once this is attained no more grievous and more thorough enemies of freedom exist than liberal institutions.

—*Friedrich Nietzsche,*
"Skirmishes in a War with the Age," 1888

Always pray that your opposition be wicked. In wickedness there is a strong strain toward rationality. Therefore there is always the possibility, in theory, of handling the wicked by outthinking them.

COROLLARY ONE: Good intentions randomize behavior.

SUB-COROLLARY ONE: Good intentions are far more difficult to cope with than malicious behavior.

—*Marion J. Levy,*
Levy's Six Laws of The Disillusionment of
The True Liberal, *1966*

9 COUNTERING THE DECLINE
OF WESTERN CULTURE

> The decline of the West, which at first sight may appear, like the corresponding decline of the Classical Culture, a phenomenon limited in time and space, we now perceive to be a philosophical problem that, when comprehended in all its gravity, includes within itself every great question of Being.
>
> —*Oswald Spengler*, The Decline of the West, *1918*

> When civilizations pass into dissolution they regularly leave behind them a deposit of universal states and universal churches and barbarian war-bands. What are we to make of these objects? Are they mere waste products, or will these debris prove, if we pick them up, to be fresh masterpieces of the weaver's art which he has woven, by an unnoticed sleight of hand, on some more ethereal instrument than the roaring loom that has been apparently occupying all his attention?
>
> —*Arnold Toynbee*, A Study of History, *1939*

> For a long time I felt a compulsion to direct myself to large issues; this was mainly due to the cant I acquired around universities about alienation. About the time that the Vietnam War broke out, it became clear to me that alienation was a state approaching to sanity, a way of being human in a monstrously inhuman world, and that feeling human was a useful form of political subversion.
>
> —*Robert Hass*, Field Guide, *1973*

The decline of the West has long been a popular theme among intellectuals. But recently the belief in the inevitability of Western decay has become widespread among the mass publics of Western democracies, particularly in America. Self-flagellation has always been an instinct of American liberals, perhaps an offspring of the Protestant ethic or the belief that everything rises or falls with the efforts or failings of the individual. Henry Fairlie, the British commentator, has even gone so far as to suggest that "Every American in each generation, it appears, must regard himself as responsible for all that his society has done, does and will do."[1] And his colleague, Peter Jenkins, has declared, "The decline of the West is an American invention."[2]

Has the decline of Western civilization become a self-fulfilling prophecy?

Are those Americans justified who feel collective guilt for the imposition of Western values and means of modernization on non-Western societies? What should America stand for in terms of Western civilization in the future and why?

Is America a New World ready for a revival? Or is it going the way of all empires before it, contracting militarily, withdrawing in economic uncertainty, losing hours in social and psychological self-reproaches that weaken its morale—like the balding man who goes crazy trying to talk his psychiatrist into making him young and attractive again. After extending adolescence as long as socially possible, Americans have been forced to grow up quickly, almost too quickly and all at once, by a set of sobering experiences. Self-pity seems like an ignoble, sentimental attitude for a society priding itself on rugged individualism and romantic self-sufficiency. But there are reasons enough for it.

Take, for example, the set of attitudes epitomized in Grant Wood's classic painting "American Gothic." There stands the self-righteous, individualistic farmer, eyes focused straight ahead in oversimplistic clarity and certainty, leaning on his pitchfork. Next to him stands his shrewd, strong wife with a glaringly hypocritical look on her face. The existential simplicity that shows through in this painting seems inappropriate in today's sophisticated world. These two individuals are set up for a fall: the school of hard knocks has become a dogmatic attitude, a self-fulfilling prophecy of doom. This attitude of individual self-sufficiency, regardless of what others might think, is as naïve as it is romantically attractive—in much the same way that Thoreau's *Walden* is. The leader of a superpower, responsible for people's needs the world over and for helping to preserve peace for everyone, cannot simply stand isolated, pitchfork in hand with an almost too determined, hypocritical wife at his side, not caring what anyone else thinks (although some leaders in America have tried). America's problems have become much too big for that, much too complex for this country to solve alone.

But does this sudden awareness of vulnerability, of dependence upon other peoples of the world, of the frustration of all efforts at self-sufficiency—does all this mean that the American empire and the Western civilization it represents are declining for good? Or does it just mean that Americans have to redefine themselves and their nation, to see their limits and even capitalize on them, to accept a certain maturity that only comes through failure in life? The bitterness of the anti-Americanism within America must be swallowed before a mature attitude toward what America should stand for in the future can be created. And for many, this kind of maturity may take some fundamental changes in philosophy.

The existential individualism of many Americans is a lonely pursuit, a deliberately isolated effort at self-sufficiency and immortality that will make a philosophical change—the admission of dependence and need for communication—difficult. Many Americans seek a form of immortality through the acquisition of money, fame, literary or technical skill, or knowledge: being for them means becoming something. Alienated from themselves as they are, they seek upward mobility from wherever they begin in the class structure; they want to "make it," and to do so they sacrifice being (both being themselves and being with others) for becoming.

Social scientist Ernest Becker has documented the tendency of individuals in Western culture to deny death. Americans, in their struggle with this repression, experience constant rootlessness, tension, feelings of unfreedom, an inability to accept themselves, and an attachment to charismatic leaders who represent the solution to their problems. The opposite of the fear of death is the desire for heroism, the crown of narcissism. Becker comments on this drive:

> To become conscious of what one is doing to earn his feeling of heroism is the main self-analytic problem of life. Everything painful and sobering in what psychoanalytic genius and religious genius have discovered about man revolves around the terror of admitting what one is doing to earn his self-esteem. This is why human heroics is a blind drivenness that burns people up; in passionate people, a screaming for glory as uncritical and reflexive as the howling of a dog. In the more passive masses of mediocre men it is disguised as they humbly and complainingly follow out the roles that society provides for their heroics and try to earn their promotions within the system. . . . The crisis of modern society is precisely that the youth no longer feel heroic in the plan for action that their culture has set up.[3]

The revolt against social meaninglessness by which Americans try to find a sense of the heroic in their own lives leads not only to extremes of assassination attempts but to the prolonged adolescence of authors and poets who make deadly dramas of their own lives. Many of America's best contemporary poets have been deathbound in exactly this narcissistic sense: John Berryman, Sylvia Plath, and Ann Sexton—all suicides—are symbols of this homage to the Wasteland. The absence of love of self, an acute sense of self-criticism, and a consequent inability to love others or to take roots—all of these are characteristic of rugged American individualists. Freedom for them becomes a risky, desperate condition rather than a positive affirmation, a self-commitment through community commitment. Walden, after all, was terribly lonely.

To create a New World Americans must actively rebel against the meaner and more selfish parts of their contemporary and traditional heritage and affirm the humanistic and sociable traditions of Jefferson and Franklin. They must create a culture and life style that uplifts, beginning with healthy blasts against excesses of authority and meaninglessness—such as those of singer Bob Dylan—to get beyond nihilism. They must affirm democracy as a state of mind that sees each human being as a person of potential, a piece of immortality, a being to be helped, nurtured, and uplifted. Elites there must be, but elites with wide human culture who are not merely power manipulators. Leaders must have a high cultural and moral vision. They must become representatives of American symbol systems that transcend the decadence of the West, turning its movement from nihilism to creative humanism, a synthesis of Western, Eastern, and Third World humanism. For a society's elites are, after all, its culture's symbols of immortality—a sobering thought.

To ask whether there are historical cycles which make the decline of all civilizations, including Western civilization, inevitable is to take the perspective of the "plum-cake historians." Ved Mehta coined the phrase to describe those metaphysically inclined thinkers, such as Karl Marx, Oswald Spengler, Arnold Toynbee, and Pitirim Sorokin, who propose an all-embracing explanation of history. In contrast, Mehta uses the term "dry-biscuit historians" to describe scholars such as R. H. Tawney and Lewis Namier, who set smaller goals for themselves and look for causal connections between religion and capitalism, Parliament and self-interest, and other such matters.[4] Charles Fair adds to Mehta's two classes a third—"shortbread historians," such as G. M. Trevelyan and C. V. Wedgwood—who focus on narrative history. Fair also notes that the dry-biscuit group is now ascendant.[5] America's present historical crisis is clearly of plum-cake proportions: dry-biscuit analysis, however badly needed, does not go far enough to satisfy, and shortbread history is too short and lightly baked, like an afternoon melodrama on television.

Consider, for a moment, the three most prominent plum-cake historians of the twentieth century—Oswald Spengler, Arnold Toynbee, and Pitirim Sorokin. All these thinkers argued that disintegrative changes occur in world history in standard cultural phases which reappear in the life cycles of different civilizations. Spengler and Toynbee, for instance, believe that civilizations pass through three cultural phases: (1) growth, spring, childhood; (2) maturity, summer; and (3) autumn, winter, disintegration. These correspond roughly to Sorokin's three cultural phases: the (1) ideational, (2) integrated (or idealistic), and (3) sensate.

According to Toynbee's vision, states are born and develop amid military activity and aggressiveness within a civilization; but a critical event occurs in the process after which wars become destructive, not creative. Exhausted, the struggling states give themselves up to an empire, which yields peace as well as domination by a master. This peace, however, is a mere interlude preceding the disintegration which is soon to follow. Peace by equilibrium thus leads to an imperial peace, which, in turn, signals the decline of civilization.[6] Some see Toynbee's vision as an apt description of America today. Kissinger proposes a peace by equilibrium, anticipating the disintegration of the American empire. Signals of Western decline seem to throb throughout the world.

Toynbee argued that unlike the decay of all civilizations before, Western civilization had the chance to regenerate itself because of its Christian faith. In contrast, Spengler viewed Christian hope (like Toynbee's) as cowardice and stressed instead the predatory nature of human beings.[7] Spengler was heavily influenced by Friedrich Nietzsche, who argued that for people of the West God is dead, that only individuals are responsible for what they do and become, that Christianity is an excuse, a rationalization for weakness and passivity. In light of Nietzsche's focus upon will, Spengler viewed science and technology as inevitable instruments of the will to power. Democratic institutions and human equality were Spenglerian signs of weakness, precipitating disintegration. Again, note the influence of Nietzsche, who wrote:

> Democracy has ever been the form of decline in organizing power. . . . In order that there may be institutions, there must be a kind of will, instinct, or imperative, which is anti-liberal to the point of malice: the will to tradition, to authority, to responsiblity for centuries to come, to the solidarity of chains of generations, forward and backward *ad infinitum*. When this will is present, something like the *imperium Romanum* is founded; or like Russia, the *only* power today which has endurance, which can wait, which can promise something—Russia, the concept that suggests the opposite of the wretched European nervousness and system of small states.[8]

Again, some hear an ominous ring of truth today in Nietzsche's words.

Like Toynbee and Nietzsche, Spengler thought that only minorities are authentically creative and can initiate cultures. But since the creative minority of the West had revealed the secrets of its power to the remainder of humanity, Spengler thought Western civilization would die, a victim of the double revolt of the white and colored masses and the resultant international struggle for dominance. Updating Spengler, one notes that Western creativity and power, from nuclear physics to nuclear biology, *have* sprung from creative minorities. And one notes sadly the spread of nuclear technology and weapons from the West to the non-Western parts of the world, not because non-Western peoples have no right to this technological development, but because of their probable inability to digest it any more wholesomely than the West has been able to.

Recall the frightening warning of Frantz Fanon, in *The Wretched of the Earth*, addressed to the Third World:

> Leave this Europe where they are never done talking of Man, yet murder men everywhere they find them, at the corner of every one of their own streets, in all the corners of the globe. For centuries they have stifled almost the whole of humanity in the name of a so-called spiritual experience. Look at them today swaying between atomic and spiritual disintegration. . . . Two centuries ago, a former European colony decided to catch up with Europe. It succeeded so well that the United States of America became a monster, in which the taints, the sickness and the inhumanity of Europe have grown to appalling dimensions.[9]

Like Spengler, Fanon is pessimistic about the prospects for Western civilization.

Pitirim Sorokin, on the other hand, supports Toynbee's more optimistic vision of the future. In Sorokin's view, the dominant culture of the contemporary world is becoming increasingly sensate, by which he means worldly and empirical. This phase will end, however, with the onset of a new religious stage—marked by the development of Christianity, through a synthesis of East and West or something else. Sorokin argues that turbulent events will characterize the transition from the sensate phase to the religious phase. In Sorokin's terminology, the sequence of events will be as follows:

Late Sensate Chaos ⟶ Increasing Polarization ⟶ Crisis ⟶ Ordeal ⟶ Catharsis ⟶ A New Religiosity.[10]

Our civilization, then, will not continue as we know it or have known it in the past, but will be terminated or painfully reborn in another form after a transitory period of chaos, irrationality, and disintegration. During this transition, some people will hold to ethical and altruistic beliefs. Others will dedicate themselves to selfish egotism, materialism, and sensualism. "Ordeal" and "Catharsis" describe this process, which culminates in the generation of a charismatic idea that will serve as the basis for an Ideational or Integrated (Idealistic) society.

Looking at America through Sorokin's lenses one senses the worldly, sensate chaos, the increasing polarization of beliefs, the continual feeling of crisis and ordeal, and the straining for a new religiosity and new forms of community. All of these are social signs that revealed themselves most blatantly in the 1960s in the counterculture.

I was an undergraduate at Stanford University when the culture storm struck. At first the signs were indirect, beneath the surface. As a philosophy major I noticed that dry-biscuit thinking had become a dogmatic monopoly in the department. Indeed, it was often difficult to find the biscuit in the mathematical symbolic logic and computer science that were required of majors. To my surprise, existentialism was banned from the philosophy department, and I had to sneak over to hear the lectures of Kurt Reinhardt in Modern Languages. Some philosophy majors were so outraged that a house for phenomenologists was established off campus, phenomenology being anathema in the department. Finally, when I could take it no more, I revolted and became an English literature major in a department where existentialism was the subject of many stimulating lectures and minds were open, if somewhat sardonic.

But the culture storm was also a political storm. As I was coming into my senior year, the war in Vietnam reached a white-heat intensity. The beautiful forms and subtleties of sensibility which I experienced in literature seemed totally incongruent with events in the real world, irrelevant to helping others or to touching base with the national crisis. So, I went into political science and international relations upon graduating, believing that here I could find the tools to make beauty, goodness, and truth into reality. Only later did I learn that political science itself was open only for being unsure of itself and was often a collection of decadent forms and theories from other disciplines, forms of "scientific" pretention. And the computer, which Theodore Geiger has aptly called "the ultimate embodiment of the Protestant ethic," was beginning to take over this field too. The rationalization of scientific technique was rampant, it seemed, throughout academia. Only the later disenchantment with Robert McNamara's sophisticated decision-making models as applied from the Pentagon upon Vietnam brought some professors back to their humanistic senses.

Meanwhile, my heart was more with novelist Ken Kesey and his merry pranksters in the Bay Area around San Francisco than with the political science courses I was taking. Writer Lorry Payne, one of Kesey's colleagues, told me bold stories of shrinking computer cards for registration at Stanford in the washing machine before handing them in, just to give the "thinking machine" something to think about. The next time I met Payne, several years later sitting on the steps of the New York University library in Greenwich Village, he was a *persona non grata* with a homestead in Canada, trying to market an antimonopoly game, which rewarded those most who became potted out fastest on their trip through the system. People like Kesey and Payne became symbols of the counterculture movement against the heavy-handed technological applications of Western rationality and against the dehumanizing consequences of Western scientism and "progress."

The counterculture in America dates back at least to the Beat movement of the 1950s and the publication of Allen Ginsberg's poem "Howl" in San Francisco. Its focus was to protest spontaneously and creatively against the repressive aspects of Western culture as it had developed in advanced technological societies like America. The ultimate political expression of the counterculture's critique of society was perhaps made by radical philosopher Herbert Marcuse in *One-Dimensional Man*. In that work Marcuse argues that American society today veils the lack of freedom in a guise of rationality:

> Domination is transfigured into administration. The capitalist bosses and owners are losing their identity as responsible agents; they are assuming the function of bureaucrats in a corporate machine. . . . The tangible force of exploitation disappears behind the facade of objective rationality. Hatred and frustration are deprived of their specific target, and the technological veil conceals the reproduction of inequality and enslavement. With technical progress as its instrument, unfreedom—in the sense of man's subjection to his productive apparatus—is perpetuated and intensified in the form of many liberties and comforts. The novel feature is the overwhelming rationality in this irrational enterprise, and the depth of the preconditioning which shapes the instinctual drives and aspirations of the individuals and obscures the difference between false and true consciousness.[11]

The significance of Marcuse's argument has largely been obscured because its use and misuse by ideological extremists such as Angela Davis have succeeded in identifying Marcuse in the popular mind as a dangerous subversive thinker, a communist threat. Such ideological extremism polarized the entire counterculture movement of the 1960s, often dividing it into "over-the-counter culture" (to use H. Nieburg's phrase) on the one hand and backwater radicalism and individual idiosyncrasy on the other.[12] Marcuse's often hidden but undeniable contribution, regardless of where one stands ideologically, was to apply a synthesis of Freud and Marx to American culture. He demonstrated that many Americans who think they are free are only participating in socially prescribed outlets of freedom, that many who believe they are alienated have been preconditioned by the media and countermedia to act out their alienation in certain conformist modes, and that many who believe they have a wide range of choice in terms of meeting their needs are actually pursuing false or artificial needs taught them by society, leaving their deepest human needs frustrated and repressed. In effect Marcuse did a psychoanalysis of the means of social control in contemporary America. Unfortunately, he left half of the job undone: he provided no alternative after dissecting the American technocratic structure with his radical critique.

Just as Marcuse was not taken seriously because of his ideological followers, the non-Marxist counterculture was largely misread in its deeper significance for being so diffuse, faddish, and sentimental. Yet the positive contributions of the counterculture of the 1960s may have provided the seeds for an alternative, humanistic, and democratic ideology for America at home and abroad. When the politics based upon the culture of control, stemming from the Cold War concern with national security and defense issues, became obsolete and self-defeating, alternative counterculture paradigms were projected for refurbishing the American community from the grassroots using the humanistic, democratic tradition of Walt Whitman and commune idealists of the past. The counterculture, in short, may have bequeathed Americans a set of value priorities and a sense of community awareness and commitment that can serve to restore American morale at home in the future.

The fundamental issue at stake is the question of social control versus individual freedom and creativity. Or put another way, for which values is social control justifiable and how is such control to be limited to protect the rights of individual citizens? In terms of Western culture, Sigmund Freud analyzed this dilemma brilliantly in his work *Civilization and Its Discontents.* First he recalled that the human personality has a three-part structure—the *id,* or human unconscious, instinctual drives; the *ego,* or human conscious rational control of desires; and the *superego,* or the social norms and rules that humans internalize through socialization at home and in the community. Then he argued that tensions between the individual ego and society's superego were inevitable, that revolts against the superego norms on the part of individuals allowed the creation of culture, and that the repression of individual drives through the voluntary submission of the ego to the superego allowed civilization to develop.[13] The consequences of this thesis are profound. If there is not enough freedom in a social order, individuals will not be spontaneous enough to create culture. But if there is not enough self-discipline or social control, superego norms decay, civilization breaks down, and anarchy, chaos, and war are the inevitable results. Thus, in *The Dying of the Light* Arnold Rogow argues that America's basic problems in the future will result from the decay of America's superego that has occurred in the past decade.[14]

The counterculture movement in America revealed that the typical American psychosocial tensions between ego and superego were resolved by repressing certain kinds of awareness and human capacities. In short, the established culture led to certain typical cultural modes and codes of behavior based upon an established consciousness or state of mind that restricted how people thought about work, pleasure, sex, time, and being. Most of all this technocratic state of mind wanted to keep things under control, to use Western science and rationality to reduce all psychosocial tensions to one consistent pattern, one "true self."

Ironically, this oversimplified belief system, which often resulted in a narrow ideological view of the world and permissible life styles, was rooted in a schizophrenia basic to Western thought itself. Individuals in Western culture often split their social universe in two, with one part against the other (creating ideology), and then try to integrate the social and psychological aspects of themselves consistently into a single, reified belief system. They do this because they believe that individual inconsistencies of personality are dangerous and result in a loss of integrity of a supposedly sacrosanct "true self." In a study of ideology and alienation among American college students in 1971, I found that typical modes of alienation and ideological extremism in contemporary America result from the tendencies toward schizophrenia and reification in Western thought itself, especially when combined with simplistic "to thine own self be true" psychoanalytic paradigms that have become so popular throughout the United States.[15]

Freud himself was a victim of this polarizing tendency of Western thought in *Civilization and Its Discontents*. Although culture is produced from the tension between ego and superego, Freud maintains that individuals remain unhappy. Their drive to give in to and create culture (the ultimate reification) is caused by a feeling of guilt derived from the superego (parent, social, and peer norms). *Normal* Western life becomes a sad case of schizophrenia—a conflict between self interest and social interest—if Freud's simplistic view is taken for granted. Alienation from this culturally preconditioned guilt causes human beings to react by a schizophrenic search for their own pleasure: "A tendency arises to separate from the ego everything that can become a source of . . . unpleasure, to throw it outside and to create a pure pleasure-ego which is confronted by a strange and threatening 'outside.' "[16]

Such a negative or escape-oriented search for pleasure describes not merely some members of the alienated counterculture movement still trapped in established cultural modes but members of the American business community as well. Capitalism is ultimately based upon a philosophy of hedonism—the individual pursuit of material satisfaction and consumption. The vital point is that Freud's view is self-fulfilling prophecy: it becomes true since people believe in it and since it fits neatly into the dichotomous thinking of Western tradition. Furthermore, more recent psychotherapists, such as Prescott Lecky and Ronald Laing, simply play new tunes on the same old schizophrenic strings. Laing does go beyond Freud in demonstrating that positivistic science further widens the splits that alienate human beings. "Man," according to Laing, is "cut off from his own mind, cut off equally from his own body—a half-crazed creature in a mad world."[17] But the first premise of Laing is unchanged: an invented false self is causing the disintegration of a real self, and the latter must overcome the former with a reintegration of perception and being.[18] The cure again is to reify half of a split (the real self). More recently, in *Knots*, Laing appears to swallow both halves of the split and stress the inconsistencies, but he does it from an alienated perspective derived from his Western background and from his original siding with one half.

Such "to thine own self be true" approaches to psychic health may actually create impossible tasks. After individuals spend a lifetime of socialization in Western dichotomies, of splitting mind from body and so forth, their attempt to define happiness as the elimination of all such splits with one integrated personality (based on a one-sided ideology or belief system) may make happiness impossible to achieve and alienation an inevitable state of "normality." Of course, if happiness is not the goal and the main social and psychological aims are power and economic production, the Western dichotomous strait jacket of constant motivating tension may be a useful means. Indeed, in writing *Individuals and World Politics,* I discovered that such a never-ceasing psychosocial tension did motivate eight great political leaders in the twentieth century: Gandhi, Lenin, Mao, Wilson, Hitler, de Gaulle, Hammarskjöld, and Kissinger.[19]

A paradox emerges which the counterculture perceptively exposed: to accept the negative, ever-striving Freudian and Faustian view of the ego is to maximize Western imperial power and technological production at the expense of Western contentment and individual happiness. If power and happiness are antithetical, then this country has much to worry about in the conflict sociologist Daniel Bell discovered between the requirements of the capitalist economic system on the one hand (greater applications of rationality, organization, and efficiency) and the direction of the capitalist culture on the other (greater emphasis upon values such as feeling, personal gratification, and the total fulfillment of the self). Social and sexual abandon, in short, may tear apart the capitalist work ethic which created the bounty making such cultural fulfillments possible—leading, perhaps, to the decline of the West.[20]

But there is another way to view the paradox at the heart of Western motivations. There is an alternative to the repressive unilinearity of the prevailing models of self that seek to eliminate all tensions, to obtain total consistency by setting low goals. One can envision a human being as a multitude of personalities rather than as just one, as an open set of options, rather than as merely one foreordained option to be discovered. The counterculture has suggested a new, higher vision of Western human development that suits the postindustrial era, that goes beyond mere efficient rationality and self-sacrifice for material production. The term "integration" is used in countries that are becoming modernized and industrialized to mean systematization on the basis of one all too efficient, consistent, and limited ideology and self-conception. However, "integration" could mean an open-ended, selfless view of self, a unity coming through the acceptance of consistencies and inconsistencies, a striving for higher tensions rather than mere tension-reduction actions. As Henry Kariel has so aptly put it, man "must first be able to welcome life's contradictory claims, seeing conflict and insecurity not as something to be transcended but as inherently valuable. He must first have understood himself as an open-ended system."[21] To explore inconsistencies is to stimulate creativity and openness, whereas to attempt to bring all psychic and social aspects of oneself into consistency too soon may be to choose a small, limited vision of self.

Advocates of inconsistent open models of self are found in artistic and creative scientific communities, the environments that make all counterculture paradigms and truly original human discovery and renaissance possible. For example, novelist André Gide wrote:

> All through my life I have never sought to know myself; that is to say I have never sought myself. It seemed to me that such seeking or rather, the success of such seeking brought with it a limitation and impoverishment of self, and that only rather poor and limited personalities succeeded in finding and understanding themselves. . . . I dislike inconsistency less than the determination to be true to oneself, and than the fear of giving oneself away. . . . The most precious part of ourselves is that which remains unformulated.[22]

Ralph Waldo Emerson made much the same point when he noted, "A foolish consistency is the hobgoblin of little minds." And psychotherapist Rollo May has demonstrated that the limited notion of the consistent self in contemporary American society represses eros, or an individual's most exhilarating sense of intentionality and fulfillment, and results in the substitution of mechanical sex and denial of intimacy in human relations: "We fly to the sensation of sex in order to avoid the passion of eros."[23] As social complexity increases and social change and future shock bear down upon individuals, they are tempted to reach for simplistic solutions—in ideology, psychotherapy, and retreat from any risk of themselves. This psychic introversion, which correlates with the national tendency toward isolationism in an era of international crisis, is defensive, reactionary, and ultimately self-defeating. The counterculture movement suggests that postindustrial Americans can grow beyond the old homeostatic model of the self, which views the individual psyche as though it were a self-adjusting thermostat of a heating system (turning itself on or off in the limited range of comfort provided by the standards of outside authorities). In short, out of apparent Western decay may come a unique opportunity for a Western renaissance.

In the Old World, cultural renaissance flowered in times of imperial decay. Italy, for example, gave the world many of its art treasures at a time of political disintegration. Should America be an exception to the rule? The flowering of the counterculture and the rapid growth of poetry, classical and folk singing, dance and the other arts in the past decade indicate that the potential for an American cultural renaissance is latent, if not manifest. The crucial questions one must ask are: What kind of cultural values should the United States represent in the world as a great power? and, Can America have its cultural renaissance and world power simultaneously?

The counterculture movement represented a new phase of development in Western culture, particularly in the United States. Rather than viewing the counterculture as a curious contradiction to capitalistic and imperial political values, perhaps it is more fruitful to see those values as the awkward parents of the movement—much as all revolutionaries depend for the meaning of their rebellion upon the existing social system which they are attempting to change. Capitalism may indeed just be a developmental phase, as Lenin suggested, yet not a mere transition to some stateless communism but a material means to a state of luxury, cultural productivity, and civilization that the world has not yet experienced.

The atrocities of Western civilization and technology are clear enough to anyone familiar with the history of the twentieth century. Counterculture poet Galway Kinnell catalogued some of them in his *Book of Nightmares*:[23]

> In the Twentieth Century of my trespass on earth,
> having exterminated one billion heathens,
> heretics, Jews, Moslems, witches, mystical seekers,
> every one of them for his own good . . . [24]

But is the answer to our Western guilt to give up our technology, which has done good as well as evil, and relinquish our power to others in the world with the benevolent assumption that everyone will be better off under their stewardship? Or is it not a sign of hope as well as of decay that Watergate, Vietnam protests, and the counterculture movement were allowed to exist, and even to flourish? The Soviet Union has to lock up, commit, or get rid of its Solzhenitsyns. The People's Republic of China bans Beethoven's music as a symbol of decadent Western individualism. Do we really want to trade our decadence for theirs? The loss in individual freedom would be undeniable, as anyone knows who has traveled to those countries and spoken with students and others who would like to travel to the United States.

To abandon the rationality and efficiency of Western technology altogether is to throw out the baby with the bath water. As C. P. Snow noted long ago, literary-minded intellectuals are often "natural Luddites," a reference to a band of workmen in the early nineteenth century who tried to prevent the use of labor-saving machinery by breaking it up and burning down factories. To try to retreat to a time before the Industrial Revolution and its technological consequences is to be as mad as Ned Lud, the first Luddite, a half-witted man who broke up stocking frames in 1779. As Snow put it so well:

Industrialisation is the only hope of the poor. I use the word "hope" in a crude prosaic sense. I have not much use for the moral sensibility of anyone who is too refined to use it so. It is all very well for us, sitting pretty, to think that material standards of living don't matter all that much. It is all very well for one, as a personal choice, to reject industrialisation—do a modern Walden, if you like, and if you go without much food, see most of your children die in infancy, despise the comforts of literacy, accept twenty years off your own life, then I respect you for the strength of your aesthetic revulsion. But I don't respect you in the slightest if, even passively, you try to impose the same choice on others who are not free to choose.[25]

Technology and industrialization, then, should not be eliminated but rather controlled with a new superego, or set of social norms that Americans respect. Such codes would allow individuals to develop in freedom and yet give them, by carrot and stick, the incentive to help others at home and abroad who are less well off than they are. The decay of the old superego in America may not be such a bad thing if it can be replaced by a rejuvenated democratic and humanistic ethos that would gain consensus at home and respect throughout the world. Philosopher Jürgen Habermas has argued persuasively that the basic political problem of postindustrial societies is that their technologically exploitable knowledge has increased much more rapidly than the democratic controls upon such knowledge.[26] Knowledge is power, and technology has overpowered democracy.

In *Politics for Human Beings* Ralph Hummel and I began with this dilemma and attempted to provide a set of standards based upon objective human needs that can be used to criticize and control technological developments.[27] Trying to demonstrate that plum-cake cycles and dry-biscuit thinking are not mutually exclusive, we suggested a cycle with three distinct sequences of political development for social relationships on all levels: creation, maintenance, and decay. The model allows individuals to locate themselves for effective action within a given society; it also led us to discover that two cycles were going on in America, grinding people between them. Traditional American rules of the political game were going from maintenance to decay, as people lost their enthusiasm for political leaders and institutions and doubted both the worth of the system and themselves. Yet simultaneously, American corporate life was going from a period of creation to a period of maintenance and institutionalization: the average American for example, does not hesitate to perceive his or her job as a first need and readily accepts the ideology of apolitics, the belief that technocratic experts and corporate oligarchies, not everyday citizens, must decide how to meet society's basic needs. Our conclusion was that according to the standards of objective human needs and democratic participation, most societies, including the United States, are unnecessarily dehumanizing. And a fundamental prerequisite for restoring a creative and democratic politics for human beings in such societies is to reform the educational system, its assumptions and curricula.

Notes

[1]Henry Fairlie, "Anti-Americanism at Home and Abroad," *Commentary*, 60, 6 (December 1975), 30.

[2]Interview with Peter Jenkins and former Prime Minister Edward Heath on the "Robert MacNeil Report," Channel 13, New York City, April 2, 1976.

[3]Ernest Becker, *The Denial of Death* (New York: Free Press, 1973), p. 6.

[4]Ved Mehta, *The New Yorker*, December 15, 1962, p. 47.

[5]Charles M. Fair, *The Dying Self* (Garden City, N.Y.: Doubleday-Anchor, 1970), p. 1.

[6]It must be noted that Toynbee stressed the heterogeneity of development of past civilizations and was well aware of the difficulties involved in comparing them. See *A Study of History* Vol. 12 (London: Oxford University Press, 1961), where this awareness is emphasized.

[7]Oswald Spengler, *The Decline of the West*, trans. by Charles F. Atkinson (New York: Knopf, 1962).

[8]Friedrich Nietzsche, "Twilight of the Idols or, How One Philosophizes with a Hammer," in *The Portable Nietzsche*, ed. by Walter Kaufmann (New York: Viking Press, 1968), p. 543.

[9]Frantz Fanon, *The Wretched of the Earth* (New York: Grove Press, 1966), pp. 252-253.

[10]Pitirim A. Sorokin, *Social and Cultural Dynamics*, vol. 1 (New York: Bedminster Press, 1962), pp. 775-779.

[11]Herbert Marcuse, *One-Dimensional Man* (Boston: Beacon Press, 1964), p. 32.

[12]See H. L. Nieburg, *Culture Storm: Politics and the Ritual Order* (New York: St. Martin's Press, 1973); *Up the Mainstream: A Critique of Ideology in American Politics and Everyday Life*, ed. by Herbert Reid (New York: David McKay, 1974); and Theodore Roszak, *The Making of a Counter Culture* (Garden City, N.Y.: Doubleday-Anchor, 1969).

[13]Sigmund Freud, *Civilization and Its Discontents* (New York: W. W. Norton, 1962).

[14]Arnold Rogow, *The Dying of the Light* (New York: G. P. Putnam, 1975).

[15]R. Isaak, "Student Alienation and Ideology: Attitude Consistency and Future Implications," a paper delivered at the 1971 Annual Meeting of the American Political Science Association in Chicago, Illinois.

[16]Freud, *Civilization and Its Discontents*, p. 14.

[17]R. D. Laing, *The Politics of Experience* (New York: Ballantine Books, 1967).

[18]R. D. Laing, *The Divided Self* (Baltimore: Penguin, 1965).

[19]R. Isaak, *Individuals and World Politics* (North Scituate, Mass.: Duxbury Press, 1975).

[20]Daniel Bell, *The Cultural Contradictions of Capitalism* (New York: Basic Books, 1976).

[21]Henry S. Kariel, *Open Systems* (Itasca, Ill.: Peacock, 1968), p. 33.

[22]André Gide, *Fruits of the Earth*, trans. by D. Bussy (New York: Alfred A. Knopf, 1949), p. 231. On creative scientific communities versus scientism, see Thomas Kuhn, *The Structure of Scientific Revolutions* (Chicago: Chicago University Press, 1962).

[23]Rollo May, *Love and Will* (New York: W. W. Norton, 1969), p. 65.

[24]Galway Kinnell, *The Book of Nightmares* (Boston: Houghton-Mifflin, 1971), p. 42.

[25]C. P. Snow, *The Two Cultures* (London: Cambridge University Press, 1969), pp. 25-26.

[26]Jürgen Habermas, *Toward a Rational Society* (Boston: Beacon Press, 1971).

[27]R. Isaak and R. Hummel, *Politics for Human Beings* (North Scituate, Mass.: Duxbury Press, 1975).

10 EDUCATION FOR WHAT?

> In training a child to activity of thought, above all things we must beware of what I will call "inert ideas"—that is to say, ideas that are merely received into the mind without being utilised, or tested, or thrown into fresh combinations. . . . Pedants sneer at an education which is useful. But if education is not useful, what is it? Is it a talent, to be hidden away in a napkin? . . . The understanding which we want is an understanding of an insistent present. The only use of a knowledge of the past is to equip us for the present. No more deadly harm can be done to young minds than by depreciation of the present. The present contains all that there is. It is holy ground; for it is the past, and it is the future.
>
> —*Alfred North Whitehead,*
> The Aims of Education, *1929*

> Do we want a society, under the impact of pervasive vocationalism, where there is a two-track work force, with the many tracked to "first jobs" and a few tracked to leadership and creativity? Clearly we cannot revert to a system from which we have so painfully emerged. To do so would be to permit the decay of democracy, whose central ideal is a thoughtful and judicious electorate.
>
> —*John C. Sawhill,*
> *"On the Problems of 'Hire Education,' "*
> The New York Times, *November 16, 1975.*

To a large extent American democracy and world power are nurtured by the American educational system. But as education has become more compulsory in the United States, to the point where a bachelor's degree is required for most of the jobs people want, there have been few corresponding efforts to make educational requirements relevant to the problems of American democratic and superpower responsibilities. Some critics have even argued that schooling may do more damage than good to many Americans in terms of their healthy functioning in later life. The belief that the more schooling and credentials a person has, the better off he or she is has been dealt a hard blow by the number of unemployed or underemployed Ph.D.'s in this country. If the recovery of American democracy and world power does indeed depend upon educating New World people, it is reasonable to ask for what they should be educated and why.

The philosophy of effective democratic government depends upon a well-educated general public. This prerequisite becomes even more critical if

157

the electorate must deal with all the sophisticated foreign policy and defense issues that world power entails. If America is to revitalize the Western tradition and compete for influence in developing countries with Soviet and Chinese alternatives, the country must produce sophisticated leaders and well-informed citizens. The alternative is disintegration domestically, an inconsistent foreign policy, and the further decline of the West.

Education involves both an ideal and a practical aim. It must develop mental awareness and receptivity to beauty and human feeling as well as provide access to useful technologies. Behind every educational system lies a psychosocial model of human development and a philosophy of education. Education is basic to other institutions—society, the economy, and the polity—which help link individual and social needs, the citizen and the nation, and the nation and the world. To fail to reveal the underlying philosophy of educational development and its consequences is to take knowledge for granted and thereby to lose its creative power. All institutions in a nation will suffer as a result.

In *Emile*, a treatise on education, philosopher Jean Jacques Rousseau described what the educational philosophy of a democratic society should be:

> There is only one man who gets his own way—he who can get it single-handed; therefore freedom, not power, is the greatest good. That man is truly free who desires what he is able to perform, and does what he desires. This is my fundamental maxim. Apply it to childhood, and all the rules of education spring from it.

Personal freedom to choose a social role in accordance with one's own needs and value preferences seems to be the ideal end for an American education, for a culture bent on encouraging individual development. But is this really the end of the existing educational system in America? Or does the existing situation make this ideal impossible to achieve?

Critics of American education today believe the latter to be the case.

In *The Night Is Dark and I Am Far from Home*, educator Jonathan Kozol poses the frightening possibility that education may in fact achieve the opposite of its ideals:

> U.S. education is by no means an inept, disordered misconstruction. It is an ice-cold and superb machine. It is only if we try to lie and tell ourselves that the true purpose of a school is to inspire ethics, to provoke irreverence or to stimulate a sense of outrage at injustice and despair, that we are able to evade the fact that public school is a spectacular device, flawed beyond

question but effective beyond dreams. The problem is not that public schools do *not* work well, but that they *do*.[2]

Kozol is not alone in this perception. Some time ago Albert Einstein said: "The teachers at the elementary school seemed to me like sergeants, the college teachers like lieutenants. It is bad when a school operates with methods of coercion and dictatorial authority. They thus destroy the pupils' honesty and self-confidence. They breed submissive people." Can any American honestly say that he or she has gone through the educational system without having thought at some time or other that the experience was wasteful?

Educational critics ranging from Paul Goodman to Ivan Illich agree with Kozol and Einstein that the maintenance of existing educational structures represses creative development and fruitful learning. In *Deschooling Society*, Ivan Illich observes:

> The pupil is . . . "schooled" to confuse teaching with learning, grade advancement with education, a diploma with competence, and fluency with the ability to say something new. His imagination is "schooled" to accept service in place of value. Medical treatment is mistaken for health care, social work for the improvement of community life, police protection for safety, military poise for national security, the rat race for productive work. Health, learning, dignity, independence, and creative endeavor are defined as little more than the performance of the institutions which claim to serve these ends, and their improvement is made to depend on allocating more resources to the management of hospitals, schools, and other agencies in question.[3]

Existing educational institutions drive out creativity in individuals. Their sole purpose seems to be not the development of the full potential of the individual but the maintenance of established social institutions. The problem is not peculiar to the United States. In France in 1976 the government issued an order for educational reform designed to steer students out of fields like social science and into fields more relevant to the technological maintenance of society, like business administration.

Americans are usually reluctant to admit that the freedom to choose what they want to be and become is limited by the aims of their technological society. But much of human life is shaped by patterns not of our own creation. Psychologist B. F. Skinner even goes so far as to to maintain that freedom is an illusion and that human behavior can be totally explained in terms of stimulus-response without reference to inner mental states.[4] We may not *believe* B. F. Skinner, but we do live his reality. We prepare for jobs and professions by going through carefully controlled mazes of curricula, contacts, and exploitative job-training experiences. Or as the feminist lawyer Florynce Kennedy put it, "Students are like mushrooms, you keep them in the dark, pile on the shit, and they grow fine."[5]

But fatalistic acceptance of social reality as it exists can only lead to alienation and a loss of creative potential. Recall that the creation of culture depends upon rejection of the status quo—the revolt of the ego against the superego, to use Freud's terminology. The revolt cannot go unchecked, however, and this gives rise to a paradox in terms of the American educational system: democracy is impossible without support for individual development, even if such support conflicts with the status quo; but the maintenance of the American political power in the world is impossible without restricting egoistic individualism through educational norms, even if these are in conflict with individual freedom. Either one must begin with American democracy as a primary objective at the risk of losing some imperial power, or begin with the maintenance of imperial power at the risk of suffocating democracy. To "resolve" the paradox by choosing either alternative is to lose.

There is an ideal solution, at least in theory, to the paradox arising from the conflict between individual freedom and state power. By viewing education as a continuous series of cycles of individual development throughout life—involving constant alternations between freedom and order, spontaneity and control, within a social framework citizens respect—it may be possible to cultivate American democracy while maintaining American influence in the world at large. However, this solution demands a great deal of individual self-discipline, social tolerance, and political understanding of the aims of education in a democratic society—prerequisites that may be hard to come by in America as it exists today.

The ideal educational solution has been summed up by philosopher Alfred North Whitehead: education must be perceived as a repetition of cycles of development, each beginning with a stage of romance (of wonder and ferment), proceeding to a stage of precision (of exactness and grammar), and ending with a stage of generalization (of synthesis and fruition).[6] Whitehead derived this rhythmic cycle of education from Hegel's three stages of progress—thesis (romance), antithesis (precision), and synthesis (generalization). The problem of education in America's technological society, as Whitehead sees it, is an undue focus upon the stage of precision. Knowledge thus becomes more dead than alive, more inert than productive:

> Education must essentially be a setting in order of a ferment already stirring in the mind: you cannot educate mind in *vacuo*. In our conception

of education we tend to confine it to the second stage of the cycle; namely to the stage of precision. But we cannot so limit our task without misconceiving the whole problem. We are concerned alike with the ferment, with the acquirement of precision, and with the subsequent fruition.'

In an era when America as a technological superpower is threatened with decay, perhaps it is inevitable that education should be preoccupied with precision and technology. But precision divorced from romance and creativity can produce nothing worthwhile. Technological forms of science become decadent in their detachment from their initial creative inspirations and brutal in their fruitless quantitative applications. And the consequences are felt in social life: community morale disintegrates, selfish interest predominates, and disenchantment with existing institutions and political leadership grows. Education, when misdirected, produces tensions that are individually and socially destructive rather than culturally constructive. Egos equipped with powerful technologies without humanistic goals, roots, or social commitment can tear apart the fabric of a democratic community. Or, as Whitehead put it, "Sensitiveness without impulse spells decadence, and impulse without sensitiveness spells brutality."

What is required, then, is a model of psychosocial development upon which an alternative American educational system can be based that allows for continual cycles of romance, precision, and generalization throughout the lives of American citizens. We must establish a way of rebelling against alienation and injustice that results in creative cultural forms and political commitment to community improvement. The precision and order of technology must not be thrown out or destroyed in Luddite fashion but adapted to creative and humane ends, to production with moral as well as material objectives in mind. We must turn out not Economic Man, nor Organization Man, nor Corporate Man, but Democratic Man.

The culture storm of the 1960s and the conservative reaction to it as a result of political and economic dislocations in the 1970s have demonstrated to Americans that the process of education is inseparable from the political environment. Models of the self are derived from the streets as well as the classroom. In these two decades of social turmoil and political trauma, a number of models of psychosocial development have emerged, largely because social psychologists needed to find models of human development that would explain the complex social change they were experiencing. Their models were sophisticated and complex because society had become that way. The simplistic ideological polarization, both left and right, and the resultant misunderstanding, violence, and human suffering of the recent past underscore the need for sophisticated belief systems that steer clear of lopsided ideologies, polarities, psychologies, or dogmatisms. If idols of the tribe we must have, they must at least be idols complex enough to merit our respect, nurture our maturity, and give us the inspiration, if not the means, to solve our problems.

Of course the models of psychosocial, moral, and educational development that emerged in the past two decades had roots in earlier psychological work—particularly Jean Piaget's studies of children in Switzerland and Erik Erikson's life cycle theories pertaining to children and society.[8] One of the most impressive and useful offspring of Piaget, Erikson, and the 1960s was Charles Hampden-Turner's model of psychosocial development.

Hampden-Turner is an Englishman, educated at Cambridge, who came to the United States to study for a Ph.D. at the Harvard Business School hoping to find some remedies to England's economic crises. Once in the United States, however, he discovered social crises worse than he had left in England. In reaction to the conservatism of the Harvard Business School, he wrote a Ph.D. thesis in business that was later published as *Radical Man: The Process of Psycho-social Development*. By 'radical,' Hampden-Turner meant going back to the roots of human motivation in social situations, so the term should not deter conservatives from examining his brilliant psychosocial synthesis. On the basis on this work, Hampden-Turner has since set up business corporations for the poor in slums and examined the psychosociology behind the rehabilitation of ex-convicts in the Delancy Street Foundation of San Francisco. He has written pathbreaking books about both of these educational experiences as well.[9] My personal experience with Hampden-Turner further confirms that he is one of the few people who applies his scientific and technological training to social needs. One might say that he is the living embodiment of what education should aim for in the future.

Hampden-Turner's model of psychosocial development is shown in the accompanying figure. In his work *Radical Man,* Hampden-Turner has demonstrated that every segment of the cycle model has been cited by five or more theorists of psychological development as a criterion for positive mental health and mature human functioning. When one person living in accord with the cycle interacts with another, a "double-helix effect" occurs, that is, each person supports and stimulates the other to make self-actualization possible for both of them. Those living according to the opposite values of each segment of the cycle are anomic or alienated: they narrow and impoverish their perception, lock in their identities, sense incompetence and anticipated loss, fail to invest authentically and intensely in their environment, devise nonsuspending, risk-reducing

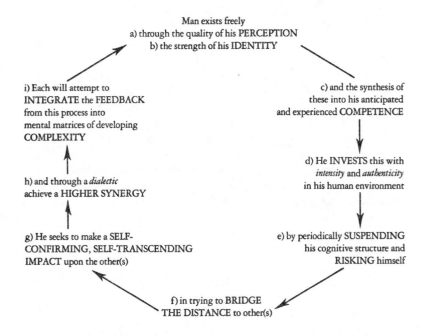

Man exists freely
a) through the quality of his PERCEPTION
b) the strength of his IDENTITY

i) Each will attempt to
INTEGRATE the FEEDBACK
from this process into
mental matrices of developing
COMPLEXITY

c) and the synthesis of
these into his anticipated
and experienced COMPETENCE

h) and through a *dialectic*
achieve a HIGHER SYNERGY

d) He INVESTS this with
intensity and *authenticity*
in his human environment

g) He seeks to make a SELF-
CONFIRMING, SELF-TRANSCENDING
IMPACT upon the other(s)

e) by periodically SUSPENDING
his cognitive structure and
RISKING himself

f) in trying to BRIDGE
THE DISTANCE to other(s)

Source: Charles Hampden-Turner, *Radical Man: The Process of Psycho-social Development* (New York: Doubleday-Anchor, 1971), p. 37. Used by permission.

strategies, avoid trying to bridge the distance to others, are unable to make a self-confirming and self-transcending impact, seek the domination of or submission to the perspectives of others, and accept little or no responsibility for feedback, resulting in disintegration and a lack of complexity in themselves and their victims.[10] In short, Hampden-Turner has provided us with a positive, creative model of Democratic Man and with a theory of psychosocial development that can help individuals to overcome the alienation forced upon them by the complex American society.

Regardless of which model of psychosocial development is finally chosen as the basis for a future American educational program, it should emphasize certain features: openness to change, self-esteem through cooperation with others, belief in self-determination and self-help, positive support of individual potential rather than negative restrictions because of class or background, enthusiasm for learning and development for its own sake, an ethical sense of demanding equal opportunity for one's self and others. These characteristics, taken together, mean that the individual is the focus of the educational system and that the maximization of his or her life chances should be its main aims in a democratic society. They do not mean that individuals should be spoiled or standards lowered. But the standards set should originate with the individual, for motivation begins with the self. And educational systems flourish by nurturing individual selves and overcoming bureaucratic apparatus that makes this appear to be an impossible task in large institutions. Order and discipline should be the appearance, creative learning should be the reality.

The American predicament caused by the conflict between democratic and great-power needs is reflected in the tension between freedom and order in the educational system. Democratic societies presuppose open systems of education that stress individual growth and creative spontaneity. Superpowers and empires, on the other hand, presuppose closed models of management that stress obedience to authority and respect for the status quo. Democratic thought tends toward the left, toward viewing the individual as the source of value, toward a radical egalitarianism and belief in the people as the source of legitimacy. Superpower thinking tends toward the right, toward viewing laws, organizations, and authorities outside the individual as the source of value, toward a secretive, managerial elitism and a belief that the elites in power and their institutions are the source of legitimacy. The classic conflict between individual democratic freedom and state law-and-order elitism is present in all democratic states, but it is heightened to fever pitch in superpower states like the United States.

Democratic thinking not only stresses individual participation but implies an educational focus upon the liberal arts, social sciences, and other fields of open, creative risk where each individual can develop his or her idiosyncratic talents to the full. In contrast, superpower thinking, which aims to maintain an *imperium*, focuses upon managerial elites and their pragmatic tools for maintaining power in the real world: business administration, management, military science, macroeconomics, computer science, and other fields of technological control. The threats to American state power from within and without are apt to lead in the future to an even greater stress upon such a technocratic curriculum at the expense of the liberal arts.

A change in this educational trend is possible, but, paradoxically, a change in the direction of radical democratization of the American educational system could actually lead to imperial domestic control by elites and a further reduction of individual freedom in the name of absolute equality. The only way out of this not improbable danger is to distinguish sharply between equality as leveling and as equal opportunity and to support a public policy that begins a massive effort to make equal opportunity a reality in both educational and socio economic terms in America. Anthropologist Ashley Montagu argues persuasively that the advent of equal opportunity will not lead to a reduction but to a great increase in the differences in achievement between human beings, since it will maximize the possibilities for the expression of each individual's uniqueness:

> It is a mistake to want to reduce differences, and a sound and humane principle to encourage the fullest expression of difference. The truth is that inequality of potentialities is the rule among humans, and that in this fact lies the great wealth of humanity; for had we all been born equal in our potentialities for achievement this would have been a very dreary world, indeed. . . . It is, therefore, desirable for us to understand that there is nothing so unequal as the equal treatment of unequals. It is wrongheaded and even cruel to treat all human beings, especially developing human beings, as if they were equal in potentialities for learning, intelligence, and achievement. In any population taken at random there exist immense differences among individuals in rates of growth and development and in the ability to absorb what is being taught. It is as unfair to teach slow developers rapidly as it is to teach rapid developers slowly. . . . Each child requires to be taught as a unique individual, with special attention to his own unique rates of growth and development. [11]

Montagu goes on to argue that to be born equal means to have equal rights to growth and the development of individual potentialities. These potentialities are not biologically but culturally determined in most cases, he argues. To eliminate inequalities of opportunity, it is necessary to eradicate the cultural disadvantages of those discriminated against so that they may take equal advantage of educational opportunities in American society. This will entail changing those socioeconomic conditions in poor or minority communities that force people to concentrate on survival, leaving no leisure time for higher-level development and leading families to stress mere money making rather than extraordinary individual achievement. Enforcing equal opportunity also requires creating conditions of good health and freedom from disease and the effects of malnutrition in disadvantaged communities, particularly during fetal and childhood development. And last but not least, meaningful equal opportunity requires adjusting educational systems to the cultural contexts of the individuals involved, so that the educational content and form are meaningful in terms of each child's traditional culture—especially if the child is black, Indian, Puerto Rican, or outside the WASP mainstream bias of existing educational and testing systems. [12]

The equal opportunity issue reveals once again the material prerequisites for democracy and the nonliberal aspects of American liberalism. Optimum psychosocial development can only occur when lower-level socioeconomic needs have been satisfied. Good educational systems that are relevant to the technological and social complexities of the modern era are expensive, both for individuals and the social system. America is one of the few countries in the world that can afford a comprehensive, democratic-elitist educational system where the higher-level educational choices are left to the individual, his or her own particular abilities, and what he or she can pay. The difficulty, of course, is that most Americans cannot afford the best possible private-school and college training. The American educational system thus perpetuates a rigid class hierarchy: private prep schools and Ivy League universities are for an elite at the top, state junior colleges and public high schools in inner-city slums for those at the bottom.

The increasingly clear-cut class hierarchy in the American educational system makes the democratic promise of equal opportunity regardless of race, religion, or sex ludicrous. To be born into a minority culture in America is to be born unequal in the competitive struggle for individual development, upward mobility, and material success. Without a restructuring of America's political economy and social structure, as outlined in the next chapter, the optimum educational model of psychosocial development may become relevant only for the children of the rich, who then must spend the rest of their lives trying to live down the guilt which this initial advantage gives them in a society with a democratic ethos.

Poet-adventurer Antoine de Saint-Exupéry gives us one of the most dramatic examples of the importance of socioeconomic class upon individual development in his work *Wind, Sand and Stars*. On a long train ride through France, Saint-Exupéry walked through the crowded third-class carriage full of Polish workers forced to leave France with their families because of desperate economic currents. One family caught his eye: the father, a lump of clay, was beaten down and hollowed out by heavy work in the mines; the mother was equally bowed and withered by a hard working-class existence. Both were the epitomé of sluggish filth and poverty imposed upon them by society from birth, and both seemed to have lost half of their human quality. But on the mother's breast lay a beautiful baby with an adorable face, a golden fruit of rugged parentage:

> I bent over the smooth brow, over those mildly pouting lips, and I said to myself: This is a musician's face. This is the child Mozart. This is a life full of beautiful promise. Little princes in legends are not different

from this. Protected, sheltered, cultivated, what could not this child become?

When by mutation a new rose is born in a garden, all the gardeners rejoice. They isolate the rose, tend it, foster it. But there is no gardener for man. This little Mozart will be shaped like the rest by the common stamping machine. This little Mozart will love shoddy music in the stench of night dives. This little Mozart is condemned. [13]

Can the richest nation of all times in absolute terms afford to ignore the development of the majority of its children, to give them less than the optimum educational environment just because they were born in the lower-middle or working class or some minority culture? As Saint-Exupéry expressed it: "What torments me is not the humps nor the hollows nor the ugliness. It is the sight, a little bit in all these men, of Mozart murdered. . . . Only the Spirit, if it breathe upon the clay, can create Man." [14]

Moral assumptions underlie all psychosocial models of individual development. It makes all the difference, for example, if one assumes that the stability of the existing social system is the greatest good rather than the freedom of individual development. This puts the existing superego (decadent or not) before the ego, the dominant political ideology of those in power before plans for social change, the interests of the state before rights and freedoms of its citizens. But a state can only be said to be meaningfully democratic if citizens' rights and freedoms are the basis of the state's legitimacy. Social order is necessary for freedom to exist, but a democracy is authentic only to the extent that it furthers the development of the majority of its citizens. The fundamental tenet of America's liberal democratic philosophy is the self-determination of the individual as the basis for the legitimacy of all political institutions. In Western democracies, self-determination is what freedom means.

Educator Lawrence Kohlberg has discovered a model of moral growth that can provide a useful basis for evaluating or changing educational systems in democratic societies. According to Kohlberg the moral development of an individual can be measured in stages, which he characterizes as follows:

Stage one: Obedience and Punishment Orientation—individual is motivated primarily by the desire to avoid punishment from a superior power: egocentric deference to avoid pain.

Stage Two: Instrumental Relativism—individual is motivated to satisfy quasi-physical needs and sometimes those of others through exchange and reciprocity.

Stage Three: Personal Concordance—individual is oriented toward approval and pleasing others, a "Good-Boy" orientation and desire to be judged by good intentions.

Stage Four: Law and Order—individual is oriented to do his duty and show respect for authority for its own sake, seeing his conformity in the larger context of a constellation of social roles, each with its conventional demands that must be obeyed.

Stage Five: Social Contract Orientation—individual sees his duty in terms of a social contract, recognizing the arbitrary nature of rules necessary for agreement and avoiding the violation of the welfare of the majority or of infringing upon the rights of others.

Stage Six: Individual Conscience or Principle Orientation—individual depends upon his own conscience, universal principles and the mutual respect of others, understanding the universal principles that underlie social commitments and attempting to apply them consistently in all moral judgments.[15]

Using this scale, Charles Hampden-Turner and Phillip Whitten have shown that differences in the political or ideological positions of middle-class Americans actually represent different levels of moral development. Young adults who see themselves as political conservatives, for example, refer to law, order, and authority maintenance (stage 4) and conformity to stereotyped roles (stage 3) in making moral judgments. Those claiming to be liberals or moderates, on the other hand, use social contract criteria (stage 5). And self-professed radicals are split: the majority cite individual conscience and principle as the basis for their moral stands (stage 6), although a large minority make egocentric judgments (stage 2). Thus, Hampden-Turner and Whitten conclude: "There is evidence to support the conservative's notion that the radical movement consists of starry-eyed idealists 'infiltrated' by Machiavellian opportunists. The same evidence, however, also justifies the radical's claim of moral superiority over both liberals and conservatives.[16]

Kohlberg's model of moral growth confronts us once more with a paradox when considering the American predicament of educating citizens to be responsible and free in a state that is a democratic superpower. Superpower equilibrium at home and strength abroad demands order, conformity, and efficiency—best achieved by encouraging the development of citizens only as far as the third and fourth stages (i.e., motivation by social approval and respect for authority). But a viable democratic society demands higher individual moral growth so that citizens can make their own determination of right and wrong behavior for each occasion on the basis of respect for others.

As young people become involved in political action and confrontations, they have a natural tendency to become aware of higher stages of moral growth and to strive to achieve these stages (although, as they become older, they often slip back to lower conventional orientations). A young French demonstrator in the student-worker movement that led to the upset of President Charles de Gaulle in 1968 noted how this happened in her case:

> It was, after all, a demonstration to obtain the release of the arrested students, so we decided to march past the Santé prison, the *symbol* of our prison society. When we got to the Santé, people started to shout, "Free our comrades!" And, suddenly, everyone started arguing, saying that it was just as disgusting for all the others who were in there; that, really, there were people who had been locked up for social reasons that were just as absurd as those for which the students had been arrested in the Sorbonne. People started shouting, "Free the prisoners!" One always rose to a higher social level. It was very interesting.[17]

Similarly the American student demonstrations against the Vietnam War in the 1960s and against the Kent State shooting of students by the National Guard in 1970 raised the moral consciousness and level of development of many individuals, turning them away from the imperial, law-and-order right and toward the democratic, individual-conscience left.

Just as people can be distinguished by conventional and postconventional moral assumptions and by left and right ideological orientations, so too can educational curricula and academic disciplines. Given today's extremely competitive job market in the United States, students are often confronted with the difficult choice of majoring in either a conventional, right discipline (like economics or business accounting) that will help them to get a job in the maintenance-oriented society of superpower America, or in a postconventional left discipline (like philosophy, literature, or art) that will help them develop creatively and morally in accordance with America's humanistic, democratic creed. Left and right are used here according to Silvan Tompkins's distinction between left-wing and right-wing ideology. According to Tompkins, those on the left tend to consider a human being as "an end in himself, an active, creative, thinking, desiring, loving force in nature," while those on the right think that humans realize themselves "only through struggle towards, participation in, conformity to, a norm, a measure, an ideal essence, basically independent of man."[18] My argument is that the democratic ethos encourages human beings to turn to the left, to see humans as ends in themselves and the source of value and creativity; but the bureaucratic state, particularly one with superpower status, requires individuals to turn to the right, to view human activity as meaningful only to the extent that it is measured by outside standards of society such as religion, social mobility in a given hierarchy, laws, or norms.

In the near future, the wise individual in America has only one sensible solution to the inevitable tension between leftist and rightist tendencies: to view these orientations as thesis (democratic left) and antithesis (statist right) in the Hegelian sense, and to strive for a synthesis of the two. Concretely, college students should major in two fields, not just one: a "democratic left" field in accordance with their own romantic, creative desires (in Whitehead's sense) and a "statist, or status quo, right" field that meets social requirements for a useful, specialized technocratic skill.

Such an educational strategy avoids the risk of the student becoming a one-dimensional person, both socially and professionally. It also gives the student the opportunity for a second career if great changes occur in either the student's goals or in the market need for his or her field. The present system advocating just one major and one minor, or a self-spawned (and often only self-relevant) interdisciplinary hodgepodge, unduly types the student in one area of competence (or none). Two majors allows him or her the possibility of developing in depth in two dimensions—one out of passion and one in order to eat.

In addition to the two majors, the undergraduate student should be able to explore as many other fields and kinds of interdisciplinary study as the system will bear. This interdisciplinary thirst for knowledge and excitement counteracts the tendency of many academic departments to produce narrow minds drunk with the self-importance of their own disciplines. Indeed, the departmental structure of most schools stifles students, frustrates creative faculty members, and mystifies knowledge unnecessarily by splitting it into parts without providing a general framework for synthesis. Short of eliminating departments (an unlikely prospect), this educational shortcoming can be alleviated by establishing interdisciplinary programs between departments.

One other practical academic reform seems necessary to better prepare students for their role in a democracy and in the world: the tendency to eliminate foreign language requirements must be reversed. In the future, international business is likely to become more important, not less so. Furthermore, America's role as a superpower will require sensitive citizen diplomacy abroad in the language of others, rather than in English, which presently serves to stoke anti-American feelings abroad. Students must be taught about other languages and cultures early in secondary school, along with world history and international relations.

America, in short, requires an alternative model of Democratic Man as the basis of a renovated educational system. A sense of individual freedom and independence can only be restored to the majority of Americans if they are given the freedom to develop their individual creative talents on the one hand and the tools to become relevant to the working world of a complex, technocratic society on the other. The alternative to the development of Democratic Man with a New World spirit of confidence and technological competence is a continuation of the present: alienation of the many and domination of decision making by a few who rule because of power, wealth, and privilege rather than because of any special skill, virtue, or wisdom.

Notes

1Jean Jacques Rousseau, *Emile* (New York: E. P. Dutton, 1933), p. 48.

2Jonathan Kozol, *The Night Is Dark and I Am Far from Home* (Boston: Houghton-Mifflin, 1975), p. 1.

3Ivan Illich, *Deschooling Society* (New York: Harper & Row, 1971), p. 1. See also Paul Goodman, *Compulsory Mis-education and the Community of Scholars* (New York: Vintage, 1962).

4See B. F. Skinner, *Beyond Freedom and Dignity* (New York: Alfred A. Knopf, 1971). See also Skinner's novel *Walden II* (New York: Macmillan, 1948).

5Florynce Kennedy, Speech at New York University, Nov. 1975.

6Alfred North Whitehead, *The Aims of Education* (New York: Free Press, 1967), chap. 2.

7*Ibid.*, p. 18.

8See Jean Piaget, *The Moral Judgement of the Child* (London: Keagan Paul, 1932); and Erik H. Erikson, *Childhood and Society* (New York: W. W. Norton, 1950).

9See Charles Hampden-Turner's three works: *Radical Man: The Process of Psycho-social Development* (Garden City, N. Y.: Doubleday-Anchor, 1971); *From Poverty to Dignity: A Strategy for Poor Americans* (Garden City, N. Y.: Doubleday-Anchor 1974); and *Sane Asylum* (San Francisco: San Francisco Book Co., 1976).

10Hampden-Turner, *Radical Man*, p. 79.

11Ashley Montagu, "Just What Is 'Equal Opportunity'?" in *Culture and Human Development: Insights into Growing Human*, ed. by Ashley Montagu (Englewood Cliffs, N.J.: Prentice-Hall, 1974), p. 34.

12*Ibid.*, p. 41.

13Antoine de Saint-Exupéry, *Wind, Sand and Stars* (New York: Harcourt, Brace, 1940), p. 305.

14*Ibid.*, p. 305.

15Lawrence Kohlberg, *Stages in the Development of Moral Thought and Action* (New York: Holt, Rinehart & Winston, 1974).

16Charles Hampden-Turner and Phillip Whitten, "Morals Left and Right," *Psychology Today*, April 1971, p. 39.

17As cited in Alfred Willener, *The Action-Image of Society—On Cultural Politicization* (New York: Pantheon, 1970), p. 7.

18Silvan Tompkins, "Left and Right: A Basic Dimension of Ideology," in *The Study of Lives*, ed. by Robert W. White (Chicago: Aldine-Atherton, 1971), pp. 391-392.

11 SOCIAL LIBERALISM: A NEW POLITICAL ECONOMY

> When the accumulation of wealth is no longer of high social importance, there will be great changes in the code of morals. We shall be able to rid ourselves of many of the pseudo-moral principles which have hag-ridden us for two hundred years, by which we have exalted some of the most distasteful of human qualities into the position of the highest virtues. We shall be able to afford to dare to assess the money-motive at its true value. . . . All kinds of social customs and economic practices, affecting the distribution of wealth and of economic rewards and penalties, which we now maintain at all costs, however distasteful and unjust they may be in themselves, because they are tremendously useful in promoting the accumulation of capital, we shall then be free, at last, to discard.
>
> . . . We shall once more value ends above means and prefer the good to the useful.
>
> . . . But beware! The time for all this is not yet. For at least another hundred years we must pretend to ourselves and to everyone that fair is foul and foul is fair; for foul is useful and fair is not. Avarice and usury and precaution must be our gods for a little longer still. For only they can lead us out of the tunnel of economic necessity into daylight.
>
> —*John Maynard Keynes,*
> *"Economic Possibilities for Our*
> *Grandchildren," 1930*

> Where bourgeois society separated the economy from the polity, the public household rejoins the two, not for the fusion of powers, but for the necessary coordination of effects. The public household requires a new socioeconomic bill of rights which redefines for our times the social needs that the polity must try to satisfy. It establishes the public budget (How much do we want to spend, and for whom?) as the mechanism whereby the society seeks to implement "the good condition of human beings."
>
> —*Daniel Bell*, The Cultural
> Contradictions of Capitalism, *1976*

In the future America will become increasingly dependent upon other nations of the world, both economically and politically. Just as one-way transfer payments, such as welfare, are breaking down the pure capitalist assumptions of the political economy at home, one-way foreign aid payments and the need for international cooperation will undermine the pure mercantilist objectives of

America's political economy abroad. Growing social demands make it clear that pure capitalism may have become obsolete since there is no guarantee that the maximization of individual self-interests or profit in a free-market economy will satisfy social needs. On the other hand, it is also clear that pure socialism is incapable of satisfying the full range of individual needs in industrial democratic societies since socialism cannot guarantee individual motivation or differentiation beyond a minimum equal level of production required by the state. An alternative political economy for America to both capitalism and socialism, social liberalism, is needed.

In terms of individual behavior, the political economy of a state is, in effect, the society's socioeconomic superego. That is, individuals are paid (or charged) for doing certain things rather than others. This "learning by paying" structure of the social system limits and directs individual development and productivity, supposedly for the sake of the whole community or state. In theory, political economic systems are supposed to represent an equilibrium of some sort that preserves the stability of the national economy while increasing national productivity and satisfying the needs of all citizens. In reality, the political economies of most advanced industrial democracies in the late twentieth century are characterized by disequilibrium of some sort, promoting uncertainty and instability in the national economy and oversatisfying the needs of the few at the expense of the many, whose needs remain unsatisfied. Clearly, what is needed is a political economy that fosters a dynamic equilibrium which encourages individual incentive and freedom and satisfies social needs. America's haphazard, rugged, individualistic capitalism of the past must be transformed into a civilized, social individualism, or social liberalism, for the future.

At the heart of America's predicament—the tension that exists between the need for individual freedom and the need for stability—are controversial assumptions about political economy. The assumption of rugged individualism that underlies Adam Smith's *laissez-faire* free-market economy has been proven historically to be inadequate to satisfy social needs. That assumption has bred greedy monopolies that antitrust legislation has failed to curb, resulting in the present domination of multinational corporations in the international economy. Yet despite its proven inadequacies, most Americans hang on to at least some belief in pure capitalism because they admire its stress upon individual freedom and initiative, its productivity, and the material economic growth and abundance it has achieved. They also perceive capitalism as the only alternative to dreaded socialism, most often seen as a prelude to communism. The fear of socialism has been so great that steps which in fact move the economy in the direction of socialism—welfare, social security, progressive tax structures, wage-and-price controls—have been thought to be mere temporary aberrations or permanent but minor exceptions to the rules of a free-market economy which has fallen on hard times.

This perception is changing somewhat today. The economic crises of the 1970s, compounded by the political traumas of Watergate and the Vietnam defeat, have served to raise American consciousness to the possibility that perhaps there are deep structural problems in their economic and political system. The 1973-1974 inflation in the United States hit Americans hard, undermining their myth of self-sufficient independence. In fact, four of the major causes of that inflation appeared to be international rather than purely domestic: the quadrupling of world crude oil prices, the explosion in world demand for food and resultant price increases, the depreciation of the value of the dollar, and the "death throes" of the Bretton Woods system of international fixed exchange rates.[1] Simultaneous recession and inflation, unemployment and political uncertainty have stimulated many Americans to begin questioning the assumptions of the American political economy and to become pessimistic about American stability at home and American influence abroad. American uncertainty and weakness have prompted Western European leaders to fear a possible "Finlandization" of Europe, which would imply increased Soviet and communist influence to offset the decline in American power and commitment. Recent communist party gains in Italy and France seem to confirm this fear.[2]

What Americans require for the future is a new form of political economy. Great nations provide great opportunities for their own people and exert great positive influence upon other peoples of the world only by representing a strong, positive ideology combined with economic, political, and military effectiveness. *Laissez-faire* captialism served America extremely well in its development into a wealthy superpower. But America has entered a higher, more civilized and social stage of development. Legitimacy at home and influence abroad can only be restored by redirecting its rugged individualism and productivity toward domestic social needs and world problems.

In *Social Choice and Individual Values,* economist Kenneth Arrow formally proved that our intuitive criteria for democratic decision making (or majority rule) cannot be satisfied unless everyone, under certain conditions, is prepared to accept a social ordering that is either imposed or dictatorial.* Arrow's

---

*Arrow illustrates the nature of his paradox as follows: "A natural way of arriving at the collective preference scale would be to say that one alternative is preferred to another if a majority of the community prefer the first alternative to the second, i.e., would choose the first over the second if those were the only two alternatives. Let *A, B,* and *C* be the three alternatives, and 1, 2, and 3 the

paradox demonstrates that strict democracy is impossible, that any democratic society initially depends upon the imposition of a social order (or what I refer to as a vision of equilibrium) at the outset.[3] The implications of the necessarily nondemocratic assumption behind all democracies are profound. In some ways Arrow's paradox seems to be a political corollary of mathematician Kurt Gödel's proof: every logical system depends for its meaning upon an arbitrary assumption outside the system.[4] The arbitrary decision rule or constitutional rules of the game imposed by the founding elite limits not merely the democratic structure of states but their political economy as well. Aristotle and S. M. Lipset said the same thing in a different way when they noted the large middle-class basis and relative wealth of successful, stable democracies.

The nonliberal basis of America's liberal democracy was not merely the Aristotelian constitution of mixed government imposed by the founders. One could argue that America's nonliberal basis also included the unique endowment of natural resources which made America rich before the nation had to become so, that provided the necessary means for industrial development and capital expansion, that permitted Americans to waste incredible amounts of raw materials and to expand production almost at will into new territories. In short, it was not only the Constitution that provided America with an initial imposed stability, but the nation's wealthy inheritance of land and resources and its ideological homogeneity, as well. From this stable basis free-market capitalism was easily developed.

Two other contemporary, stable, democratic, capitalist states have an even less liberal basis for their imposed stability or equilibrium. The fascist heritages of West Germany and Japan, including the heavy interpenetration of businesses and banks with the state, gave them the structural stability and "arbitrary outside assumption" upon which their successful free-market economies (or more cynically, systems of democratic mercantilism) could be erected. For example, in explaining the West German "economic miracle" of recovery after the war, economist Georg Küster noted:

> The recovery of the economy was greatly helped by two factors: by substantial initial state aids for private industry; and by the fact that the

---

three individuals. Suppose individual 1 prefers *A* to *B* and *B* to *C* (and therefore *A* to *C*), individual 2 prefers *B* to *C* and *C* to *A* (and therefore *B* to *A*), and individual 3 prefers *C* to *A* and *A* to *B* (and therefore *C* to *B*). Then a majority prefer *A* to *B*, and a majority prefer *B* to *C*. We may therefore say that the community prefers *A* to *B* and *B* to *C*. If the community is to be regarded as behaving rationally, we are forced to say that *A* is preferred to *C*. But in fact a majority of the community prefer *C* to *A*. So the method just outlined for passing from individual to collective tastes fails to satisfy the condition of rationality, as we ordinarily understand it." K. Arrow, *Social Choice and Individual Values* (New York: John Wiley, 1966), p. 3.

old prewar structure of capital and wealth in Germany was almost wholly retained. In 1948, the Federal Republic began with a private economy whose structure was the same as, and whose degree of concentration was only minimally lower than, that under the rule of National Socialism; and this private economy was left to the "free play of forces."[5]

On the basis of the Japanese and West German models, one might well predict that Spain's transition from fascist stability to democratic capitalism is apt to be successful as well, particularly if American capital investment continues.

I should note at this point that I am not happy whatsoever about discovering the nonliberal bases of successful democratic capitalist states. But wishing things were otherwise does not make them so. And the inevitable conclusion from both formal logical proofs and actual empirical findings appears to be that successful democratic capitalism depends upon the initial imposition of a stable social order or vision of equilibrium, upon which the luxury of free-market, individualistic capitalism can then be allowed to operate—particularly if there are plenty of markets and sources of raw materials available abroad (which made the incredible economic growth of the United States, Japan, and Germany possible through their policies of neomercantilism).[6]

The basic question in establishing a democracy, whether a capitalist or a socialist democracy, is what kind of social order or vision of equilibrium is to be imposed at the outset. Democratic capitalisms accent the primacy of the individual and the value of freedom (the model provided by Locke and Hobbes); whereas socialist democracies stress the social community as primary and the value of equality (the Marxist-socialist model).

These two basic types of democracy have developed with extremely different assumptions of social order. J. L. Talmon calls them the liberal and totalitarian schools of democracy and notes:

> The essential difference between the two schools of democratic thought as they have evolved is not, as is often alleged, in the affirmation of the value of liberty by one, and its denial by the other. It is in their different attitude to politics. The liberal approach assumes politics to be a matter of trial and error, and regards political systems as pragmatic contrivances of human ingenuity and spontaneity. It also recognizes a variety of levels of personal and collective endeavor, which are altogether outside the sphere of politics. The totalitarian school, on the other hand, is based upon the assumption of a sole and exclusive truth in politics. It may be called political

Messianism in the sense that it postulates a preordained, harmonious and perfect scheme of things, to which men are irresistibly driven, and at which they are bound to arrive. It recognizes ultimately only one plane of existence, the political. It widens the scope of politics to embrace the whole of human existence. It treats all human thought and action as having social significance, and therefore as falling within the orbit of political action.[7]

Talmon, here, is deliberately drawing an extreme contrast. Recent political experience has indicated both that social democracies exist which are not totalitarian and that capitalist democracies are often less than liberal. The deeper question is why a particular nation chooses one form over another, or alternatively, why certain conditions are more apt to lead to capitalist than socialist democracy. My thesis is that this may largely be a question of the stage of political development of a society combined with the nature of the resources and philosophical beliefs it inherits. What is most remarkable about the modern era is, perhaps, not so much the differences between capitalist and socialist democracies in large, postindustrial technocratic societies, but their similarities—the relative unfreedom and social injustice of both forms. Such observations have led theorists to postulate a convergence of capitalist and socialist forms of society at their highest stage of development. The larger either form of society becomes, the more individual freedom seems to diminish and the more inevitable state control and imperialist tendencies appear to become. Social relationships turn into social physics because quantity increases so greatly as to substantially change quality. Technocratic domination displaces both capitalist and socialist ideological objectives.

The postindustrial, technological stage of social development renders both the capitalist and socialist forms of political economy obsolete in terms of an optimum balance between the values of individual freedom and social equality. Pure capitalism does not perform the social welfare function well, whereas pure socialism, in the name of social equality, does not provide sufficient individual motivation to produce beyond a certain level.

The alternative to capitalism and socialism, social liberalism, must remedy the defects of both systems: it must combine individual freedom and the incentive for production and distinction with maximum satisfaction of social need. It must also take into account Kenneth Arrow's demonstration that any democratic society depends upon the imposition of a social order to establish an equilibrium at the outset. Consistent with these aims, the political economy of social liberalism should be based upon the following propositions.

Proposition 1. An imposed social order is only justifiable if it balances individual freedom with social justice and harmony.

Social stability is inconceivable without imposing some social order or vision of equilibrium. And the nature of individual freedom depends upon the kind of order against which it is set. In imposing a social order, John Stuart Mill's words in *On Liberty* should be kept in mind:

> Neither one person, nor any number of persons, is warranted in saying to another human creature of ripe years that he shall not do with his life for his own benefit what he chooses to do with it. . . . The interference of society to overrule his judgment and purposes in what only regards himself must be grounded on general presumptions which may be altogether wrong and, even if right, are as likely as not to be misapplied to individual cases, by persons no better acquainted with the circumstances of such cases than those are who look at them merely from without. . . . In the conduct of human beings toward one another it is necessary that general rules should for the most part be observed in order that people may know what they have to expect; but in each person's own concerns his individual spontaneity is entitled to free exercise.[8]

Without the existence of such individual freedom an imposed social order destroys individual initiative and dampens economic productivity.

Proposition 2. A productive economy requires unequal rewards for accomplishment.

Unequal skill or productivity should be recognized by unequal rewards in order to provide motivation for maximum individual development and social productivity in society. An increase in growth, wealth, and productivity in a national economy presupposes an acceptance of meritocracy. This, in turn, means that issues of social justice and equality in such a productive economy must focus upon equality of opportunity rather than equality of reward. The distinction between the two forms of equality is clearly made by Professor Frank Parkin in his incisive work, *Class Inequality and Political Order—Social Stratification in Capitalist and Communist Societies*:

> On what grounds, it is asked, is it morally legitimate to give greater economic and social benefits to one set of occupations than to another, when each in its own way contributes to the social good? Generally, egalitarians have espoused a view of social justice which asks that men be rewarded in accordance with their individual social needs, family responsibilities, and the like, rather than in accordance with their role in the division of labour. The meritocratic critique of the class system, on the

other hand, is less concerned about inequalities of reward accruing to different positions than about the process of recruitment to these positions. The prime objection raised is against present restrictions on the opportunities for talented but lowly born people to improve their personal lot. Seen from this angle, social justice entails not so much the equalization of rewards as the equalization of opportunities to compete for the most privileged positions.[9]

Inequalities arise in a class system through the allocation of rewards to different positions, on the one hand, and through the process of recruitment to these positions, on the other. A democracy with a productive economy and individual freedom must open up the process of recruitment to desired social positions without lowering the standards of skill required for the positions. Equality of opportunity is achieved by replacing inherited privilege and undue advantages with strict skill and merit criteria—a tall order given the heavy educational and socioeconomic subsidies required to make equal opportunity real for minority groups and poor people in American society. However, without making such equal opportunity a reality, the economy will lose a great deal of its potential individual initiative and creativity that is presently buried and repressed in disadvantaged segments of the population.

Proposition 3. The market structures the economic choices that lead to individual productivity; society limits individuals' pay to achieve social harmony; government's role is to intervene to maintain a balance between freedom and equal opportunity in this given system of structures and limits.

The necessary social equilibrium for a productive economy can be maintained only if the freedom of individual initiative is balanced by social norms and government laws that assure the satisfaction of social needs and steady economic development as well as individual gratification. The needs of the existing world market determine the range of the economic choices for the individual that are productive, given resource and other limitations. Imposed social norms and government controls narrow this freedom of productive choice even further. Hence, all existing individual freedoms in a society are loaded, biased by the initial limits to freedom imposed by the social structure and political economy. The critical questions for government decision makers are: Toward which values and whose needs are these freedoms loaded in the existing social economy? and, Toward whose needs and which values should they be biased in the future to make equal opportunity real for the disadvantaged while yet maintaining individual initiative and economic productivity? For example, the United States government discovered in the 1960s (and the Indian government in the 1970s) that there was a point of diminishing returns in taxing the very rich for the sake of equal opportunity. Both found that by reducing the highest income tax bracket (in the 90 percent range) significantly, they could increase the inflow of money into government coffers by stimulating the rich to produce. But this upper limit must be weighed against overdue American tax reform legislation that would make the burden for subsidizing the poor fall less heavily on middle-class wage earners and more upon upper and upper-middle class investors.

Proposition 4. To justify restrictions of individual choice in terms of the social responsibilities of government, material rewards and social status must be geared to society's welfare; individual income and status should be greatest for those individuals whose productivity is most oriented toward a hierarchy of social needs called "the social welfare function."

Without a clear-cut hierarchy of social needs and values, it is unjustifiable to impose any kind of restriction on individual freedom. Yet in the political economies of most existing industrial democracies, there is no such clear-cut value or need hierarchy. This situation leads to a rugged, competitive individualism aimed at satisfying private wants rather than social needs and giving undue advantage to the rich and the privileged. Social status and prestige in such societies are based upon the success of an individual not in satisfying social needs but in fulfilling selfish, private wants. An individual's status is determined by asking such questions as, "What do you earn?" "What is your title?" "How many people do you have under you?" and, "What are your chances for advancement?" And an individual's wants usually go beyond what he or she actually needs, for wants are insatiable and unlimited. An individual's needs—the physical, psychological, and social prerequisites for human health—are, on the other hand, limited and satisfiable. In a world of material scarcity, the task of a social liberal economy is to set up the economic payoffs of the social system so as to encourage individuals both to limit their wants to what they really need and to work to satisfy the needs of others in the community. Rugged individualism must be replaced by social individualism.

"The social welfare function" refers to the hierarchy of values and community needs in a society that gives the government an objective basis for its legitimacy and social contract with its citizens. Kenneth Arrow has defined the social welfare function as a process of social choice or ordering through individual preferences which constitutes a *constitution* for the community of people in question.[10] But this definition is too vague. The process of social choice in a community includes not only the constitution, formal laws, and decrees of society but also the class system of the political economy which tilts formal laws in the direction of established interests. To be legitimate and effective, social liberalism must be based upon a specific, empirically grounded hierarchy of social needs. Psychologist Abraham Maslow has demonstrated that such a need hierarchy exists for the individual. The five levels of individual human need which he recognizes, in order of priority, are physiological needs, security needs, love needs, self-esteem needs, and self-actualization needs.[11] Because of the lack of a clear-cut, objective, empirically based *social* need hierarchy, elites and politicians of the past and present have imposed a so-called social welfare system which frustrates more needs than it satisfies, leading most citizens to see nothing but its faults. Changing that system has proved impossible because the democratic majority cannot get together at the appropriate time to agree on any other concrete alternative.

But assuming that a legitimate empirical hierarchy of social needs can be spelled out, the political problem is then to create positive and negative rewards in the economy which encourage individuals to limit their insatiable wants and to work to satisfy their own limited needs and those of others. A simple principle for social behavior is needed that accomplishes the task of motivating individuals to work for social needs regardless of the particular social need/value hierarchy agreed upon by the community.

Philosopher John Rawls tried to do this with his difference principle. But as noted in chapter 3, his stress upon equality of reward has a counterproductive leveling effect because it discriminates against the most skillful and productive members of society. Rawls's difference principle appears to search out weakness and compound it rather than seeking to encourage strength in terms of individual productivity for the sake of the social good. To avoid this negative effect of an otherwise admirable moral principle, social liberalism accents the positive. Its basic tenet is: the highest wages and social status should go to those who orient their productivity toward society's greatest needs in terms of its existing social welfare hierarchy, whatever that may be. Adherence to this principle would encourage the most competent and ambitious members of society to find self-fulfillment by working for those most in need or by fulfilling those functions needed most by society (whether economic growth, medical care, or other social services). The alternative is to maintain the merely selfish, materialistic ethic of private gain that supports the status quo. The rich will get richer (for the sake of riches and the prestige they bring), the poor poorer, and no one will necessarily be better off for the failure to change the rules of the game.

Proposition 5. Social priorities should be established by a representative democratic government using the services of technical experts; to balance the opinion of the majority, the advice of appointed or elected elites with relevant technical backgrounds should be sought.

Kenneth Arrow, Robert Dahl, and other social scientists have demon strated the logical inadequacy of any system based upon pure majority rule.[12] Chapter 4 sketched many of the prerequisites needed for a stable, democratic political system—including Aristotle's suggestion of balancing democratic and elitist forms of authority. The United States was founded upon Aristotle's principles, as modified by the suggestions of John Locke and Montesquieu, and its stability as a democracy is undoubtedly due in part to this wise constitutional choice. But with the recent abuses of government power by executive elites and security agencies, the unworkable concept of pure democracy may well be raised as a standard. That concept suffers from the same intellectual utopianism as pure communism: the state and its elites refuse to wither away. No political society has ever existed without elites. The question is not, then, whether elites should be tolerated but how these elites should be selected, what their qualifications should be, and how their necessary powers should be checked by other governmental bodies representative of the people.

The initial balance of the executive, legislative, and judicial branches of government has served the American people well as a whole as far as it goes. But a new imbalance has arisen—because of the increasing dependence of America's democratic form of govenment upon self-proclaimed technocratic elites for the solution of its public problems—which requires new constitutional and educational checks. Without explicit constitutional checks upon possible abuses of power and influence by technocratic elites and a massive educational program to inform citizens how best to test technocratic advice in terms of their own true individual and social needs and values, Americans may come to believe in the extreme ideology of apolitics at the expense of democratic principles and individual freedoms.

Proposition 6. Qualified elites and technocratic experts should be elected or appointed on the basis of their proven competence at social need satisfaction.

Postindustrial, technocratic societies like the United State have an abundance of talent capable of filling any of the elected or advisory posts in the government. Yet few Americans take the time to determine whether those individuals selected for public office are either technically qualified for their jobs or experienced in applying their skills to the satisfaction of social needs. The technological development of American society has solved the problem of knowing who is qualified to be a technocratic advisor to some extent, but has had little or no effect upon making clear the qualifications sought in elected officials. Moreover, in neither case has the critical criterion of social liberalism been applied, namely, whether a nominee has actually used his or her technological or political skills in an effective manner to satisfy pressing contemporary social needs. Technocratic experts are often selected as economic, political, or social advisors on the basis of their theoretical writing or academic backgrounds exclusively, without ever having been tested on their knowledge under actual field conditions, or without ever having demonstrated their success in satisfying social needs. Politicians, of course, are notorious for blowing up any vaguely related past political experience as a form of qualification for their electability. But voters rarely analyze these claims in terms of actual effectiveness in satisfying specific social needs. Additionally, important technocratic advisory appointments should be rotated with limited terms of service to prevent a monopoly on the jobs by career bureaucrats. Further steps should be taken to assure equal opportunity for appointment of qualified candidates from all sectors of society to assure fresh blood and an open elite.

Proposition 7. Social liberalism is a political economy that combines values and technology in such a way as to maximize individual freedom of choice at different levels of individual development while supporting most (by economic and social rewards) those individuals whose choices and productive labor most satisfy social needs.

This basic tenet of social liberalism calls for Americans to reform their political economy in order to balance individual freedom with the satisfaction of social needs. On the one hand, the economy should never restrict any individual from doing what he or she wants to do as a career or occupation; on the other, it must give the highest wages and social status to those who work for the satisfaction of social needs. Such a reform in the pay-off structure of America's political economy would be a vast improvement over the present inequitable stew of private free-market greed, large corporate monopolies, and nonproductive welfare payments. The positive aspects of free-market individualism are retained because maximum individual freedom is allowed at each stage of personal and career development; at the same time, the social need criterion pulls this individual energy toward the common good, transforming rugged individualism into social individualism. Adam Smith's great motivator of self-interest and private financial gain is fully exploited but skewed toward the dominant social needs of the country at each particular moment. A National Social Needs Research Center should be established in Washington, D. C., to centralize all empirical social needs research in the nation and to develop acceptable criteria for setting social need priorities.

Proposition 8. The scope of economic organizations must be limited through decentralization to assure the satisfaction of the individual's full range of needs; but this decentralization must be balanced by centralization in the national social welfare system such that the needs of the majority are always satisfied before the needs of any particular minority.

Calls for decentralization and limiting the size and scope of business organizations make sense in human terms. A small-size organization is more conducive to meaningful participation by all working in the firm, gives management a clearer view of its task at the top, and puts managers more quickly in touch with the grassroots human needs of both workers and the members of the community in which the firm is located.[13] On a national basis, limiting the size and scope of business firms can create more equal opportunity and fairer competition by preventing the development of monopolies and unwieldy, dehumanizing bureaucracies.

Of course, decentralization can also be pushed to extremes in a large, industrial superpower like America upon which so much of the world economy depends for vitality. For example, in his charming *Small Is Beautiful—Economics As if People Mattered,* E. F. Schumacher advocates a governmental policy of requiring all companies over a certain size to issue 50 percent of their stock as equity shares which would become publically owned. Public influence would be exercised through local social councils with advisory powers, but not voting powers, in the companies' management meetings. These equity shares would take the place of present taxes upon corporate profits of large firms and yet would initially act as deterrents for small firms, discouraging them from becoming too large.[14] But charm is also expensive. Although Schumacher's ideas have definite applicability for smaller, underdeveloped countries, if his extreme decentralization plan was adopted by all American corporations, America's economic growth rate would be apt to slow significantly—certainly in the initial long period of transition—with negative costs both at home and abroad. As economist Simon Whitney has noted about Shumacher's plan:

> He is careless in suggesting that large corporations should be encouraged to pay more in dividends to the "public" than now in profit taxes. Consider a representative corporation: it earns $100 million, pays 48 million in profit taxes, pays out 31.2 million in dividends, reinvests 20.8 million. Under his plan, it earns $100 million, of which 50 million accrues to the public shares, but it pays the public shares more than 48 million in dividends, and is obliged by law to pay its other shareholders the same amount; this leaves about $2 million or so for reinvestment. Expansion would be pretty much impossible. . . . His assumption is that the big corporations . . . [can] operate on a local, or at most a "district," basis. Farewell to mass production and mass distribution, and thus to the modern standard of living.[15]

But the flaw in Whitney's argument is that, although the legal rate of corporate income tax is 48 percent, the effective rate is often far less than that. For example, in 1973, General Motors had sales of $35 billion and paid taxes amounting to $3 billion—9 percent of sales. At present the corporation is free to declare dividends on its shares at any rate it wishes. If it chose, it could declare dividends up to 60 percent on all shares, meaning that the public and private shares would split that amount equally (the government still coming out ahead because the present effective tax rate is so low) and the corporation would still have 40 percent for reinvestment. And this appears to be the thrust of Schumacher's argument.

From the viewpoint of the romantic individualist, small is beautiful and decentralization is seductive. But from the perspective of national and global social needs, the freedom permitted by decentralization must be balanced in large, industrial societies with government centralized standards, planning, organization, communication, and management. Although large is not always efficient, as critics of the American oil companies have accurately noted, total decentralization might just spread out present injustices (keeping the rich and strong, rich and strong in their smaller grass-roots environments without necessarily improving the lot of the poor and weak). And if an extreme decentralization program did lead to a decline in economic growth, the lower standards of living and lesser need satisfaction would hit those hardest who can least afford it—the lower class poor (both at home and abroad). A stoic trend toward belt-tightening and less consumption may well be healthy for many Americans. But the potential negative consequences upon national economic growth and the subsequent reductions in goods and services of all kinds are rarely spelled out by the "new politicians of the old austerity" (such as Governor Jerry Brown of California and the no-gn wth fatalists discussed in Chapter 2).

To be effective for the entire national community, the worthy principle of decentralization must itself be limited. Areas that require national centralization of organization must be maintained in order to satisfy the individual and social needs for the majority of citizens—even at the expense of freedom and advantage for any one particular minority. Individual freedom must be balanced with social equality, small-is-beautiful with large-is-efficient, and all policy extremes with Admiral Groshkov's motto: " 'Better' is the enemy of 'good enough.' "

Proposition 9. The political economy of social liberalism at home can become the basis of an ideology of political development abroad in American foreign policy, competing effectively with Russian, Chinese, and other models.

One of the great advantages of Russian and Chinese foreign policy is that both of these nations have definite political economic models they can export and use as a basis for giving advice and foreign aid. America's Cold War negativism was perceived as reactionary by many developing nations, not offering positive applicable principles with which they could easily identify. And recently America's political and economic principles seem confused to many: capitalism is recommended for those who can afford it, foreign aid and arms are given haphazardly to the needy or to our allies regardless of the principles of political economy they follow. Cynical self-interest is not an influential political ideology but the sign of the absence of one. The "demonstration effect" of a clear-cut political-economic philosophy of social liberalism which Americans can believe in may encourage lesser-developed nations to increase their capacity for self-support and allow them to retain enough savings to underwrite badly needed economic growth. It could stimulate American corporations to invest badly needed capital in poor countries that need it the most, and could become the basis for a realistic model of modernization that promises freedom as well as equality, a "New World" doctrine that could compete effectively with the Russian and Chinese programs.

Notes

[1]Edwin L. Dale, "Inflation That Wasn't Bred at Home," *The New York Times*, May 2, 1976.

[2]See Flora Lewis, "The View from Europe Is of a Receding U.S.," *The New York Times*, April 18, 1976; and William F. Buckley, Jr., "The New Isolationism," *The New York Post*, April 20, 1976.

[3]Kenneth Arrow, *Social Choice and Individual Values* (New York: John Wiley, 1966).

[4]See E. Nagel and J. R. Newman, "Gödel's Proof," *Scientific American*, 196, 6 (June 1956), 71-86

[5]Georg H. Küster, "Germany," in *Big Business and the State*, ed. by Raymond Vernon (Cambridge, Mass.: Harvard University Press, 1974), p. 65.

[6]See David Calleo and Benjamin Rowland, *America and the World Political Economy* (Bloomington, Ind.: Indiana University Press, 1973).

[7]J. L. Talmon, *The Origins of Totalitarian Democracy* (New York: Frederick A. Praeger, 1965), pp 1-2.

[8]John Stuart Mill, *On Liberty* (New York: Bobbs-Merrill, 1956), p. 93.

[9]Frank Parkin, *Class Inequality and Political Order—Social Stratification in Capitalist and Communist Societies* (New York: Frederick A. Praeger, 1971), p. 13.

[10]Arrow, *Social Choice and Individual Values*, pp. 104-105.

[11]For how Maslow's need hierarchy can be applied in collective political action and policy evaluation, see R. Isaak and R. Hummel, *Politics for Human Beings* (North Scituate, Mass.: Duxbury Press, 1975).

[12]See Kenneth Arrow and Robert Dahl, *A Preface to Democratic Theory* (Chicago: University of Chicago Press, 1956).

[13]See Peter Drucker, *Management* (New York: Harper & Row, 1974), pp. 572-602.

[14]F. F. Schumacher, *Small Is Beautiful—Economics as if People Mattered* (New York: Harper & Row, 1975), pp. 272-297.

[15]Simon Whitney, "Comments on 'Social Liberalism: A New Political Economy'," personal typed communication, May 24, 1976. For Whitney's own perspective on such matters, see his *Economic Principles* (Columbus, O.: Grid, 1975).

Part IV

HOW AMERICA COULD GO

By 2076 people sensibly may not want to grow much richer, but for quite a few years yet most people most definitely will. And this is a main reason for worry at America's 200th birthday. There is a danger that the Americans, with all their power, for dynamism and good, may be about to desert what should be their manifest and now rather easy destiny of leading the rest of us towards a decent world society and an abundant cheap lunch. If they do, the leadership of the world may be yielded from American to less sophisticated hands, at a perilous moment.

—*Norman Macrae, "America's Third Century"*,
The Economist, *1975*

We shall not all sleep, but we shall be changed.
—*Galway Kinnell*, The Book of Nightmares, *1971*

12 THE FUTURE OF THE NEW WORLD

I know no safe depository of the ultimate powers of the society but the people themselves; and if we think them not enlightened enough to exercise their control with a wholesome discretion, the remedy is not to take it from them, but to inform their discretion.

—*Thomas Jefferson,*
"Letter to William Charles Jarvis,"
September 28, 1820

Even if in many respects a concern for efficiency suggests *initiatives* by the advanced nations, *solutions* will almost invariably require the full participation of the less advanced, if only because many of their problems—from population to genocide, from industrialization to pollution—cannot be "decoupled" from the world of the rich. At any rate, nothing could backfire more disastrously than a division of world politics along degrees of development, whether a common front of the underdeveloped emerges from a confrontation with a coalition of "advanced nations," or as a reaction to "benign neglect." A manageable world requires the fragmentation of the highly heterogeneous Third World into its different components, issue by issue; either overt decoupling or promoting a bloc of advanced nations would have the opposite effect.

—*Stanley Hoffmann,*
"Choices," Foreign Policy,
Fall, 1973

The time has come for us to seek a partnership between North America, Western Europe and Japan: Our three regions share economic, political and security concerns that make it logical that we should seek ever-increasing unity and understanding.

—*Jimmy Carter,*
speech in New York City,
New York Times, *June 24, 1976*

Tough-minded compassion is no longer a luxury but the ultimate wisdom for a nation with the strength of Goliath and the ideals of David. Torn between a conservative empire and a democratic creed, Americans may become participants in tragedy if they cannot find a political philosophy and program that uses the power and wealth of the United States to promote humanistic goals at home and abroad. Unaccustomed to tragedy as a nation, many Americans have viewed the political disasters of the Vietnam-Watergate era as exceptions to the rule rather than as natural outgrowths of deep-seated contradictions between intentions and behavior in American policy making. Democratic and humanistic rhetoric has too often been used to cover a diplomacy of cynical realism and short-term national interest. But this very rhetoric makes the gap between America's democratic empathy for the weak and its material, technological power more apparent to the world, leading many to look not to what America stands for today but for what it has stood for in the past. Americans no longer tend to think of themselves as citizens of the New World, and the cynical manipulations of American policy makers make it increasingly difficult to distinguish the American spirit from the decadent Old World spirit against which Americans once defined themselves.

Perhaps the most pessimistic of the dominant world views held by American policy makers is that of the strong man's club. Henry Kissinger's advocacy of a strategic triangle or a superbalance of power between the United States, the Soviet Union, and the People's Republic of China symbolizes this world-view. In a multipolar world of increasingly interdependent countries on the one hand and small-state rebellions on the other, the assumption of the strong man's club is that the only way for the United States to maintain the strength of a Goliath is to neutralize its most powerful potential enemies, Russia and China, by entangling them in a stable equilibrium of spheres of influence, which Kissinger calls a "structure of peace" and the Third World labels a "superpower condominium." Ideologically, Kissinger has gloomily predicted the decline of Western democratic forms of government and the inevitable spread of socialism throughout the world. With America's long-term future apparently lost, only reactionary, short-term gains are seen as possible: if the Old World balance of power of the nineteenth century cannot be restored, at least a dynamic equilibrium can be maintained by limiting violence at the nuclear level and forestalling other explosive conventional wars before they threaten to upset the status quo.

A second vision of America's future held by many in the policy-making community, which is less pessimistic but equally short-sighted, is that of the rich man's club. The Trilateral Commission's advocacy of an economic triangle or private alliance between North America, Western Europe, and Japan symbolizes this world view. According to trilateralism's best-known spokesman Zbigniew Brzezinski, the preservation of America's power in the world depends upon unifying the democratic capitalistic countries of the West, which can then negotiate as a successful economic force with the anticapitalist superpowers on the one hand and the poor Third and Fourth World countries on the other. In his work *Between Two Ages*, for example, Brzezinski argues that only the "technotronic" societies of Western Europe, Japan, and the United States have the global consciousness capable of using modern technology to bring a peace through prosperity to the world. At the end of this book, published in 1970, Brzezinski suggested the creation of a trilateral framework among the elites of these technotronic societies to discuss the major policy problems of our time, a suggestion that was carried out in 1973 with the establishment of the Trilateral Commission. About the same time Brzezinski began to send Jimmy Carter books, articles, and briefings. Carter joined the Trilateral Commission as Governor from Georgia and has since advocated many of its ideas in public speeches. The moderate reformism that the commission recommends is distrusted by many socialists who see the approach as an attempt to to preserve the status quo from the threats of radical social change.

Sensing a domestic political threat from the world view of the rich man's club, Secretary of State Kissinger modified the confrontational tactics implied by his strong man's club viewpoint in 1975 and 1976. He sought to negotiate with the Third and Fourth World after organizing preliminary "bloc" meetings with Western European and Japanese leaders. By expanding his own vision to include that of the rich man's club, Kissinger made it certain that America's foreign policy in the next decade will seek to combine the strategic American-Soviet-Chinese triangle on the one hand with the economic American-Western European-Japanese triangle on the other. But the end remains the same: to maintain the declining power of the American empire by stabilizing the global status quo both strategically and economically, thus heading off revolutionary change and making this conservative policy into a moral, self-righteous stance backed by a united Western front. The strong men and the rich men will shake hands to preserve their national strategic and economic interests first, regardless of the social needs of the majority of nations standing outside the two elitist triangles (see chapters 5 and 7).

The nuances of the strong-man and rich-man world views have been left out here to highlight their basic common purposes: to shore up the strength of the American Goliath against all those who take potshots at the American empire from the Second (communist), Third, and Fourth Worlds. The democratic and humanistic principles of the American creed are forgotten in the attempt to build strategic and economic power. Yet, ironically, even these traditional Old World objectives of American diplomacy will be frustrated if the strong-rich-man policies are continued, for they are based on faulty assumptions.

First, the strong-rich-man synthesis assumes that the security needs of the strong superpowers and the political economies of the rich Western industrial states are the same. This assumption of similarity allows policy makers to split foreign policy objectives from domestic political and economic problems and to think in abstract terms of blocs of rich or powerful states. But in reality, the security objectives of the strong and rich nations are more dissimilar than identical. And the world economic crises of the 1970s have made it clearer than ever that foreign policy objectives cannot be separated from domestic political and economic conditions.

The Strategic Arms Limitations Talks (SALT), for example, have been continuously frustrated because the psychological insecurity of the Soviet Union appears to be greater than that of the United States, leading the Soviets to strive for nuclear and conventional superiority over the United States regardless of official declarations and agreements. Even if some final ceiling on all weapons systems was agreed to by these two superpowers, disarmament would still be a distant goal and the threat of nuclear proliferation and revolutionary terrorism would still be present throughout the globe. Indeed, the closer the apparent harmony between the United States and the Soviet Union in the eyes of the rest of the world, the greater the possibility that other nations would attempt to develop their own nuclear and conventional capacities for protection or blackmail against the Soviet-American condominium.

Likewise, the rich, industrial, Western democracies also exhibit more dissimilarities than similarities among themselves. Many of the Western European democracies are considerably to the left of the American political system, particularly Italy and France, and some of the Western European members of the Common Market are more advanced than the United States in the development of social and health services, which results in greater centralization of the state bureaucracy and more limitations upon free-market capitalism. The interlocking of economic and political elites in Japan and the Japanese people's relatively greater stress on community values distinguish that country markedly from the United States. In short, the political economies of the three trilateral Western regions appear to be so different in conditions and values that no natural long-term cooperation can be taken for granted among them. For example, as soon as the oil crisis struck, France made separate agreements with the oil producers in spite of Western guidelines advocating unified Western European action.

This does not mean that cooperation between democratic, capitalistic states should not be attempted. On the contrary, it means that such cooperation must begin at the beginning, with a rigorous analysis of the differences between Western political economies and the implications for Western diplomacy. As long as no major wars involving the West are in progress, foreign policies will be hopelessly interlocked with domestic political and economic objectives. Ideological conflicts, therefore, will not become less significant but ever more important. More than ever, America's Western allies will be concerned not merely with where the United States stands internationally but with what it represents domestically in terms of its economic plans, social policy, and basic ideology. The great challenge of America's future is to create a domestic ideological consensus, which can serve as a model and strong basis for American diplomacy abroad. Social Liberalism could become the key to such a consensus and provide the means for Americans to resolve the contradiction between the conservative strong-man-rich-man objectives of the American empire on the one hand and the democratic, humanistic ideals of social justice and equality on the other.

Social liberalism could be seen as one of the few ways to save capitalism from obsolescence. Or it could be interpreted as a way to save America from the obsolescence of socialism. For pure capitalism lacks the human, social appeal to become a widespread ideology in the future, no matter how effective it may be in producing unevenly distributed material prosperity. And pure socialism appears to promise too much and result in too little in terms of economic growth, if existing socialist states are any indication of future trends. That a coherent ideology or political economy should exist between the extremes of pure capitalism and socialism seems to make common sense. But common sense is rarely all that common. The complexity of such a third alternative confounds the political philosopher and threatens to be difficult to sell to the average citizen, who seeks simple solutions to difficult problems.

The idea of social liberalism originated as a response to my uncomfortable discovery that the most successful democratic capitalistic systems—the United States, Germany, and Japan—required the imposition of a nonliberal social order, or equilibrium, before they could function efficiently (see Chapter 11). If success depended upon some sort of imposed equilibrium, the critical question became: What *kind* of imposed equilibrium could justify the sacrifice of an individual's freedom of action to the society and state? That is, if one is born into a state with a social order not of one's own making, why should one obey its laws and customs rather than rebelling?

The optimum answer to this question (indeed, the only satisfactory answer I could conceive) is a basic proposition of social liberalism: restrictions of individual choice in terms of the existing imposed social order can be justified only to the extent that such restrictions benefit the social needs of the whole community, including the individual who must make the sacrifices. In order to make this condition meaningful, another basic tenet of social liberalism must be followed: those individuals who produce to meet society's greatest needs should receive the highest wages and social status. Only if principles such as these are accepted as the basis of a political economy will social individualism become a reality, for only then will people discover that it pays more to maximize their own interests in harmony with community interests than to aim merely for their own selfish profit regardless of the consequences for the community. Individual freedom, in short, must be balanced with social justice and equality of opportunity to make any imposed social order or equilibrium justifiable.

It is possible to view world history as a sequence of passing equilibria, or as one set of disequilibria being replaced by another. This perspective is appealing since it provides a basis for explaining historical change without assuming that such change necessarily results in progress, as Hegel suggested, or decline, as Spengler predicted. Powerful empires then represent the dominant military equilibria of their times, and productive economies, the most dynamic economic equilibria. Not accidentally, a dominant empire often combines military and economic strength. But history cannot be explained in terms of military and economic factors alone. Social, cultural, and philosophical factors play a critical role, particularly when the world is passing from the domination of one imperial and cultural equilibrium to another. Indeed, the fundamental reason for the widespread belief in the present decay and decline of Western civilization and values is probably the general sense of cultural malaise and philosophical bankruptcy. Hedonistic and nihilistic values often seem to displace positive social and humanistic goals in the West, culminating in dramatic violence that alone seems to satisfy people's longings for significance. *The Wasteland, The Last Tango in Paris, The Godfather,* and *A Clockwork Orange*— these are not cultural artifacts that inspire confidence in Western values either at home or abroad.

In the post-Vietnam, post-Watergate era, a recovery of cultural and political dynamism can only occur in the West if humanistic social goals replace selfish individualism. It is as if the pessimistic views of Sigmund Freud were coming true: the release from repressions of individual drives have led Americans to social chaos and the meaningless pursuit of pleasure and consumption. We must recover the positive Western individualism of the Renaissance and the Enlightenment. The great attraction which the People's Republic of China holds as a political system for many people the world over is that it provides a cultural and moral meaning for the individual's sacrifice for the community. People consider the loss of liberalism or individual freedom as more than made up for by the gain in social equality and community commitment.

Americans should not underestimate the difficulty in competing with the Chinese (or even the Russian) model abroad. With few material resources and an attractive ideology that placed people (not machines) first, Mao reconstructed China displaying a political brilliance that the world is only now beginning to appreciate fully. Mao's imposed equilibrium seems to derive its cohesion and dynamism at least as much from its social, cultural, and philosophical aspects as from its military and economic components. The liberal capitalist argument, in contrast, often seems to have an old-fashioned, decadent ring to it when compared to the revolutionary fervor and poetic symbols of Maoism.

But this need not be the case. If Americans replace their rugged *laissez-faire* version of liberalism with a more realistic social liberalism that better suits the needs and temper of the times, they can provide a model of social justice for the world that can be shown to benefit the community more effectively than the communist or socialist models. The American accomplishment of the recent past can lend credence to that model. Thus, progress toward racial equality in this country gives Americans a certain moral authority to speak about majority rule in Africa: our own Third World dilemma can be related to theirs, particularly if we have a coherent program that is imitable. Similarly, increasing social and economic mobility within the United States gives Americans a right to speak about a new international economic order and a dialogue among the Old Rich, the New Rich, and the Poor in the world. Even the very survival of the American Constitution after the military and political traumas of recent times puts Americans in an advantageous position to discuss democracy in general. But to make such potentially strong arguments effective in the ideological debate with other countries in the world, America must first have a clear-cut ideology that underlies these arguments. The political economy of social liberalism may provide the basis for an ideological consensus.

Not accidentally, social liberalism asks the basic political questions of democracy today: What should the hierarchy of social needs be and who should determine it? But social liberalism goes beyond traditional left-right ideological labels in leaving the definition of that social need hierarchy open, to be filled in by elected democratic representatives advised by relevant economic and technological experts who have had previous experience in meeting the needs of various publics. For example, this group of policy makers might decide that the main economic problem of the American system is that transfer payments to individuals, such as social security payments and unemployment compensation, have risen at a rate of more than 9 percent in real terms every year for twenty years, faster than real total budget expenditures. To dampen this great increase in nonproductive government spending, such policy makers might determine that a policy of fiscal conservatism is in order and that spending limits must be stressed in all federal programs. But simultaneously social liberalism would advocate that those individuals be given the greatest government support or tax advantages who do the most to solve the social problems of the unemployed and the aged, disabled, and dependent *within* these limits.

Two kinds of problem solvers would immediately benefit: those who work to curb rising inflation rates, which hit those of fixed incomes hardest, and those who work to lower unemployment rates, which would lower the transfer payments from the government in the form of unemployment insurance. Government intervention to achieve an equilibrium between the pressures of inflation and unemployment would be given more clear-cut democratic legitimacy. Such grassroots legitimacy could be made concrete every four years with a national referendum that ranked the ten greatest national social needs perceived by the American people at the time of presidential elections. This bypassing of the American party bureaucracies would give independent voters a greater feeling of democratic participation in their national government and clarify those areas of social need on which winning candidates should concentrate. The establishment of a National Social Needs Center for centralizing empirical research on social need priorities could complement this presidential election year referendum, pressuring elected officials to be more consistent.

Without some innovations such as these to bring back a sense of popular political participation on the issues, American politics will remain both too personality oriented (threatening democracy with charismatic demagoguery) and too abstracted from the concerns of the everyday citizen (who comes to believe "my vote doesn't matter much anyway"). The only way to build enthusiasm for democracy at home is to restore the people's confidence in their own political significance. Only if such enthusiasm is generated on a widespread scale for a democratic ideology within America can an exportable body of ideas be brought together that will influence nations abroad.

It is just as senseless for Americans to deny that they constitute a strong and rich elite in the world as it is to deny that they belong to an empire. Yet their democratic creed makes it difficult for Americans to think of themselves in these terms. Perhaps the reason that the visions of the strong-man club and rich-man club are popular with American foreign policy makers is that Americans have never fully accepted the fact or responsibility of being strong and rich elites in the world, and what cannot be taken for granted must be constantly reasserted as policy to make the public conscious of their status. Consequently, American policy makers have become involved in clumsy actions of strategic overkill in CIA operations and the Vietnam War, undermining public confi dence in the government and tying the hands of future foreign policy makers because of negative domestic and world opinion. Fluctuating between extreme isolationism and interventionism, this country has developed an image abroad of unsteadiness and indecisiveness. An elite that is unsure of itself gives up its status by default to more tenacious groups that appear to be more reliable and therefore more powerful.

By coming to a broad consensus as to what kind of democracy and political economy they want at home, Americans will automatically develop criteria for the kinds of regimes they should be supporting abroad, giving the American role in world affairs more coherence and intelligibility. Without the development of such an ideological coherence, American policy makers will find it difficult to rally public support for their policies on defense and foreign aid, and American allies will increasingly question the credibility of American commitments.

Kissinger has argued that ambiguity is an important attribute of effective foreign policy, and in tactical negotiations with nondemocratic regimes he is undoubtedly correct. But if such elite flexibility is to be effective over the long run, it must be based on specific objectives that can gain strong domestic support. And the American educational system must prepare Americans to evaluate the policies of their leaders and to assume a role of leadership themselves as representatives of a superpower.

As it stands, the educational system does not adequately prepare Americans to be democratic citizens or to accept the responsibilities of being superpower elites. Courses in politics, economics, government, international relations, and the history of Western civilization must be introduced much earlier into the curriculum than they are at present. And foreign language requirements should be stiffened and started at a very tender age, or the anti-Americanism aroused by the ethnocentric attitudes of American travelers and business people who demand that all others speak English will become even worse. Americans should strive to create that good will that comes only from an international cosmopolitanism of people well versed in other languages and cultures.

The educational system also has a role in helping Americans recover their belief in the New World spirit, that rough and ready democratic will to struggle for equality, humanism, and individual distinction and the rights of others to do the same. The schools' rekindling of confidence in Democratic Man—combined with their provision for those concrete tools necessary for upward mobility and equal opportunity in a complex competitive society—can help to counter the widespread pessimism that has infected American beliefs and contemporary Western values. Nietzsche noted that democratic states give rise to a feeling of *ressentiment*—a bitter envy of the success of others stemming not from a concrete jealousy of not having or being something in particular but from the guilt one feels at voluntarily accepting a role that limits the expression of one's full potential. This general feeling of bitterness, of being used, is particularly prevalent among lower-class functionaries in society but has spread with the economic recession of the 1970s to the middle and upper classes as well. Too many Americans are educated only far enough to feel the unfulfilled promise of upward mobility and the American Dream. They do not come to the point of realizing that they are born with greater life chances than any other people in the world and that their ethical responsibilities stemming from this enormous advantage in the global context are proportionally greater. Gratitude for one's privileges and self-sacrifice for the sake of others less well-off should be the moral posture of a rich and strong elite that is enlightened in the best sense of that term. But, alas, many Americans have been raised to expect more from the social system than from themselves.

And the feeling of bitter *ressentiment* at home is nothing compared to that felt by foreigners toward Americans abroad. In both Western and non-Western countries, rich and poor alike feel betrayed by Americans for promising the world so much with their New World democratic ideology and technological power, only to deliver disappointment after disappointment—politically, economically, morally, and culturally. Whether such feelings abroad are justified is beside the point. Americans must live with this widespread anti-Americanism as an existential fact for the rest of the twentieth century. The only way to change such attitudes is for Americans individually to represent the best potential of their culture. We must replace the rugged individualism of pioneering days with sophisticated social individualism, which seeks to create a New World for all of humanity. We must become tough-minded, compassionate idealists who call a spade a spade and then go on to use our power and skills to improve the human condition in spite of itself.

The possibility remains that Americans will choose to shape their future by continuing to mimic the decadence of the Old World. Assuming, for a moment, that Old World policies are continued, that some blend of the strong-man and rich-man world views prevails, one can anticipate the probable trends that await us.

First, we can expect increasing polarization between left and right at home and abroad. The left will stress social equality, government subsidy, and the dangers of unemployment, while the right will focus upon individual freedom, corporate profits, fiscal conservatism, and the dangers of inflation. This split will make a stable domestic consensus unlikely, aggravating political tensions caused by increasing social demands on the one hand and the reluctance of the taxpayer to support them on the other.

Ideological polarization is apt to be accompanied by increasing bureau-cratization and stratification in American institutions. The class system will thus be stabilized, and the easy upward mobility of less advantaged groups will be prevented. "Decentralization" may just be used as a catchword by those who promise the return to power of those at the grassroots level, but who in fact seek to freeze the status quo.

American educational institutions are likely to become even more "segre-gated" along class lines because of the increasing expense of private and college education, resulting in a more rigid social class system and conservative social hierarchy. The present retreat from education supported by the deschooling critics on the left and the opposition to massive college enrollments expressed by those skeptical of universal education on the right may result in a fiscal conservatism that undermines equal opportunity for upward mobility. Students from the upper and upper-middle classes who can pay or take out loans will get the best educations and best jobs. Those from lower classes who cannot afford a quality education will be relegated to lower, more menial tasks in their working careers. The alienation and powerlessness that will result—the feeling of "being made" by existing class backgrounds and social structures rather than making it on one's own—will soon be felt socially. The erosion of self-confidence will lead to greater disenchantment with Western culture, including the power of reason itself, and the escalation of hedonistic escapism and violence.

Old World policies at home and abroad may be expected to increase selfishness and hedonism in America and other Old Rich Western democracies with similar policies. The effort by policy makers to mimic Old World decadence will encourage individuals to increase and refine their material consumption. Many Americans will work harder to keep what they have rather than taking healthy, long-term risks to increase wealth so that others less fortunate than themselves at home or abroad can share in it.

Old World policies can also be expected to increase anti-Americanism and anti-Westernism abroad. Although the advocates of both the strong-man and rich-man world views often speak about the need to help the Third World and to improve the dialogue between the countries of the northern and southern hemispheres, this is largely rhetoric designed to keep the world stable, not to restructure it fundamentally. Take Kissinger's Rhodesian plan resulting from negotiations in southern Africa during 1976, for example. This package, if accepted by all parties, calls for a billion-dollar Western fund to help finance the departure of whites and bring Rhodesia to majority rule within two years

Clearly the United States will be called on to foot most of this bill. What Bdoes America get in return? Even if the peace plan prevents some bloodshed in the two transitional years, America will be identified not so much with the new black African government as with the repressive white colonial regime. American dollars are all too clearly to be spent on whites leaving rather than on blacks remaining in the country. In effect, American taxpayers are being asked to finance Ian Smith's retreat. Kissinger's *rhetorical* policy—siding with black Africans against white racism in southern Africa—appears *behaviorally* to prolong white rule and to pay off the white losers, even imparting Western respectability to the government of South Africa and its apartheid policy. The continuing split in government policy between liberal words and conservative deeds is implicitly based upon the cynical assumption that no one of any importance will notice the contradiction or care, that the American masses are either indifferent or ignorant when it comes to such diplomacy, and that elites can continue to be as inconsistent as they like.

America's policies toward racial minorities at home and abroad take on particular significance when one realizes that in the future an increasingly higher percentage of the world's population will be made up of non-Westerners. This trend, taken in conjunction with the projection that an increasingly higher percentage of the American population will be made up of older people, implies that the American voting public is likely to become more conservative and increasingly defensive about its minority position relative to the population explosion occurring in the non-Western world. Political elections will be affected by this trend: with respect to domestic affairs social security, health, and pension issues will become increasingly dominant themes; on foreign policy issues, national security concerns are apt to overwhelm badly needed foreign aid and world economic reform.

Indeed, in terms of the world economic system, past and present American policies may have already caused irreparable damage to the system and America's position in it. The breakdown of the international monetary system in 1971, resulting from the unilateral decisions of Richard Nixon and John Connally, set the stage for an international fashion of economic mercantilism. Hidden under the euphemism of "a system of floating exchange rates" is the attempt to transfer to other countries the economic problems of one's own nation. In terms of balance-of-payments deficits, rich nations export their deficits to poor countries that can least afford them. Not surprisingly, Nixon's mercantilist economic policy stimulated an angry counterpolicy in the Third World, most dramatically manifested in the quadrupling of oil prices by oil producers. Most significantly, the entire Third World has been mobilized against the First World of the Old Rich—particularly the United States. This animosity has, in turn, led to the suggestion by trilateral advisors that the industrial West coordinate its policies. The Old Rich nations prepare for possible economic warfare with the New Rich and the Poor. If economic stability is lost in the process, it is the Old Rich with the greatest stake in the existing status quo who will lose the most.

In the area of relations with communist powers, reactionary Old World policies are proving to be just as disastrous for the United States. As the Communist parties of Italy and France gain increasing power and legitimacy, the Old World anticommunist rationale of the North Atlantic Treaty Organization (NATO) is undermined from within. The reasonable thing to do, it would seem, is to declare frankly that NATO is an anti-Soviet (as opposed to anticommunist) alliance. But to do this would be to undermine the entire American policy of *détente*, not to mention the West German *Ostpolitik* (policy of accommodation with Eastern Europe) and the 1975 Helsinki accords. The only way out of this complex dilemma is for the leaders of the West to sit down and to analyze exactly what kind of political economy and ideology they think NATO should be defending in the West.

Although the alternative of social liberalism suggested here was designed to be useful for solving such dilemmas as that of NATO, present Old World policy makers in the United States and Western Europe, never noted in the first place for their abilities in political philosophy, are unlikely to risk the new. They prefer to hang on to the psychological and political security they find in old, stock ideological responses. Politics for Old World politicians in the decadent West has come to mean keeping the old system going as long as it lasts. Old World politics requires maintenance men—administrative bureaucrats who specialize in staving off decay, not in creating solutions to critical problems or in designing a New World political economy.

READINGS ON AMERICA

A selective list of readings on America's past, present, and future may be useful to those who want to delve further into some of the themes of this book. America's predicament, in terms of the contradiction between a democratic heritage and a conservative role in the world as a superpower, has been touched upon indirectly in Robert Tucker, *Nation or Empire?* (Baltimore: Johns Hopkins Press, 1968); Carl Oglesby and Richard Shaull, *Containment and Change* (New York: Macmillan, 1967); Ronald Steel, *Pax Americana* (New York: Viking Press, 1970); Lincoln Bloomfield, *In Search of American Foreign Policy: The Humane Use of Power* (New York: Oxford University Press, 1974); Zbigniew Brzezinski, *America in a Hostile World* (New York: Basic Books, forthcoming); and George Ball, *Diplomacy for a Crowded World* (Boston: Little, Brown, 1976).

For the history of the ideas that helped form American values and the American image, begin with Vernon L. Parrington, *Main Currents in American Thought* (New York: Harcourt Brace, 1927) and Ralph Henry Gabriel, *The Course of American Democratic Thought* (New York: Ronald Press, 1940). On the frontier thesis, turn to Frederick J. Turner, *The Early Writings*, compiled by Everett Edwards (Madison, Wisc.: University of Wisconsin Press, 1938) and to the provocative Henry Nash Smith, *Virgin Land—The American West as Symbol and Myth* (Cambridge, Mass: Harvard University Press, 1950). To understand why Americans have such a difficult time comprehending or becoming what they have not experienced, see the brilliant work by Louis Hartz, *The Liberal Tradition in America* (New York: Harcourt Brace, 1955) and H. Mark Roelofs, *Ideology and Myth in American Politics: A Critique of a National Political Mind* (Boston: Little, Brown, 1976). For an effort to provide contemporary empirical support for Hartz's thesis that America's political ideology is shot through and through with eighteenth-century Lockean liberalism, see Donald Devine, *The Political Culture of the United States* (Boston: Little, Brown, 1972). The thesis that material abundance is the crucial variable in explaining Americans is propounded in David Potter, *People of Plenty: Economic Abundance and the American Character* (Chicago: University of Chicago Press, 1968). Contemporary public opinion on American values is summarized in William Watts and Lloyd Free, *Changing Values of Americans: The State of the Nation* (New York: Potomac Associates, Universe Books, 1977) and Louis Harris, *The Anguish of Change* (New York: W. W. Norton, 1973). For conflicting projections of America's future and value changes, see Nicholas Rescher, *Values and the Future: The Impact of Technological Change on American Values* (New York: Free Press, 1969); Donella Meadows et al., *The Limits to Growth* (New York: Universe Books, 1972); Herman Kahn et al., *The Next 200 Years* (New York: William Morrow, 1975); Robert Heilbroner, *An Inquiry into the Human*

Prospect (New York: W. W. Norton, 1974); and Arnold A. Rogow, *The Dying of the Light* (New York: G. P. Putnam, 1975).

To comprehend the roots of the debate over capitalism and socialism one should begin with the classics: Adam Smith's *An Inquiry into the Nature and Causes of the Wealth of Nations* and the works of Karl Marx (both in various editions). These should be followed by a reading of the more contemporary classics: R. H. Tawney, *Religion and the Rise of Capitalism* (New York: Harcourt Brace Jovanovich, 1954) and *Equality* (London: Allen & Unwin, 1964); John Dewey, *Individualism Old and New* (New York: Capricorn Books, 1962); Thurman Arnold, *The Folklore of Capitalism* (New Haven, Conn.: Yale University Press, 1964); and, Friedrich A. Hayek, *The Road to Serfdom* (Chicago: University of Chicago Press, 1944).

The contemporary debate over individual freedom and social justice as epitomized by ʾcapitalist and socialist ideologies is carried on by John Rawls, *A Theory of Justice* (Cambridge, Mass.: Harvard University Press, 1971); Robert Nozick, *Anarchy, State and Utopia* (New York: Basic Books, 1974); Daniel Bell, *The Cultural Contradictions of Capitalism* (New York: Basic Books, 1976); Jürgen Habermas, *Toward a Rational Society* (Boston: Beacon Press, 1970); Michael Harrington, *Socialism* (New York: Saturday Review Press, 1972); R. N. Berki, *Socialism* (New York: St. Martin's Press, 1975); Frank Parkin, *Class Inequality and Political Order—Social Stratification in Capitalist and Communist Societies* (New York: Frederick A. Praeger, 1971); Peter Drucker, *Concept of the Corporation* (New York: John Day, 1972); David Linowes, *The Corporate Conscience* (New York: Hawthorn Books, 1974); and E. F. Schumacher, *Small Is Beautiful—Economics As if People Mattered* (New York: Harper & Row, 1975).

On democracy and elitism, begin with Aristotle's *Politics* and Alexis de Tocqueville's *Democracy in America* (both in various editions). For a more contemporary comparative perspective on the economic and social bases for stable democracies, read Seymour Martin Lipset, *Political Man* (Garden City, N. Y.: Doubleday-Anchor, 1963); Daniel Lerner, *The Passing of Traditional Society* (New York: Free Press, 1958); and Barrington Moore, *Social Origins of Dictatorship and Democracy* (Boston: Beacon Press, 1966). For a provocative treatment of the contradiction between the urge for individual liberty and the desire for a final salvationist order—as envisioned in eighteenth-century democratic ideologies—see J. L. Talmon, *The Origins of Totalitarian Democracy* (New York: Frederick A. Praeger, 1965). A brilliant, lucid, and short treatment of contemporary theories of Western and non-Western democracy and their economic and philosophical assumptions can be found in C. B. Macpherson, *The Real World of Democracy* (London: Oxford University Press, 1966). In *Toward a Rational Society* (Boston: Beacon Press, 1970), Jürgen Habermas demonstrates that the effects of the rapid growth of technology and "purposive-rational" action have overwhelmed efforts by democratic forms of government to control them. Even more pessimistic is the 1975 Report to the Trilateral Commission, "The Governability of Democracies," which asserts that social demands are apt to become so great that the democratic systems of America, Western Europe, and Japan may soon no longer be able to cope with them—published by Michel Crozier, Samuel Huntington, and Joji Watanuki as *The Crisis of Democracy* (New York: New York

University Press, 1975). And on current and future dilemmas that American democracy will face, see the bicentennial issue of *The Public Interest*, 41 (Fall 1975).

Value conflict in the world political economy between the Old Rich, the New Rich, and the Poor is a classic theme that academics and policy makers have suddenly rediscovered following the decline of national security problems in the Kissinger era. The Arab oil embargo and world recession of the 1970s brought political economy to center stage at home and abroad. Provocative overviews of global political economic problems that surfaced in this period include David P. Calleo and Benjamin M. Rowland, *America and the World Political Economy* (Bloomington, Ind.: Indiana University Press, 1973); Harald Malmgren, *International Economic Peacekeeping in Phase II* (New York: Quadrangle Books, 1973); Richard Barnet and Ronald Müller, *Global Reach: The Power of the Multinational Corporations* (New York: Simon & Schuster, 1974); David Blake and Robert Walters, *The Politics of Global Economic Relations* (Englewood Cliffs, N. J.: Prentice-Hall, 1976); Raymond Vernon, *Sovereignty at Bay* (New York: Basic Books, 1971) and Joan Spero, *The Politics of International Economic Relations* (New York: St. Martin's, 1977).

In relating world economic problems to the tensions between public opinion and foreign aid, begin with two classics: Barbara Ward's *Rich Nations and Poor Nations* and Walter Lippmann's *The Public Philosophy* (both in various editions). For the contemporary debate, read Gunnar Myrdal, *The Challenge of World Poverty* (New York: Pantheon, 1970); Robert Walters, *American and Soviet Aid* (Pittsburgh: University of Pittsburgh Press, 1970); Steven Weisman (ed.), *The Trojan Horse: A Radical View of American Foreign Aid* (San Francisco: Ramparts Press, 1974); and an essay by Robert Nisbet, "Public Opinion Versus Popular Opinion," in *The Public Interest*, 41 (Fall 1975).

On the historical background of America's stake in the superpower sweepstakes with Russia and China, read the lucid work of John G. Stoessinger, *Nations in Darkness: China, Russia and America* (New York: Random House, 1971). For the European context of superpower rivalry, see Robert S. Jordan (ed.), *Europe and the Superpowers* (Boston: Allyn & Bacon, 1971). For an historical and theoretical analysis of the interactions between great powers and small powers with radically different ideologies in a time of revolutionary change, see Kyung-Won Kim, *Revolution and International System* (New York: New York University Press, 1970). The theory and practice of deterrence can be found in Alexander George and Richard Smoke, *Deterrence in American Foreign Policy* (New York: Columbia University Press, 1974). Provocative essays on the contemporary situation include Raymond Vernon, "Apparatchics and Entrepreneurs: U.S.-Soviet Economic Relations," *Foreign Affairs*, 52, 2 (January 1974); Theodore Draper, "Appeasement and Détente," *Commentary*, 61, 2 (February 1976); Stanley Hoffmann, "Choices," *Foreign Policy*, 12 (Fall 1973) and "Weighing the Balance of Power," *Foreign Affairs*, 50, 4 (July 1972); and Zbigniew Brzezinski, "U.S. Foreign Policy: The Search for Focus," *Foreign Affairs*, 51, 4 (July 1973). For the role of rhetoric, see Thomas Frank and Edward Weisband, *Word Politics: Verbal Strategy among the Superpowers* (New York: Oxford University Press, 1972).

On isolationism and interventionism, read Walter Laqueur, *Neo-Isolationism and the World of the Seventies* (New York: Library Press, 1972); Ronald Steel, *Pax Americana* (New York: Viking Press, 1970); Robert Tucker, *A New Isolationism: Threat or Promise?* (New York: Universe Books, 1972); and Geoffrey Goodwin and Andrew Linklater (eds.), *New Dimensions of World Politics* (New York: John Wiley, 1975). Essays on the contemporary situation that are stimulating include: Bayless Manning, "Foreign Intervention in Civil Strife," *Stanford Journal of International Studies*, 3 (June 1968); Graham Allison, "Cool It: The Foreign Policy of Young America," *Foreign Policy* (Winter 1970-1971); Peter Berger, "The Greening of American Foreign Policy," *Commentary*, 61, 3 (March 1976); C. Fred Bergsten "The Response to the Third World," *Foreign Policy*, 17 (Winter 1974-1975); Robert Tucker, "Egalitarianism and International Politics," *Commentary*, 60, 3 (September 1975); and Henry Kissinger, "Building an Enduring Foreign Policy: Creative Leadership in a Moment of Uncertainty," reprinted in *Vital Speeches of the Day*, 42, 6 (January 1, 1976).

Those interested in the decay of Western culture and its possible recent revival in counterculture movements should start with the three critical classics: Oswald Spengler's *The Decline of the West*, Arnold Toynbee's *Study of History*, and Pitirim Sorokin's *Social and Cultural Dynamics* (all in various editions). One of the most provocative explanations for the pending decline of Western civilization is found in Sigmund Freud's short, brilliant essay *Civilization and Its Discontents* (New York: W. W. Norton, 1962). A recent interpretation of Freud's theory of the superego, which sees its decline as the basis for the decay of American culture, appears in Arnold Rogow, *The Dying of the Light* (New York: G. P. Putnam, 1975). The psychosociology of the decay of Western institutions and systems of control, using the ideas of Max Weber, Karl Marx, and Sigmund Freud as takeoff points, has been treated in Herbert Marcuse, *One-Dimensional Man* (Boston: Beacon Press, 1964); Fred Weinstein and Gerald Platt, *The Wish to Be Free: Society, Psyche, and Value Change* (Berkeley: University of California Press, 1969); and Ralph Hummel, *The Bureaucratic Experience* (New York: St. Martin's Press, 1977).

For the relationship of historical cycles to Western decay and America's possible rejuvenation, see Charles M. Fair, *The Dying Self* (Garden City, N.Y.: Doubleday-Anchor, 1970) and R. Isaak and R. Hummel, *Politics for Human Beings* (North Scituate, Mass.: Duxbury Press, 1975). On the counterculture movement in America in the 1960s and its heritage as an alternative value system for the West read H. L. Nieburg, *Culture Storm: Politics and the Ritual Order* (New York: St. Martin's Press, 1973); Theodore Roszak, *The Making of a Counter Culture* (Garden City, N. Y.: Doubleday-Anchor, 1969); Herbert Reid (ed.), *Up the Mainstream: A Critique of Ideology in American Politics and Everyday Life* (New York: David McKay, 1974); Ronald Laing, *The Politics of Experience* (New York: Ballantine Books, 1967); Galway Kinnell, *The Book of Nightmares* (Boston: Houghton-Mifflin, 1971); and Kriyananda, *Cooperative Communities: How to Start Them, and Why* (Nevada City, Calif.: Ananda Publications, 1970).

On education as a vehicle for positive cultural change, begin with three classics: Plato's *Republic*, Jean Jacques Rousseau's *Emile*, and Alfred North Whitehead's *The*

Aims of Education (all in various editions). For contemporary educational criticisms, read Jonathan Kozol, *The Night Is Dark and I Am Far from Home* (Boston: Houghton-Mifflin, 1975); Ivan Illich, *Deschooling Society* (New York: Harper & Row, 1971); Paul Goodman, *Compulsory Mis-education and the Community of Scholars* (New York: Vintage, 1962); and B. F. Skinner's novel, *Walden II* (New York: Macmillan, 1948).

Profoundly stimulating psychosocial theories of educational development can be found in Jean Piaget, *The Moral Judgement of the Child* (London: Keagan Paul, 1932); Erik H. Erikson, *Childhood and Society* (New York: W. W. Norton, 1950); Lawrence Kohlberg, *Stages in the Development of Moral Thought and Action* (New York: Holt, Rinehart and Winston, 1974); and the three works of Charles Hampden-Turner, *Radical Man: The Process of Psycho-social Development* (Garden City, N. Y.: Doubleday-Anchor, 1971), *From Poverty to Dignity: A Strategy for Poor Americans* (Garden City, N. Y.: Doubleday-Anchor, 1974); and *Sane Asylum* (San Francisco: San Francisco Book Co., 1976). See also the provocative essay by Charles Hampden-Turner and Phillip Whitten, "Morals Left and Right," in *Psychology Today,* April 1971. On the cultural prerequisites for meaningful equality of opportunity in education, see Ashley Montagu (ed.), *Culture and Human Development* (Englewood Cliffs, N. J.: Prentice-Hall, 1974).

In terms of the sociology of knowledge, my notion of social liberalism as an alternative form of political economy was inspired, in part, by T. H. Green, *Lectures on the Principles of Political Obligation* (various editions). Green's thought, in turn, was partially derived from post-Kantian German philosophy. The central problem of the idealist revision of liberalism, the tradition Green represents, was the interdependence of the structure of personality and the cultural structure of the social milieu. Green noted, for example, that "the self is a social self," and that ethics rested on the mutual dependence of the individual and the social community. Merely working for one's own sake, in short, cannot be "good" unless its consequences for the community are taken into account.

However, the assumption of mutuality between the individual and society raises innumerable paradoxes. One of the most intriguing is Kenneth Arrow's paradox of majority rule, which is demonstrated in *Social Choice and Individual Values* (New York: John Wiley, 1966). The paradox, in brief, is that majority rule cannot exist without the imposition of some arbitrary social order, undemocratically imposed. If, then, there must be inequalities of some sort, philosopher John Rawls argued, in his *Theory of Justice* (Boston: Harvard University Press, 1971), that such inequalities are justifiable only to the extent that they maximize the interests of those least advantaged in the society— Rawls's "difference principle." Yet as Robert Nozick noted in his provocative *Anarchy, State and Utopia* (New York: Basic Books, 1974), Rawls's difference principle discriminates against those who begin with intelligence, skill, or wealth through no fault of their own. Rather than letting this observation lead to the legitimization of existing property rights and contractual agreements, as does Nozick, Elliot Richardson makes the moderate proposal, in *The Creative Balance: Government, Politics and the Individual in America's Third Century* (New York: Holt, Rinehart & Winston, 1976), that "Those who have been fortunate in genetic endowments or social advantage have a moral duty to employ their talents in the service of the least advantaged." Although agreeing with Richardson's ethic (which is consistent with T. H. Green's), I was pessimistic about the probabilty that Americans, brought up in the cultural milieu of rugged individualism, would adopt it voluntarily unless paid to do so. In sum, social liberalism is a system of political economy that constructs a payoff structure (or "learning system") to encourage individuals to voluntarily produce for the social welfare and receive monetary and social rewards in return.

This enforcement structure of social liberalism is based upon the assumption that the only way to preserve the intelligence, efficacy, and productivity of the capitalist incentive system is to demonstrate in individual cases that the system can function for the good of all—or at least work in this direction, rather that in the direction of rapacious individualism. Several recent works helped to inspire the development of the propositions of social liberalism. The most significant were Kenneth Boulding, *The Economy of Love and Fear* (Belmont, Calif.: Wadsworth, 1973); Daniel Bell, *The Cultural Contradictions of Capitalism* (New York: Basic Books, 1976); and Frank Parkin's *Class Inequality and Political Order—Social Stratification in Capitalist and Communist Societies* (New York: Frederick A. Praeger, 1971). In reacting to the chapter on social liberalism, economist Charles Kindelberger recommended Mancur Olsen, *A Theory of Collective Action* (New York: Schocken Books, 1964), in which I discovered further support for my belief that individuals in a group or community will not automatically pursue the group interest in the same way that they might be expected to pursue their individual interests. Finally, in reading E. F. Schumacher, *Small Is Beautiful* (New York: Harper & Row, 1973), I found support for the notion that economics can be designed as if people mattered, although I remain skeptical about the proposition that small is always beautiful for the many, who depend upon mass production and industrialization for their economic well-being and social opportunities. In short, given America's privileged position, American liberalism must become more social to survive as an ideology or basis for political economy both at home and abroad.

For those interested in speculating further about possible futures for the New World, Henry Kissinger's alternative is implied in *A World Restored* (New York: Grosset & Dunlap, 1964). The trilateral alternative of a more cohesive alliance between America, Western Europe, and Japan is explored in Zbigniew Brzezinski, *Between Two Ages: America's Role in the Technotronic Era* (New York: Viking Press, 1970). The role of *ressentiment*, distinction, and liberty in America's democracy is discussed in Edgar Friedenberg, *The Disposal of Liberty and Other Industrial Wastes* (Garden City, N. Y.: Doubleday-Anchor, 1975). A perceptive book on the tendency to revert to a "conservative impulse" when beseiged by too much change at once is Peter Marris, *Loss and Change* (New York: Pantheon, 1974). For a melioristic view of the future development of America and Western Europe, read Theodore Geiger, *The Fortunes of the West: The Future of the Atlantic Nations* (Bloomington, Ind.: Indiana University Press, 1973). For an optimistic view that puts perhaps too much weight on technological rationality and too little on philosophical and cultural change, read Herman Kahn et al., *The Next 200 Years* (New York: William Morrow, 1975). And for a pessimistic version of America's future, see Robert Heilbroner, *An Inquiry into the Human Prospect* (New York: W. W. Norton, 1974) and Aleksandr Solzhenitsyn, *A Warning to the West* (forthcoming).

INDEX